Dostoevsky and the Epileptic Mode of Being

LEGENDA

LEGENDA, founded in 1995 by the European Humanities Research Centre of the University of Oxford, is now a joint imprint of the Modern Humanities Research Association and Maney Publishing. Titles range from medieval texts to contemporary cinema and form a widely comparative view of the modern humanities, including works on Arabic, Catalan, English, French, German, Greek, Italian, Portuguese, Russian, Spanish, and Yiddish literature. An Editorial Board of distinguished academic specialists works in collaboration with leading scholarly bodies such as the Society for French Studies, the British Comparative Literature Association and the Association of Hispanists of Great Britain & Ireland.

MHRA

The Modern Humanities Research Association (MHRA) encourages and promotes advanced study and research in the field of the modern humanities, especially modern European languages and literature, including English, and also cinema. It also aims to break down the barriers between scholars working in different disciplines and to maintain the unity of humanistic scholarship in the face of increasing specialization. The Association fulfils this purpose primarily through the publication of journals, bibliographies, monographs and other aids to research.

Maney Publishing

Maney Publishing is one of the few remaining independent British academic publishers. Founded in 1900 the company has offices both in the UK, in Leeds and London, and in North America, in Philadelphia. Since 1945 Maney Publishing has worked closely with learned societies, their editors, authors, and members, in publishing academic books and journals to the highest traditional standards of materials and production.

Dostoevsky and the Epileptic Mode of Being

❖

Paul Fung

LEGENDA
Modern Humanities Research Association and Maney Publishing
2015

Published by the
Modern Humanities Research Association and Maney Publishing
1 Carlton House Terrace
London SW1Y 5AF
United Kingdom

LEGENDA is an imprint of the
Modern Humanities Research Association and Maney Publishing

Maney Publishing is the trading name of W. S. Maney & Son Ltd,
whose registered office is at Suite 1C, Joseph's Well, Hanover Walk, Leeds LS3 1AB

ISBN 978-1-909662-08-7

First published 2015

Printed in Great Britain

Cover: 875 Design

Copy-Editor: Nigel Hope

CONTENTS

FOR MY PARENTS

ACKNOWLEDGEMENTS

The earliest form of this book can be dated back to my doctoral dissertation at the University of Manchester in 2007. I intended to conduct a comparative study on the conceptualization of the Other in Bakhtin, Lacan, and Levinas. The theoretical approach to the Other later became the background for rethinking Dostoevsky's novels, specifically their representations of epilepsy. This book could not have been completed without the support of Hang Seng Management College. I would like to thank in particular my departmental colleagues, Thomas Luk and Joel Swann, for their encouragement and comments on the manuscript.

The core of this book was completed at the University of Manchester. I received invaluable advice and support from my teachers, colleagues, and friends. I would like to express my gratitude to Jeremy Tambling, whose comments on my research were tremendously helpful and inspiring. I would also like to thank him for encouraging me to do the PhD. Galin Tihanov's supportive and caring words, especially his comments on my conference papers on Dostoevsky, have been an invaluable source of motivation for my pursuit of Russian literature. I am also grateful to Galin for providing me with the opportunity to study Russian at the University. Hal Gladfelder's meticulous reading of my chapters has been helpful in polishing the book's presentation. I also thank him for letting me teach literature as a graduate teaching assistant, from which I have learnt a lot. David Shepherd and Daniela Caselli's in-depth questions and comments on this book's earlier version gave me the confidence to pursue its publication. Thanks also to other professors at Manchester: Jerome De Groot, Malcolm Hicks, Kevin Parker, Alan Rawes, Michael Sanders, Robert Spencer, and Anastasia Valassopoulos. Their encouraging words and openness to critical thoughts were fantastic sources of motivation.

The theory reading group, led by Jeremy Tambling and initiated by James Smith, gave me the chance to engage with the intensely exciting work of thinkers such as Maurice Blanchot, Jacques Lacan, and Walter Benjamin. The group discussion inspired the theoretical aspect of this book.

My thanks to Carolyn Broomhead for listening to my chapter on *The Idiot* and J. T. Welsh for commenting on my work on cinema and the representation of death. The talks with Iain Bailey and James Smith about literature and the future were very useful and uplifting. My study trip to St Petersburg would not have taken place without my friend Federico's help. My neighbour Maksim Samuilov helped me to overcome some of the lowest periods. The conversations with Vincenz Serrano were energizing. With him I was able to express my fragmented ideas. Lucia Nigri was caring and sensible. Her presence was indescribably important to my life in Manchester. My thanks also to those who read the drafts of the book. Their support in the last stage of my research was vital: Irene Huhulea, Rebecca Pohl, James Smith, Joel Swann, and J. T. Welsh.

Lastly, I would like to express my gratitude to Venus Wong, whose unconditional support has made the completion of this book possible. This book is for my parents.

P.F., Hong Kong, August 2014

NOTE ON TEXTS

Throughout the book, I have quoted Dostoevsky in English. In some circumstances, I have added the Russian original text in order to emphasize a phrase or sentence. To be consistent, most of the quotes are from the translations by Richard Pevear and Larissa Volokhonsky. Their editions have explanatory notes and they have preserved much of the style of the original texts. For the texts they have not translated, I have used other translations published by Penguin, Oxford, and Northwestern University Press (see below). Please refer to the Bibliography for a list of other editions I have studied. References to Dostoevsky's novels generally include part, chapter, and page number. For example, '1.2.3' refers to page 3 of chapter 2 of part 1; 1:2 refers to page 2 of volume 1 of the complete works of Dostoevsky in Russian.

Dostoevskii, Fedor Mikhailovich, *Polnoe sobranie sochinenii v tridtsati tomakh*, ed. by V. G. Bazanov and others, 30 vols (Leningrad: Nauka, 1972–90)

Dostoevsky, Fyodor, *Poor Folk and Other Stories*, trans. by David McDuff (Harmondsworth: Penguin, 1988)

—— *Uncle's Dream and Other Stories*, trans. by David McDuff (Harmondsworth: Penguin, 1989)

—— *The Brothers Karamazov*, trans. by Richard Pevear and Larissa Volokhonsky (London: Vintage, 1992)

—— *Crime and Punishment*, trans. by Richard Pevear and Larissa Volokhonsky (London: Vintage, 1993)

—— *Notes from Underground*, trans. by Richard Pevear and Larissa Volokhonsky (New York: Alfred A. Knopf, 1993)

—— *Demons*, trans. by Richard Pevear and Larissa Volokhonsky (London: Vintage, 1994)

—— *A Writer's Diary*, trans. by Kenneth Lantz, 2 vols (Evanston; IL: Northwestern University Press, 1994)

—— *Winter Notes on Summer Impressions*, trans. by David Patterson (Evanston; IL: Northwestern University Press, 1997)

—— *Memoirs from the House of the Dead*, trans. by Jessie Coulson (Oxford: Oxford University Press, 2001)

—— *The Idiot*, trans. by Richard Pevear and Larissa Volokhonsky (New York: Vintage, 2003)

—— *The Adolescent*, trans. by Richard Pevear and Larissa Volokhonsky (London: Vintage, 2004)

—— *The Double and The Gambler*, trans. by Richard Pevear and Larissa Volohonsky (New York: Alfred A. Knopf, 2005)

—— *Humiliated and Insulted*, trans. by Ignat Avsey (Surrey: Oneworld Classic, 2008)

INTRODUCTION

❖

For in fact Dostoevsky always represents a person *on the threshold* of a final decision, at a moment of *crisis*, at an unfinalizable — and *unpredeterminable* — turning point for his soul.

MIKHAIL BAKHTIN, *Problems of Dostoevsky's Poetics*, p. 61

Thinking involves not only the flow of thoughts, but their arrest as well. Where thinking suddenly stops in a configuration pregnant with tensions, it gives that configuration a shock, by which it crystallizes into a monad.

WALTER BENJAMIN, *Illuminations*, p. 254

Let us go in together,
And still your fingers on your lips, I pray.
The time is out of joint: O cursed spite,
That ever I was born to set it right!
Nay, come, let's go together.

SHAKESPEARE, *Hamlet* 1.5.186–90

Approaching the Epileptic Mode of Being

This book intends to reread Fyodor Dostoevsky's novels from the perspective of the 'moment'. By the 'moment' I mean an indivisible instant, a caesura or a break, during which consciousness is abruptly cut off. In the moment the flow of thoughts of the Dostoevskian subject is suspended; the intensive dialogues of different voices — no matter whether they happen within consciousness or among several characters — come to a halt. The rupturing moment finds its most graphic and bodily form in an epileptic seizure. This book positions epilepsy as a metaphor: Dostoevsky's writing is 'epileptic' as it is punctuated by moments of caesuras and breaks.

The centre of this book is not a single and definite image of epilepsy which the reader can keep referring back to in his or her experience in reading Dostoevsky. The centre is constructed by gaps, breaks, and silences in the texts. One of my aims is to show, metaphorically speaking, how the Dostoevskian hero reacts to the sudden removal of the ground. His reaction will be understood as characteristic of an epileptic mode of being, which is crucial for understanding how it is like to be in the world of Dostoevsky.

This book argues that Dostoevsky's novels can be understood in terms of an incessant anxiety to experience this critical moment. But at the same time, that infinitely short period of time is beyond the reach of lived experience and therefore eludes the subject who desires to control it. The writing of epilepsy will therefore be understood as doubly structured: it refers to the radical and uncontrollable rupture of experience, a caesura in the course of narrative which suspends representations. But it also articulates the fearful attraction to that rupture. Put another way, an active force which aims to master experience is met with a sudden attack of epilepsy which throws the subject into passivity. The subject is both active and passive, and yet these two tendencies do not cancel each other out. They create continual disappointment, as the moment is always missed and being sought after.[1]

The moment, around which epilepsy is structured, eludes the desiring subject. It interrupts lived experience, nullifying a sense of self-possession and completeness. It is also comparable to the way in which caesura functions in Greek tragedy. Here I refer specifically to Friedrich Hölderlin's understanding of the term in his notes on Sophocles' *Oedipus the King*. The poet says that in tragedy the development of ideas, feelings, and reflections operates on the principle of 'counterpoise' rather than 'pure succession'.[2] He suggests the idea of caesura as such a counterbalancing mechanism:

> For the tragic transport is actually empty, and the least restrained. — Thereby, in the rhythmic sequence of the representations wherein the transport presents itself, there becomes necessary what in poetic meter is called caesura, the pure word, the counter-rhythmic rupture — namely, in order to meet the onrushing change of representations at its highest point, in such a manner that not the change of representation but the representation itself very soon appears.[3]

The passion ('tragic transport') expressed in characters is interrupted by a sudden surge of sobriety. Such moment reveals that the tragic transport in the play is but representation. The rhythmic flow, representing life and time, has been arrested in caesura. The act of representation suspends; what becomes clear to the reader is the concept of representation itself. The critic Walter Benjamin sees in Hölderlin's quotation 'fundamental significance for the theory of art in general' (340). What interests Benjamin is not the harmonious representation of life and time in the play but the moment when such making of beautiful appearance becomes paralysed. Only through this moment of suspension can the understanding of art be complete. Benjamin called the power in front of which all kinds of representation come to a halt the expressionless: in the caesura, 'every expression simultaneously comes to a standstill, in order to give free reign to an expressionless power inside all artistic media' (341). The expressionless (*das Ausdruckslose*) can be seen as a kind of singularity: it is not subsumed under any form of totalistic understanding of art. Benjamin describes the beautiful semblance in the common understanding of an artwork as 'the false, errant totality'. In fact, 'only the expressionless completes the works, by shattering it into a thing of shards, into a fragment of the true world, into the torso of a symbol' (340).[4]

This book will take epilepsy as the moment of suspension, where all kinds of grandiose ideas, feelings, and visions lose their expressive power. The moment will be discussed with attention to specific episodes in Dostoevsky's post-Siberian novels: mystic terror which destroys rationalization (*Humiliated and Insulted*); the alienating and suppressive Petersburg which is described as 'epileptic' (*Crime and Punishment*); an image of the guillotine in which the convict is on the border between life and death (*The Idiot*); a suicide project motivated by the obsession with self-will (*Demons*); hysterical fits which mark the repressed history of paternal violence (*The Brothers Karamazov*).

Dostoevsky's heroes keep coming back to the moment, trying to comprehend and even master it in their consciousness. This desire to seize upon what is unseizable characterizes what I call the 'epileptic mode of being', a description borrowed from a chapter in Robert Lord's book on Dostoevsky.[5] However, the way I understand the phrase will be different from Lord's. He perceives epilepsy as something that keeps the subject in check. He suggests, for instance, that Prince Myshkin's epilepsy in *The Idiot* is a delimiting force which prevents the realization of the destructive alter ego. Epilepsy resembles a buffer, which keeps the Prince in check, making sure that he does not actualize his 'monstrous potentiality':

> If epilepsy can be said to be a release of tension, it becomes thereby a form of human limitation. If these moments were to endure for more than a second of time, the epileptic would be transformed into a god, or into a superhuman monster (Kirilov), or simply annihilated. An epileptic, then, is pre-eminently one who founders and miscarries, one who is compelled to stop short of a goal, which will remain unattainable for the very reason that his personality is (to use a currently fashionable term) 'structured' in a particular way. Epilepsy, subjectively viewed, is that which limits and holds in check. (94)

The epileptic seizure is preceded by moments of ecstasy, or as the narrator in *The Idiot* describes, 'sublime tranquillity', 'harmonious joy', 'ecstatic, prayerful merging with the highest synthesis of life' (2.5.227). These moments are both rapturous and unbearable. To endure it one has to become a man-god, which is the theory of Kirilov in *Demons*. It is true that the intensified consciousness is curtailed by the seizure. But to say that the self is 'compelled to stop short of a goal' or that his personality is '"structured" in a particular way' runs the risk of reducing the complexities of the epileptic experience. The ecstatic moments are instants when the subject desires to transgress, to think the impossible, and to confront his alter ego. The seizure, rather than playing the role of a guard or a safety valve, represents a much more radical moment where all these desires are destroyed. I agree with Lord that Dostoevsky's epilepsy is the building-up of an intense consciousness and the cancellation of it. But the epileptic figure is not compelled to 'stop short of a goal'. His desires to think the impossible are always already excessive before they are stopped by the seizure. If Lord's reading is informed by a structuralist approach, my reading will be a post-structuralist one. That is to say, Dostoevsky's epilepsy marks the desire to dissolve the structure, to transgress the economy of pleasure. Yet, this incessant desire to go beyond one's own limit is punctuated by sudden seizures, which turn an active repetition into a passive one. The desire to conquer an experience is at the same time a subjection to the uncontrollable seizure. The epileptic wakes up from a seizure only to be anxious that another one is impending. This particular state of anxiety characterizes the epileptic mode of being, which is always subject to the annihilation of existence.

My approach to epilepsy differs from that of Alex de Jonge's *Dostoevsky and The Age of Intensity*. In chapter 11, 'Intensity and Time', he discusses Prince Myshkin's meditation on the moment of epileptic fit, arguing that it is the experience of 'pseudo-mystic ecstasy and oneness, a kind of *paradis artificiel*'.[6] For de Jonge, the Prince's comment on epilepsy shows an intense nostalgia for having full meanings and a sense of eternity, which is symptomatic of nineteenth-century European literature (he compares Dostoevsky with Baudelaire throughout the book). This reading of the Prince's epilepsy overlooks two points: first, the onset of an epileptic seizure is painful, terrifying, and it annihilates consciousness; second, after one seizure, the next one is impending, suggesting repetition in the experience of epilepsy. In other words, epilepsy is not entirely an intensive experience; it comprises intensity and its effacement. The alternation of these two phases marks the experience of the epileptic, and it is the infinite alternation that makes epilepsy traumatic. This book focuses on this contradictory pattern of epilepsy. If de Jonge is interested in reading the nineteenth century as the age of intensity, my book explores how the relationship between intensity and its disappearance suggests a kind of postponement, a subjectivity which is infinitely deferred.

The Introduction will be in three parts. First, I will look at how epilepsy was perceived in history and how these opinions might be helpful for us to understand Dostoevsky's own reading of epilepsy in terms of the disruptive moment. I will discuss Mikhail Bakhtin's idea of polyphony to demonstrate the ways in which different historical and literary references to epilepsy are amalgamated in Dostoevsky's works. The coexistence of the 'epileptic voices' necessitates a reading which does not impose a single meaning to the illness. Instead of giving a definitive meaning to epilepsy and having it tested throughout Dostoevsky's works, this book aims to explore the specific implications of epilepsy in each of the major post-Siberian novels. The second part of the Introduction will examine Dostoevsky's medical reports and how the epileptic writer perceives his own epileptic condition. He describes his epilepsy in terms of the approaching of death and 'mystic terror'. He also uses the latter phrase to describe the moment just before he was supposed to be executed by firing squad in 1849. The mystic terror refers both to Dostoevsky's fear of what is unknown in epilepsy and death, and to the anxiety to make sense of it. In this way, I will suggest that Dostoevsky is driven by the desire to comprehend and write the incomprehensible.

The History of Epilepsy

The word 'epilepsy' originates in Greek (*epilēpsis*), meaning to 'take hold on' or 'to seize upon', and thereby already suggests something about the moment. One of the earliest records of the word was found in the Hippocratic medical writings collected in *On the Sacred Disease*.[7] Epilepsy was called the 'great disease' or 'sacred disease' originating in the brain. It was sacred because a deity had sent a demon which had entered the patient, or he had sinned against the moon (hence 'lunacy').[8] Plato also understood epilepsy as a sacred disease which disturbs the revolutions in the head.[9] Epilepsy was also called the 'falling sickness', which visualizes the symptom of falling on the ground during a seizure.

The 'falling sickness' is used in Shakespeare's *Julius Caesar* to describe Caesar's epilepsy when he is offered the crown: 'the rabblement hooted and clapped their chapped hands and threw up their sweaty night-caps and uttered such a deal of stinking breath because Caesar refused the crown that it had almost choked Caesar;

for he swooned and fell down at it...' (1.2.243–46).[10] Casca goes on to say: 'He fell down in the market-place, and foamed at mouth, and was speechless', to which Brutus responds: ''Tis very like: he hath the falling sickness' (252). Cassius disagrees with Brutus and says that it is not Caesar but 'we' who have the falling sickness, implying that the republic is actually falling apart: 'No, Caesar hath it not; but you and I, and honest Casca, we have the falling sickness' (253–54).

Shakespeare's details about Caesar's epilepsy come from Plutarch, who refers to three occasions of Caesar having the falling sickness in his *Lives*.[11] The figure of Caesar is central for rereading Dostoevsky, who prefers the phrase falling sickness (падучая) to epilepsy (эпилепсия) when he refers to the epileptics in his novels.[12] For instance, Raskolnikov, the impoverished law student who murders a pawnbroker and her sister in *Crime and Punishment*, justifies his crime by appealing to the 'Napoleonic theory', an idea originally formulated in Napoleon III's 1865 book, *The Life of Julius Caesar*. Retrospectively, Raskolnikov elaborates his theory through his article 'Concerning Crime', saying that mankind is divided into two classes — the ordinary majority and the extraordinary minority. While the ordinary ones must be subject to authority and the law, the extraordinary ones have the right to commit any crime and break any law just because they are extraordinary (3.5.259–61). Later in the novel, Raskolnikov says that he wants to make himself a Napoleon and that is why he killed the pawnbroker (5.4.415). The young man, among other justifications, sees himself as one of the extraordinary minority such as Napoleon or Caesar, who has the right to shed blood:

> The lawgivers and founders of mankind, starting from the most ancient and going on to the Lycurguses, the Solons, the Muhammads, the Napoleons, and so forth, that all of them to a man were criminals, from the fact alone that in giving a new law they thereby violated the old one, held sacred by society and passed down from their fathers, and they certainly did not stop at shedding blood either, if it happened that blood (sometimes quite innocent and shed valiantly for the ancient law) could help them. (3.5.260)

The law-breakers suggest transgression, which brings us back to the novel's title: the word 'crime' in Russian (преступление) literally means 'stepping-over'. Although there is no mention of Raskolnikov being an epileptic, it is significant that he identifies himself with the 'Napoleonic theory', which is based upon the great epileptic figure in history (Julius Caesar), suggesting the point that Raskolnikov is an 'epileptic' character even if he is not literally an epileptic.[13]

The 'Napoleonic theory' is later refracted in the voice of Shigalyov, one of the revolutionaries in *Demons*, who envisages a utopian society in which one tenth of the population must enjoy absolute freedom and have the right to control the remaining ninth-tenths (2.7.403). Both Raskolnikov and Shigalyov's theories aim to solve social problems in biological terms, which was a burgeoning discourse in nineteenth-century Europe.[14] The Italian criminologist Cesare Lombroso (1836–1909), for instance, proposed that a born criminal is a special type of man whose biological structure is very similar to that of the epileptic. He also argued that the born criminal type often has cerebral irritability, which can create great original intellectual and psychic power as well as nervous disorder. This theory led him to the conclusion that the epileptic has the potential to be not only a criminal but also a genius. In his book *The Men of Genius* (1891), Lombroso shows that many men of genius experienced headaches, loss of memory, and morbid irritability, which are suggestive of having epilepsy. These figures who expressed 'the epileptoid nature of genius' included Julius Caesar, Napoleon, Molière, Petrarch, Peter the Great, Mohammed, Handel, Swift, Richelieu, Charles V, Flaubert, St Paul, and Dostoevsky.[15] In fact, the criminologist quotes the famous passages on epilepsy from *The Idiot* and *Demons* at length, saying that one might call the kind of fit they describe 'psychic epilepsy'.[16]

Friedrich Nietzsche called the epileptic genius the 'active man'. The philosopher wrote that Dostoevsky is the only psychologist 'from whom [he] had anything to learn'.[17] It has been proved that Nietzsche had read Dostoevsky's novels and it is likely that his comment on the epileptic was inspired by his experience of reading Dostoevsky.[18] In the preface of *Daybreak: Thoughts on the Prejudices of Morality* (1881), for instance, Nietzsche writes that his reader will discover a 'subterranean man' who 'tunnels and mines and undermines', an image which is readily comparable to the Underground Man in *Notes from Underground*, which Nietzsche had read in French.[19] In the entry 'Flight from Oneself', Nietzsche says that men such as Byron and Alfred de Musset have strong impulses for actions. These men cannot 'endure to remain within themselves' and long to dissolve into something 'outside'. He refers to four famous epileptics at the end:

> Those men given to intellectual spasm — Byron and Alfred de Musset are examples — who are impatient and gloomily inclined towards themselves and in all they do resemble rampaging horses, and who derive from their own works, indeed, only a short-lived fire and joy which almost bursts their veins and then a desolation and sourness made more wintry by the contrast it presents — how should such men endure to remain within *themselves*! They long to dissolve into something *'outside'*; if one is a Christian and is possessed by such a longing one's goal is to be dissolved into God, to 'become wholly at one with him'; if one is Shakespeare one is satisfied only with being dissolved into images of the most passionate life; if one is Byron one longs for *action*, because action draws us away from ourself even more than do thoughts, feelings or works. And so could all impulse to action perhaps be at bottom flight from oneself? — Pascal would ask. And the proposition might indeed be demonstrated in the case of the supreme examples known to us of the impulse to action: for consider — in the light of the experience of psychiatry, as is only proper — that four of the most active men of all time were epileptics (namely Alexander, Caesar, Mohammed and Napoleon), just as Byron was also subject to this complaint.[20]

A 'short-lived fire and joy' almost bursts in the 'active men' who cannot 'endure to remain within themselves'. The passage uses 'dissolve' to describe the 'flight from oneself', suggesting a process of dissolution of subjectivity. The passage compares this dissolution with the Christian ideal of longing to be dissolved into God. The same image also appears in the moment before the attack of epilepsy in *The Idiot*, during which the epileptic Prince Myshkin experiences 'ecstatic, prayerful merging with the highest synthesis of life' (2.5.226).

Nietzsche suggests that the four epileptics — Alexander, Caesar, Mohammed, and Napoleon — are also great active men. This can be explained from the fact that they were all ingeniously active figures who founded entirely new orders that marked decisive moments in history. These moments are the threshold moment of action and transformation, where the world is 'turned upside down'. A subjective and subversive decision changed the whole of objective reality. Nietzsche asks: 'Could all impulse to action perhaps be at bottom flight from oneself?' This question presupposes a man who desires action and wants to go beyond his own limit, to overcome the self. The four great epileptics in history were able to do this. To what extent can Dostoevsky's 'epileptic' heroes achieve that? In the opening page of *Crime and Punishment*, Raskolnikov, who is rehearsing his crime, says to himself that what people are most afraid of is 'a new step, their own new word' (1.1.4). The 'epileptic' figure in the world of Dostoevsky is continually troubled by whether he can speak the 'new word', to do what is unprecedented, that is, to transgress one's own limit, to flee from oneself.

For Nietzsche, one of the four great active epileptics is Mohammed, whom Raskolnikov sees as one of the transgressors who stepped-over and made a new law. There is no evidence showing that Mohammed was an epileptic. But it is said that a remarkable incident in his early youth is suggestive of epilepsy. When he was living under the care of his wet-nurse Halima, two angels approached Mohammed, split open his abdomen, and removed a black clot of blood. Mohammed was cleansed with melted snow in a golden basin. Then they weighed him, and his weight surpassed that of a thousand people.[21]

Determining whether this story ever actually happened is beyond the scope of this book. But it is true that Christian Byzantium, which was often at war with the Arabs, reduced Mohammed's story of visions to simply the signs of physical illness, that is, epilepsy.[22] The perception of Mohammed having visions became more accepted in the West in the nineteenth century, which possibly had to do with the emergence of the discipline of psychiatry.[23] Thomas Carlyle, for instance, in his lecture on heroes and hero worship, takes Mohammed as an example to illustrate the hero as a prophet.[24] Dostoevsky also has a positive view on Mohammed's vision and compares his own epileptic condition with one of the visionary moments recorded in the Koran, when Allah brings Mohammed by night from the 'Inviolable Place of Worship (Mecca) to the Far Distant Place of Worship (Jerusalem)' (17:1).[25] A similar story says that Mohammed was awakened one night by the archangel Gabriel, who, as he pushed against a jug of water with his wing, brought him to Jerusalem, and from there Mohammed rose into the seven heavens where he spoke with angels, prophets, and Allah, visited the fiery Gehenna, and came back in time to keep the jug from spilling. In *The Idiot*, Prince Myshkin compares this infinitely brief period of time to the ecstatic moment just before the attack of epilepsy, saying that in those moments 'time shall be no more' (2.5.227, Revelation 10:6). The Prince reflects on these moments, which, like Nietzsche's flight from oneself, have to do with the loosening of boundaries (the word 'ecstatic' derives from *ekstasis* in Greek, meaning 'standing outside'). But on the other hand, he knows that those moments will be followed by the annihilative seizure.

Apart from the 'falling sickness', epilepsy is also called St. Vitus's dance in *The*

Idiot. The saintly, childish, and epileptic Prince Myshkin is described in the opening page of the novel:

> [...] he had indeed been away from Russia for a long time, more than four years, [...] sent abroad of illness, some strange nervous illness like the falling sickness or St. Vitus's dance, some sort of trembling and convulsions. (1.1.6)

St. Vitus's dance originally referred to a kind of dancing mania (*choreomania*) in the Middle Ages, which became a psychic epidemic seizing thousands of men and women and made them dance till they fell down in exhaustion. People who carried out the dance showed similar symptoms to those of an epileptic, such as frothing at the mouth, limb jerking, and the loss of consciousness. St Vitus was an epileptic who became a patron saint of actors, comedians, dancers, and also epileptics. During the dance, music was played on drums and pipes, which served a dual purpose: it provoked madness and sought to cure it.[26] The dance was supposed to commemorate St Vitus and celebrate the holiness of epilepsy. But the choreography itself could be madness-inducing. That St Vitus's dance implies both 'falling' and 'uplifting' (maddening and celebratory) reiterates the ambivalence of epilepsy in Dostoevsky's texts.

In the European Renaissance, natural phenomena were often understood as expressions of physical illnesses. For Paracelsus (1493–1541), the Swiss occultist and physician, epilepsy was associated with natural phenomena such as thunderstorms and earthquakes due to their conceptual similarities with splitting and distortion.[27] The epileptic seizure resembles the thunderstorm which 'splits' the cloud; the peculiar scream resembles an earthquake which cracks the shell. In *Humiliated and Insulted* (1861), a thunderstorm breaks out when the protagonist Nelly is explaining her traumatic family history, after which she has an epileptic seizure: 'At that instant a fairly loud clap of thunder resounded, and torrential rain began to beat heavily against the window panes; it went dark in the room' (4.8.318). In *The Idiot*, the thunderstorm also approaches during the Prince's solipsistic reflection. He is about to enter the hotel where he will have the seizure: 'It was at that moment very dark: the storm cloud came over, swallowing up the evening light, and just as the prince was near the house, the cloud suddenly opened and poured down rain' (2.5.233). When he reaches the top of a spiral staircase, the Prince is attacked by his 'spiritual brother' Rogozhin, who is about to stab him with a garden knife. At this moment, the Prince has an epileptic fit:

> His consciousness instantly went out, and there was total darkness. He had had a fit of epilepsy, which had left him very long ago. It is known that these fits, *falling fits* [падучая] properly speaking, come instantaneously. In these moments the face, especially the eyes, suddenly becomes extremely distorted. Convulsions and spasms seize the whole body and all the features of the face. A dreadful, unimaginable scream, unlike anything, bursts from the breast; everything human suddenly disappears, as it were, in this scream, and it is quite impossible, or at least very difficult, for the observer to imagine and allow that this is the man himself screaming. It may even seem as if someone else were screaming from inside the man. At least many people have explained their impression that way, and there are many whom the sight of a man in a falling fit

> fills with a decided and unbearable terror, which even has something mystical in it. (2.5.235, 8:195)

The passage describes the seizure in detail: convulsion, spasm, frothing, screaming, and, most importantly, the impairment of consciousness. Like the thunderstorm which splits and the earthquake which cracks, consciousness instantly collapses as the fit arrives. The seizure also causes 'everything human suddenly [to] disappear' and create a sense of mystical terror.

In his essay 'The "Uncanny"' (*Das Unheimliche*, 1919), Freud suggests that the sight of an epileptic seizure resembles the movement of an automaton and evokes the uncanny, a peculiar and mixed feeling of the familiar and unfamiliar (homely and unhomely). In his discussion of E. T. A. Hoffman's tale 'The Sand-man', a text Dostoevsky may have read, Freud suggests that the falling of the eyeballs from the automaton Ophelia is uncanny and evokes the fear of castration.[28] Freud does not directly discuss epilepsy in the essay, but the seizure — which causes extreme distortion, the 'doubling' of screaming and 'decided and unbearable' terror — suggests the peculiar feeling of being familiar and unfamiliar at the same time. Dostoevsky's emphasis on the image of the falling of the Prince recalls the reference to Caesar's falling sickness, which can be seen as the 'castration' of male ruling power. Alyosha is described as being 'cut down' in an epileptic seizure (*The Brothers Karamazov*). A huge machine is said to have devoured the body of Christ in a painting (*The Idiot*). In the same context, Prince Myshkin reflects feverishly on the guillotine. He has a presentiment that he will be stabbed to death. Castration recurs in the novels and represents a destructive force which attracts and repels the subject.

In her book *Unconscious Structure in The Idiot: A Study in Literature and Psychoanalysis*, Elizabeth Dalton provides a psychoanalytical reading of the Prince's epilepsy in a section entitled 'An Epileptic Mode of Being', which she borrows from Robert Lord. She understands epilepsy as a psychic battlefield among the id, ego, and superego:

> The sexual and aggressive feelings usually experienced by Myshkin in the disguised masochistic form of suffering rush into the ego with an effect of ecstatic joyful release. But the ego cannot tolerate the force of these energies in their original unmodified form, nor can it allow their meaning to rise into conscious awareness. The moment of orgiastic release is followed by the total eclipse of the ego in the epileptic seizure. The fit is also the revenge of the superego, which can be deposed only temporarily; for the uninhibited release of sexual and aggressive energy it exacts the talion penalty of symbolic castration and death. The instinctual drives are once more experienced under the negative sign of superego, in the form of asceticism and suffering.[29]

Dalton suggests that the ecstatic moments represent the animalistic tendency which has been repressed in the id. Neither the ego nor the superego can tolerate these primitive desires. Therefore the seizure is evoked to 'punish' the id. Dalton's reading makes a parallel between a psychic structure and epilepsy. It presumes that epilepsy has to do with moral judgment: the seizure represents the punishment of the release of animalistic instinct.

Dalton does for Prince Myshkin what Freud does for Dostoevsky. In his 1928 essay 'Dostoevsky and Parricide', published as the preface to a German edition of *The Brothers Karamazov*, Freud suggests that the writer is driven by a 'very strong destructive instinct', which is comparable to that of a sinner or criminal:

> His personality retained sadistic traits in plenty, which show themselves in his irritability, his love of tormenting and his intolerance even towards people he loved, and which appear also in the way in which, as an author, he treats his readers.[30]

This observation was also made in the essay 'A Cruel Talent' (1882) by the critic and sociologist N. K. Mikhailovsky, who argues that Dostoevsky not only enjoyed tormenting his literary characters, but was also compelled to torment his readers with his ideas and long-winded narrating style.[31]

On the other hand, Freud elaborates on Dostoevsky's 'cruel talent', saying that the writer showed a 'great need of love and enormous capacity for love', which seems opposed to the idea that he was a sadist. Freud resolves the contradiction by saying that the destructive instinct is turned towards the writer himself, characterizing Dostoevsky as a moral masochist: 'Thus in little things he was a sadist towards others, and in bigger things a sadist towards himself, in fact a masochist — that is to say the mildest, kindliest, most helpful person possible' (236). The masochist, subservient to the superego, acts 'against his own interest' and ultimately 'destroys his own real existence'.[32] For Freud, the epileptic seizure is an expression of the destructive instinct turned inward. The destructive instinct in Dostoevsky anticipates one of the most controversial concepts in Freudian psychoanalysis, that is, the death drive, which Laplanche and Pontalis call the drive *par excellence*.[33] I will come back to Freud's idea of sadomasochism in my discussion of *Humiliated and Insulted*. I will also discuss the psychoanalyst's theories on dream, hysteria, and memory. The use of Freud in rethinking Dostoevsky throughout this book is based on the premise that the epileptic mode of being is unthinkable without involving the analysis of the body. The seizures that appear in the novels are not only the end result of an intensified consciousness, but also a symptom which points to what has been denied, disavowed, or repressed in the texts. Rethinking Dostoevsky with Freud therefore implies a multilayered understanding of the texts. These layers are most often in contradiction. They form the basis of a confused and decentred self, which distinguishes the epileptic mode of being.

The destructive tendency in Dostoevsky's epilepsy can be further explained with another literary reference. In Euripides' tragedy *Bacchae*, Pentheus, the king of Thebes, forbids his people to worship Dionysus, who later punishes Pentheus by burning his palace and having him ripped to shreds by the maenads. Dionysus wanders all over the world, accompanied by Silenus and a wild army of satyrs and maenads. He makes his followers celebrate him by dancing insanely, like the psychic epidemic of the St Vitus's dance. Part of the chorus reads:

> And with shouts [Dionysus] rouses the scattered bands,
> Sets their feet dancing,
> As he shakes his delicate locks to the wild wind.
> And amidst the frenzy of song he shouts like thunder:
> 'On, on! Run, dance, delirious, possessed!'[34]

Dionysus is seen as the god of thunderstorms and more than once is he called 'Bromius' by the chorus ('noisy', 'boisterous'; *βρέμειν* means 'to roar'), which suggests the noise of thunder.[35] The moment when the maenads rip Pentheus into pieces marks his 'thunderous', disintegrating power.

Nietzsche makes a similar connection between epilepsy and Dionysus. In *The Birth of Tragedy*, he discusses Raphael's last painting, *Transfiguration* (1520), in terms of the Dionysian and Apollonian forces. Apollo is the god of light, prophecy, and medicine, and is associated with discipline, beauty of form, and individual identity.[36] On the other hand, Dionysus is the god of wine and tragedy, and his worship, recalling Euripides' *Bacchae*, involved intoxication, violence, madness, and the loss of identity.[37] Nietzsche sees the Apollonian and the Dionysian as two competing and complementary forces at work in Greek art.

Raphael's *Transfiguration* combines two scenes in the Bible: the upper part shows Christ's transfiguration on the high mountain and the lower part depicts an epileptic boy with his parents and other disciples in awe. After the transfiguration, Christ encounters a crowd of people. One of them approaches Christ and asks him to cure his epileptic son:

> Master, I have brought unto thee my son, which hath a dumb spirit; And wheresoever he taketh him, he teareth him: and he foameth, and gnasheth with his teeth, and pineth away [...] when he saw him, straightway the spirit tare him; and he fell on the ground, and wallowed foaming. And he asked his father, How long is it ago since this came unto him? And he said, Of a child. And ofttimes it hath cast him into the fire, and into the waters, to destroy him [...] When Jesus saw that the people came running together, he rebuked the foul spirit, saying unto him, *Thou* dumb and deaf spirit, I charge thee, come out of him, and enter no more into him. And *the spirit* cried, and rent him sore, and came out of him: and he was as one dead; insomuch that many said, He is dead. But Jesus took him by the hand, and lifted him up; and he arose. (Mark 9: 17–27)[38]

In the parallel narrative of St Matthew the father describes the son as a 'lunatic'. Lunacy and epilepsy were understood as synonymous by the Church fathers, who affirmed that both were due to unclean spirits. The 'spirit' causes the young boy to jump into fire and waters, fall on the ground and to froth — all these symptoms were identified as those of epilepsy by ancient physicians.[39] The 'dumb and deaf' spirit (or 'deaf and mute') can be seen as a self-destructive 'epileptic spirit'. In fact, the 'deaf and dumb' spirit is referred to in *The Idiot* to describe the Prince's second epileptic seizure: a 'wild shout of the "spirit that convulsed and dashed down" the unfortunate man' (4.7.554).[40] And in *Crime and Punishment*, Petersburg's cityscape is described as 'deaf and dumb', suggesting the city is 'epileptic' by nature: 'An inexplicable chill always breathed on [Raskolnikov] from this splendid panorama; for him the magnificent picture was filled with a mute and deaf spirit' (2.2.114). In *Transfiguration*, the 'deaf and dumb' spirit which destroys the epileptic boy represents violence, grotesque, and the loss of identity. As Nietzsche writes:

> the lower half with the possessed boy, his despairing bearers, and the helplessly fearful disciples, shows us the reflection of eternal original suffering, of the sole ground of the world: 'appearance' here is the reflection of the eternal contradiction, of the father of things.[41]

The lower part, which shows pain and chaotic emotions among the disciples, is in contradiction with the upper part, which shows the sublime and lofty image of Christ, allowing 'a brilliant hovering in purest bliss and painless contemplation through beaming wide-open eyes' (31). The upper part recalls the Underground Man's phrase 'the refinement of everything beautiful and lofty' (1.4.13). Nietzsche continues: 'Here we have before our eyes, rendered in the highest symbolism of art, that Apollonian world of beauty and its substratum, the horrific wisdom of Silenus, and we understand intuitively their reciprocal necessity' (31). Although Dionysus is not mentioned, we know that Silenus was a companion and tutor of the wine god. In *Bacchae*, he wanders all over the world along with Dionysus and a wild army of satyrs and maenads. In other words, the lower part of *Transfiguration* reflects the Dionysian 'horrific wisdom' — chaos, contradictions, violence, and dissolution of identity — which is crystallized in the wild scream of the epileptic boy who is yet to be healed in the picture.

Epilepsy and the Moment

I have discussed the historical and literary references to epilepsy in Dostoevsky's works, suggesting that these references in various ways point to the disruptive, fracturing, and violent moment of the attack of epilepsy. I have called the previous section 'The History of Epilepsy', but I am not so much interested in tracing a linear and homogeneous history of Dostoevsky's epilepsy as showing how multiple references to the illness are presented polyphonically in his works. My approach to the history of epilepsy follows that of Oswei Temkin, the author of the classic study, *The Falling Sickness: A History of Epilepsy from the Greeks to the Beginnings of Modern Neurology* (1945, 1971). In the preface, he writes:

> There is no unanimity about the range of the concept of epilepsy, and the nature of the disease is as yet obscure. For, on the one hand, there are many organic diseases which may lead to the same syndrome as it exhibited in 'genuine' epilepsy; on the other hand, it is very difficult, if not impossible, to draw a distinct borderline between epilepsy and certain cases of severe hysteria. The broader the point of view from which epilepsy is studied, the more the condition tends to lose its identity and merge into the domain of convulsive states, encompassing many 'epilepsies' of different origin.[42]

The history of epilepsy is different from, to use Temkin's example, the history of tuberculosis. In the latter case, the historian can apply a critical standard to the past and be able to say whether a medical case is actually tuberculosis or not. But in the former case, there is hardly a progressive or linear development in the study of epilepsy before the rise of modern neurology: 'we may easily decry as false what the future will prove to be true' (ix). Thanks to the massive and divergent receptions of epilepsy in the past, Temkin's encyclopaedic study is that of 'the opinions of laymen, philosophers and theologians, as well as those of physicians' (ix). The book is a collection of historical fragments about epilepsy rather than a teleological reading of the disease's development. It should be also noted that Temkin begins *The Falling Sickness* from Hippocrates and finishes with the psychiatrist Charcot. The history of epilepsy came to a point of epistemological shift by the end of the nineteenth century: it was then treated in accordance with scientific knowledge derived from methods such as statistics, hospital observation, and pathological anatomy. Temkin writes: 'Thus we can say that until the nineteenth century, the history of epilepsy was the history of the falling sickness' (x). With the emphasis on 'the falling sickness', Temkin's book archives the social and ideological opinions of epilepsy until the end of the nineteenth century, enabling a diversified range of 'voices' to be represented in the illness's long history.

As one Dostoevsky critic puts it, the meaning of epilepsy is always mediated by one's health, diet, and psychological stress. The epileptic seizure is 'dependent on history, intelligence, imagination and the responses of the others'.[43] Instead of seeing how the present-day understanding of epilepsy illuminates Dostoevsky's novels, this book is more interested in the writer's subjective reading of the disease, and the way in which he makes use of relevant medical opinions from different periods to represent the illness. As the previous section has shown, Dostoevsky's references to epilepsy are not restricted to a particular discipline or period. The world of epilepsy in Dostoevsky is a constructed mixture of opinions from the Greeks, the Bible, medieval and Renaissance scholarship, and modern criminology. Such creative referentiality in the writing of epilepsy would be another way of thinking Mikhail Bakhtin's proposition that Dostoevsky is the creator of the polyphonic novel.[44] That is to say, the author's view of his own epileptic condition does not dominate the other historical opinions of epilepsy. The non-hierarchical interaction between the two sides of views creates an unfinalized reading of epilepsy in Dostoevsky's works, which the following chapters intend to explore.

It is true that references to epilepsy from multiple historical periods permeate Dostoevsky's works. But it is also true that Dostoevsky makes them depict one particular moment, that is, the moment of an epileptic seizure, during which consciousness collapses. As I have discussed in the opening, this book takes that moment of seizure as the caesura that suspends the flow of representation. Epilepsy in this book therefore will be understood as being outside the realm of historical action. That is to say, epilepsy cannot be historicized in the world of Dostoevsky due to its repetitive and disruptive quality.

If consciousness ceases when the seizure arrives, how can the writer possibly describe it? Put another way, if the caesura is unrepresentable, how can the writer possibly speak of it? We could find illuminations from Mikhail Bakhtin's comment on Dostoevsky's representation of death, which I understand as analogous to that of epilepsy. In his notebooks for the second edition of his book on Dostoevsky, Bakhtin writes:

> Dostoevsky *never* depicts death from within. Final agony and death are observed by others. Death cannot be a fact of consciousness itself. [...] Death from within, that is, one's own death consciously perceived, does not exist for anyone: not for the dying person, nor for others; it does not exist at all. Precisely this consciousness for its own sake, which neither knows nor has the ultimate word, is the object of depiction in Dostoevsky's world.[45]

Bakhtin contrasts Dostoevsky with Tolstoy, who is interested in 'what it feels like to die inside the person who is dying'.[46] This is absent in Dostoevsky, because consciousness collapses when a person dies. The writer is primarily interested in depicting the activities of consciousness. As I have shown earlier in the passage from *The Idiot*, just when the epileptic seizure breaks out, the narrative's point of view switches from within the Prince's consciousness to outside it. Just as death is never depicted from within, an epileptic seizure is never depicted from within the epileptic's consciousness.

And yet, before the attack of the seizure, the Prince keeps coming back to reflect on the seizure, fantasizing it as evoking eternity (he says he finally understands the extraordinary phrase 'time shall be no more' from the Book of Revelation when he has his last seizure (2.5.227)). Bakhtin goes on to say: 'In Dostoevsky's world death finalizes nothing, because death does not affect the most important thing in this world — consciousness for its own sake' (290). On the one hand, epilepsy and death point to the annihilative moment, which cannot be consciously perceived. On the other hand, Dostoevsky's heroes anxiously and continually imagine that particular moment. Epilepsy, like death, finalizes nothing; it creates infinite possibilities for consciousness and does not predetermine personalities. Bakhtin argues that 'Dostoevsky always represents a person *on the threshold* of a final decision, at a moment of *crisis*, at an unfinalizable — and *unpredeterminable* — turning point for his soul'.[47] How do we relate this argument to epilepsy and death? Or, how do we relate the concept of infinitude in relation to finitude? This book takes the concept of 'unfinalizability' as a starting point, not only reading it as a structural characteristic in Dostoevsky, but also as a mode of modern existence distinguished by compulsion and excess. In the following chapters, Dostoevsky's writings will be understood as incessant depictions of consciousness which are always punctuated by a rupture, that is, the moment which cannot be consciously perceived but which the subject is anxious to capture, master, and beautify. Such anxiety to grasp the ungraspable is often marked by a kind of 'mystic terror' recorded in both the writer's novels and his medical records, to which I shall now move.

Epilepsy and Mystic Terror

The sources of the following seizure records are James Rice's *Dostoevsky and the Healing Art* (1985), Jacques Catteau's *Dostoyevsky and the Process of Literary Creation* (1989), and Joseph Frank's five-volume biography.[48] Rice sees epilepsy as an isolated disease which is central to understanding the significance of Dostoevsky's creations. His book is mainly a biographical study of the moments when major epileptic fits took place in the writer's life. One-third of the book also suggests the nineteenth-century medical literature Dostoevsky might have read. Rice argues that the writer's significance 'lies not in the denial of illness but in its acceptance and mastery, and in the discovery (and invention, to be sure) of polymorphous and polyphonic values precisely within his pathological condition, which he consciously and ingeniously negotiated through art'.[49] It is true that Dostoevsky keeps coming back to the subject of illness in his novels, and it is also true that the writing of epilepsy, as I will argue, is frequently represented as a way of gaining mastery over experience. But whether this attempt at mastery succeeds or becomes a therapeutic art is questionable.

Besides, Rice's book offers few in-depth textual analyses of the novels in proving the point. Jacques Catteau's book provides invaluable information on Dostoevsky's medical history, particularly his selection of two medical reports which record the writer's 'mystical terror', a crucial phrase for understanding the writer's response to his condition.[50] Catteau's chapter makes an interesting comparison between the epilepsy in the writer's life and the epilepsy in his works. But, as Edward Wasiolek puts it, the chapter did not develop a substantial argument out of the comparison.[51] Catteau did not give detailed analysis of Dostoevsky's novels, but his views are insightful. For instance, connecting epilepsy with the process of creating the novels, he says that Dostoevsky's writings are driven by a 'violent and convulsive' impetus and are inclined to a form of excess.[52] My book further explores Catteau's view by rethinking Dostoevsky's works not only in terms of the obsessive impetus to think about a particular moment or an idea, but also by considering the sudden rupture of that impetus. Catteau puts his emphasis on the former, whereas mine is on the latter, what I called the caesura, the break, the collapse of consciousness. Joseph Frank's biography has been very helpful in terms of Dostoevsky's biographical details. Particularly useful is his discussion of the execution of the Petrashevsky Circle in 1849 and the Petersburg novel *Humiliated and Insulted*. The above studies take a biographical approach to Dostoevsky's epilepsy. They treat the process of literary creation as a way for the writer to cope with or accept his own illnesses. My project works in a different direction: it explores new meanings of epilepsy in the created works and suggests how they can help us to rethink Dostoevsky's life. By the writer's life I refer to two aspects in particular: the ideas that he was haunted by epilepsy and that he was haunted by death after his survival from a mock execution in 1849.

From the age of twenty-six, Dostoevsky had an epileptic seizure almost once every three weeks until he died of a haemorrhage at the age of sixty. Thinking retrospectively, Dostoevsky said to Vsevolod Solovyev (brother of the philosopher Vladimir Solovyev):

> Two years before Siberia, at the time of my various literary difficulties and quarrels, I was the victim of some sort of strange and unbearably torturing nervous illness. I cannot tell you what these hideous sensations were; but I remember them vividly; it often seemed to me that I was dying, and the truth is — real death came and then went away again.[53]

The year when 'real death came and then went away again' was 1847. The writer was twenty-six and suffering from some kind of severe and progressive mental illness, which only when he was in the army in 1856 did he realize was epilepsy. He often had a fit while he was asleep which left him bloody and battered upon awakening. This kind of attack made him uncertain whether he would survive the night. After each seizure, he was haunted by 'objectless fear', 'mystic depression', and a 'sense of guilt from a crime not remembered'.[54] It is not unreasonable to suggest that the writer saw epilepsy as a form of death.

During the early years (1846–49), Dostoevsky read a wide range of medical literature concerning the brain, the nervous system, and the psyche by borrowing books from his physician and close friend Dr Stepan Dmitrievich Yanovsky (1817–97).

Apart from that, he had daily meetings with the doctor two times per day to discuss medicine and other subjects such as religion. Although Yanovsky did not mention epilepsy when Dostoevsky suffered from apoplectic fits, the writer himself might have thought about the possibility of having epilepsy.[55]

In 1846, after publishing *Poor Folk*, Dostoevsky was under enormous pressure to maintain his newly established reputation. Possibly because of that he began to suffer from what he called 'a severe shock to the whole nervous system'.[56] Regarding his nervous disorder, Dostoevsky recorded that someone was snoring beside him at night. It turned out that it was actually a hallucination, which anticipated the onset of apoplexy (*kondrashka*), which is a kind of stroke.[57] The phrase *kondrashka*, as Rice points out, was a popular term for a sudden death.[58] That same phrase was used in the short story 'Mr Prokharchin' (1846), in which the hero is stricken by 'a fainting spell, paralytic stupor, or *kondrashka*'.[59] Because the fits made him appear dead Dostoevsky was very anxious about being buried alive. His friends and brother reported that he was always disturbed and terrified by the idea of 'lethargic sleep', a phrase which is found again to describe Stavrogin napping mysteriously in *Demons* (2.1.229–30).

Previously, I have quoted the passage from *The Idiot* showing that the sight of the Prince's falling fit arouses in the observer a 'decided and unbearable' horror (2.5.235). Although Dostoevsky could not see himself having the fit, he experienced immense horror every time before and after the seizure. Among the various states he had gone through, I would like to draw attention to the one he called 'mystic terror'. In the medical report of 1870, he used the phrase twice in two consecutive entries:

> At three o'clock in the morning a fit of extreme violence, in the lobby, while awake. Fall and wound on the forehead. Without remembering anything and without being aware of it, I carried the lighted candle in a perfect state into the bedroom, closed the window and only guessed later that I had had a fit ... I was beginning to calm down when I suddenly had another fit ... When I regained consciousness I had a horrible headache and was unable to speak properly for a long time. Anya spent the night with me (*Extreme mystic terror*) ... *Impossible to think of work; profound hypochondria during the night* ... (10 February)
>
> Fit during sleep, I had just gone to bed at ten past five in the morning ... weak ... although the consequences of the fit (that is, *heaviness and even pain in the head, nervous disturbance, nervous laugh and mystic terror*) last longer than before ... (23 February)[60]

In the first passage, the writer records consecutive seizures, after which he experienced 'extreme mystic terror' and lost the ability to work. Mystic terror refers to the extreme fear of death or the fear of one's own destruction. This is confirmed by the fact that Dostoevsky uses the same phrase to describe the moment before his expected execution in 1849. On the morning of 23 April 1849, Dostoevsky was arrested for participating in the revolutionary Petrashevsky Circle. The group studied and disseminated writings by Fourier and Saint-Simon, the leading figures of French utopian socialism. The writer, besides accusations of bearing 'the spirit of opposition to the government' and 'a desire to alter the existing state of things', was charged specifically for reading an outraged letter written by Belinsky to Gogol,

FIG. 1. The mock execution of the Petrashevtsy (the members of the Petrashevsky Circle). From *Feodor Mikhailovich Dostoevsky v portretakh, illyustratsiyakh, dokumentakh*, ed. V. S. Nechaeva (Moscow, 1972)

calling the latter a traitor to the cause of reform.[61] Dostoevsky and other members were confined in the Peter and Paul fortress for eight months. They were found guilty of 'plotting to subvert public order' and sentenced to death by firing squad before a crowd of 3,000 people on Semenovsky Square.[62] The names of the circle members were read out. Fifteen of them were condemned to death, and a priest invited them to confess to their crimes and repent.[63] Tsar Nicholas had decided to revoke the death sentence, but he ordered the soldiers to act as if it was real up until the last minute. At the end, the death sentence was commuted to four years of hard labour in Siberia and four years of military service.

Among the victims who were supposed to be executed, Nikolai Grigoryev, who had already suffered a mental derangement in the fortress, never recovered his senses after the reprieve and remained a mental invalid for the rest of his life. In another account, a colleague who stood next to Dostoevsky recalled the writer's behaviour:

> Dostoevsky was quite excited, he recalled *Le dernier jour d'un condamné* of Victor Hugo, and, going up to Speshnev, said: '*Nous serons avec le Christ*' (we shall be with Christ). '*Un peu de poussière*' (A bit of dust) — the latter answered with a twisted smile.[64]

A word of faith was met with nihilistic sarcasm.

In his short story 'The Meek Girl' (1876), Dostoevsky calls *Le dernier jour d'un condamné* (*The Last Day of a Condemned Man*) a masterpiece.[65] He goes on to write:

> [Victor Hugo] permitted [the fantasy] that a man who has been condemned to death would be able (and have the time) to make notes not only on his last day, but even in his last hour and, quite literally, at his very last moment. (254)

As it is described, Hugo's short story is about a condemned man writing from a first-person perspective his thoughts until he is sent to the guillotine. It is not surprising that Dostoevsky recalled the story at the critical moment of life and death. The critic Liza Knapp suggested that the writer could have in mind a particular passage from Hugo's story. Hugo's condemned man writes:

> Condemned to death!
> Well, why not. *Men* — I remember reading in some book where that was the only good part — *men are all condemned to death with indefinite stays of execution.* How is my situation now any different?[66]

Hugo's ingenious statement not only captures the straightforward fact that everyone is subject to natural death, but it can also be read as a commentary on Dostoevsky's life, which had been traumatized by epilepsy. Epilepsy, appearing as death which advances and retreats unexpectedly, causes in Dostoevsky the state of 'indefinite stays of execution'. Despite the fact that the writer said he would be with Christ, the moment before his supposed death was by no means peaceful. Many years later, according to the writer's friend Orest Miller, Dostoevsky described the memory of that last moment from a very different perspective: 'He felt only a mystic terror, and was completely dominated by the thought that in perhaps five minutes he would be going to another unknown life'.[67] The phrase 'mystic terror' returns. Twenty years after the mock execution, Prince Myshkin in *The Idiot* speculates on what a condemned convict has in mind in the last moment of the beheading. The convict is also horrified by the unknowable when death takes place: 'The ignorance of and loathing for this new thing that would be and would come presently were terrible' (1.5.61). The passage illuminates the meaning of the mystic terror: death is fearful mainly because it is beyond human experience and cannot be known. Dostoevsky could be right that he will be with Christ, but there is no guarantee. In this way, mystical terror has to do with the fear of ignorance of the moment in the future. The subject — who is in the indefinite stays of execution and knows nothing about the moment — is petrified and placed into an inert position. Perhaps that is why Dostoevsky later writes in *A Writer's Diary* (1873) that mystic terror is 'the most colossal power over the human soul. [...] A sense of horror is something pitiless; it withers the heart and hardens it toward any lofty or tender feeling' ('Vlas', 1.165).

Writing the Impossible

On the one hand, the moment of an epileptic seizure evokes the fear of death. On the other hand, it is described as ecstatic, resembling the state of 'eternal harmony'. Dostoevsky's friend Strakhov wrote in 1883:

> Many times F. M. told me that before an attack he would have minutes of an enraptured state. 'For several instants', he would say, 'I experience a happiness that is impossible in an ordinary state, and of which other people have no conception. I feel full harmony in myself and in the whole world, and the

> feeling is so strong and sweet that for a few seconds of such bliss one could give up ten years of life, perhaps all of life'.[68]

In the memoirs of Sophie Kovalevsky (whose older sister Dostoevsky had wished to marry), the professional mathematician reported a private conversation she had with the writer:

> 'I felt', said F.M., 'that heaven descended to earth and swallowed me. I really attained God, and was imbued with him. "Yes, God exists!" I cried. And I recall no more'. 'All of you healthy people,' he continued, 'don't even suspect what happiness is, that happiness which we epileptics experience for a second before an attack. Muhammad avows in his Koran that he saw Paradise and was in it. All the wise fools are convinced that he is simply a liar and deceiver. But no! He does not lie! He actually was in Paradise during an attack of epilepsy, from which he suffered just as I do. I don't know whether that blessedness lasts seconds or hours or months, but trust my word, all the joys which life can give I would not take in exchange for it!'[69]

Initially, we would have thought the epileptic seizure meant only pain and meaninglessness to Dostoevsky. But here a new meaning is added to it. The moment is not only a form of simulated death, but according to the writer, it is also inseparable from a certain ecstasy. This epileptic moment, which consists of the experience of death and the pleasure of eternal harmony, suggests *jouissance*, which I understand as an interruption of consciousness, an orgasmic, even violent form of pleasure that is removed from language and disconfirms identity.

There is hardly any empirical evidence that Dostoevsky did experience the ecstatic moment. Both James Rice and Jacques Catteau quote a study carried out by the French epileptologist Henri Gastaut, who argued that Dostoevsky 'never experienced the ecstatic aura he gives to Prince Myshkin and which was attributed to him by two of his contemporaries'.[70] Jacques Catteau picks up on Gastaut's point, arguing that Dostoevsky's epileptic visions

> may be no more than a sensation of vertigo rationalized after the event, like an elevation or assumption. Possibly it was Dostoevsky's secret inclination towards themes of universal harmony, eternity, God, which gave the aura [sic. the moment before the attack of epilepsy] its feeling of happiness and joy. In short, Dostoevsky may have mythologized the aura so as to experience a transcendence which he could not reach by other means.[71]

Whether the epileptic writer really had a vision just before the onset of a seizure is immaterial. Rather, what I am interested in is the fact that Dostoevsky keeps returning to this ecstatic moment in his writings. It should be remembered that consciousness collapses immediately after the infinitely brief moment of ecstasy. Dostoevsky is fascinated by this rupture, this moment of incomprehensibility. Perhaps it is because the moment is incomprehensible and outside the realm of experience that the writer becomes anxious to speak, to write and even to mythologize it. In this way, Dostoevsky's works are driven by the compulsion to represent the unrepresentable.

At the beginning of this chapter I have suggested that Dostoevsky's novels can be understood in terms of an incessant anxiety to experience the moment of epileptic ecstasy. But the attempt is always destroyed by the seizure which is inseparable from the ecstasy. I have also suggested that the ecstasy could be an imaginary construction that would enable the subject to master an unknown experience. It is this quixotic desire to experience the impossible and its continual failure that are at the heart of the epileptic mode of being. The following chapters further examine this desire through five of Dostoevsky's novels, which were written after his survival of the mock execution. That Dostoevsky is placed in indefinite stays of execution is integral to his epileptic condition, which has been described as death which constantly comes and goes. This is not to say that the pre-Siberian novels cannot be read as epileptic texts. In fact, the very first instance of epilepsy takes place in an early short story.[72]

The following chapters discuss references to epilepsy in each of the major novels and show how they illuminate a new perspective in rethinking Dostoevsky's works. The chapters take epilepsy as a trope for discussing the unrepresentable moment, during which idealistic expressions are subject to destruction. Chapter 1 examines *Humiliated and Insulted*, looking at the romantic idealist figure Vanya (Ivan Petrovich). On the one hand, he is an impoverished writer who pursues philanthropy and moral ideals. He sacrifices his personal interest in exchange for other people's benefits. Apparently, he is the selfless, naturally good figure of Dostoevsky. On the other hand, in his meeting with Prince Valkovsky, whose principal interest is sensual pleasure, Vanya's project of philanthropy is called into question.

By focusing on a dialogue between Vanya and the Prince, I will show that philanthropy — which the novel connects with the state of being humiliated and insulted — is no less pleasurable than the Prince's libertinism. The difference between the Prince's libertinism and Vanya's philanthropy is only an apparent one. The Prince likes to mock what he calls the 'Schillerian types', giving them a shock by unveiling his own obscene habits. The chapter suggests that Vanya is in recurring horror, as his philanthropic project is constantly being challenged and problematized. The protagonist is petrified by the mystic terror every night when he writes his novel. I take the mystic terror as the 'epileptic' force, which, together with the terror caused by the Prince, challenges and suspends Vanya's philanthropic ideal. The chapter will further explore the problem of philanthropy by linking it with Kant's categorical imperative, looking at the ways in which Vanya does good for the sake of duty. The chapter will also discuss Sigmund Freud's 'The Economic Problem of Masochism' and Jacques Lacan's essay *Kant with Sade*, suggesting that Vanya's philanthropy involves moral masochism and repression under the institution of the moral law.

Chapter 2 continues with the rereading of idealism by examining *Crime and Punishment*, in which the Petersburg cityscape is described as 'deaf and dumb' when Raskolnikov has a vision on the river Neva. The chapter examines this vision to find out why the city receives such description. I will look at the city's eclectic architecture, which creates an effect of disorientation for the Petersburgers. Their subjectivity is always decentred and figuratively seized upon by the chaotic cityscape. I will also compare the eclecticism in architecture to Eisenstein's conception of cinematic montage, suggesting that Dostoevsky's Petersburg is pre-cinematic. Images of the city are discrete and yet pieced together in the novel.

Montage becomes another way for thinking how the epileptic city creates the split subject.

This chapter also looks at Raskolnikov's dreams, showing how the schismatic state of being is marked there as well. In fact, there is not much difference between Dostoevsky's dreams and his Petersburg. I will focus on the mare-beating dream to show that 'crime' and 'punishment' coincide and implicate each other. Raskolnikov says he wants to kill like a Napoleon and speak the 'new word'. But every time he thinks of transgressing by killing the pawnbroker, he is also haunted by the desire for punishment. The 'Napoleonic theory' is nothing but an ideal which Raskolnikov uses to justifies his murder. But the schism of the protagonist shows the limit of that ideal. Both the city's architecture and Raskolnikov's interiority show that Dostoevsky's Petersburg and its inhabitants are consistently schismatic and therefore 'epileptic'.

Chapter 3 examines *The Idiot* and further spells out the problem of idealism. Prince Myshkin, as the Introduction has shown, contemplates the moment just before the seizure, fantasizing about the possibility of having an eternal life. Similarly, the Prince is obsessed with a convict's thoughts in the final moments before he is decapitated by the guillotine blade. This last moment is also what happened to Dostoevsky himself in 1849. For the Prince, the convict, though terrified, is compelled to contemplate an afterlife before the guillotine blade strikes. The Prince keeps reflecting on this last moment, hoping to freeze it and turn it into eternity. But the wish is immediately cut off as the seizure breaks out or the blade falls. The idealistic wish for an eternal life is always dwarfed by the material aspect of the seizure and the execution. This will be further illuminated by the nihilist Ippolit's discussion of Hans Holbein's *The Body of the Dead Christ in the Tomb* (1521). The vivid deadliness of Christ in the painting leads Ippolit to think that the Resurrection will not happen. The religious ideal is once again countered by materialism.

Chapter 4 looks at the political novel *Demons*, showing the ways in which the failure of revolution is integral to the failure of the will. Kirilov, one of the revolutionary group members, plans to commit suicide in order to prove his absolute freedom and his insubordination to God. He says he will become a man-god if he manages to kill himself of his own volition. Similarly, he experiences the ecstatic moments which Prince Myshkin also has just before an epileptic seizure. Kirilov contemplates the possibility of overcoming those moments and extending the ecstasy to eternity. In both cases — the suicide and his fantasy of epilepsy — Kirilov is driven by the desire to freeze, to seize upon the moment. But continuing the argument in Chapter 3, I will show that Kirilov's will to possess death and epilepsy is insatiable. This is because both the moment of death and the epileptic seizure are by definition beyond the realm of experience. In this way, Kirilov's will to death and epilepsy is continually unfulfilled and postponed. This chapter will also look at Stavrogin's confession and Shatov's discussion of nationalism in relation to the failure of the will. I will also bring in the French writer Maurice Blanchot's discussion of Kirilov in *The Space of Literature*, Nietzsche on nihilism in *On the Genealogy of Morals*, and his notebook's commentary on *Demons*.

Chapter 5 examines Dostoevsky's final novel, *The Brothers Karamazov*, suggesting how the epileptic seizure is understood as the moment at which a violent and silenced family history is unveiled. When the father gives an account of how he sexually abused his wife, the youngest brother, Alyosha Karamazov, has a hysterical seizure, which is identical to his mother's. The chapter will take Alyosha's hysteria as a form of 'feminine' epilepsy. I will discuss Breuer and Freud's *Studies in Hysteria*, showing how the male hysteric suffers from his reminiscences. By reminiscences I mean the memory of the father's sexual violence which has been repressed. Only through rereading the hysterical seizure are we able to rearticulate the repression of violence as well as the violence of repression. This chapter follows Walter Benjamin's discussion of history in his *Theses on the Philosophy of History*, treating the hysterical seizure as 'a moment of danger' during which a repressed past flits by. To reread *The Brothers Karamazov* means to reread symptomatically a family history that is violent and repressed.

The Conclusion will show that the epileptic mode of being — characterized by the alternation between the continual desire to seize upon the moment and the annihilation of that desire — is marked by what I call an infinite postponement. I will revisit Dostoevsky's mock execution in 1849 and compare it with the young man who survives an execution in Maurice Blanchot's *The Instant of My Death*. The young man turns out to be Blanchot himself, who survived a German military shooting in 1944. Both writers survived the executions, but the instant of their death stays with them, recalling Dostoevsky saying that his epilepsy is like death which comes and goes, or Hugo's condemned man saying that men are thrown into indefinite stays of execution. The writers' death sentences are infinitely postponed, causing their writings to be 'posthumous'. Likewise, the desire to comprehend, to possess, to master the moment is infinitely postponed, producing a Dostoevskian subject which is deferred and unfinalized.

Notes to the Introduction

1. I find the following studies of Dostoevsky's novels most helpful to my research: Mikhail Bakhtin, *Problems of Dostoevsky's Poetics*, ed. and trans. by Caryl Emerson (Minneapolis and London: University of Minnesota Press, 1984). Jacques Catteau, *Dostoyevsky and the Process of Literary Creation*, trans. by Audrey Littlewood (Cambridge: Cambridge University Press, 1989), rather fragmentary in structure, but often insightful; Robert L. Jackson, *Dostoevsky's Quest for Form: A Study of his Philosophy of Art* (New Haven: Yale University Press, 1966), helpful in explaining the writer's 'fantastic realism' (the appendix 'Dostoevsky and the Fine Arts' informs the discussion of Holbein's *Dead Christ* in the following chapter on *The Idiot*); Richard Peace, *Dostoyevsky: An Examination of the Major Novels* (London: Bristol Classical Press, 1992); Edward Wasiolek, *Dostoevsky: The Major Fiction* (Cambridge, MA: MIT Press, 1964). For biographical studies of Dostoevsky, see Joseph Frank, *Dostoevsky*, 5 vols (Princeton: Princeton University Press, 1976–2002); Leonid Grossman, *Dostoevsky: A Biography*, trans. by Mary Mackler (London: Allen Lane, Penguin, 1974); Konstantin Mochulsky, *Dostoevsky: His Life and Work*, trans. by Michael A. Minihan (Princeton: Princeton University Press, 1973).
2. Friedrich Hölderlin, 'Notes on the *Oedipus* and Notes on the *Antigone*', trans. by Jeremy Adler, in *Comparative Criticism*, v, ed. by William Shaffer (Cambridge: Cambridge University Press, 1983), 205–44 (p. 231).
3. Walter Benjamin, 'Goethe's *Elective Affinities*', trans. by Stanley Corngold, in *Selected Writings 1913–1926*, ed. by Marcus Bullock and Michael W. Jennings, i (Cambridge, MA and London: Harvard University Press, 1996), pp. 297–360 (pp. 340–41).

4. For further discussion of Benjamin's concept of the expressionless, see Winfried Menninghaus, 'Walter Benjamin's Variations of Imagelessness', *Critical Horizons: A Journal of Philosophy & Social Theory*, 14 (2013), 407–28.
5. Robert Lord, 'An Epileptic Mode of Being', in *Dostoevsky: Essays and Perspectives* (London: Chatto & Windus, 1970), pp. 81–101.
6. Alex de Jonge, *Dostoevsky and the Age of Intensity* (London: Secker & Warburg, 1975), p. 175.
7. For the historical facts of epilepsy, I have consulted Owsei Temkin, *The Falling Sickness: A History of Epilepsy from the Greeks to the Beginnings of Modern Neurology*, 2nd edn (Baltimore and London: Johns Hopkins Press, 1971). For the development of epilepsy since the beginning of modern neurology, see Walter J. Friedlander, *The History of Modern Epilepsy: The Beginning, 1865–1914* (Westport, CT and London: Greenwood Press, 2001).
8. See Temkin, 'The Doctrine of Epilepsy in the Hippocratic Writings', *Bulletin of the History of Medicine*, 1 (1933), 277–322.
9. Plato, *Timaeus*, trans. by R. G. Bury (Cambridge, MA and London: Harvard University Press, 1929), 85a–b, p. 228.
10. William Shakespeare, *The Norton Shakespeare*, ed. by Stephen Greenblatt, Walter Cohen, Jean Elizabeth Howard, and Katharine Eisaman Maus, Andrew Gurr (New York: W. W. Norton, 2008), pp. 1557–1613 (p. 1564).
11. See Terence Cawthorne, 'Julius Caesar and the Falling Sickness', *Proceedings of the Royal Society of Medicine*, 51 (1957), 1–4. Othello is another epileptic figure in Shakespeare. See John P. Emery, 'Othello's Epilepsy', *Psychoanalytic Review*, 46 (1959), 30–32. For other literary references in English literature, see Peter Wolf, 'Epilepsy in Literature', *Epilepsia*, 36 Supplement (1995), 12–17.
12. See Richard Pevear's note in *The Brothers Karamazov*, p. 783.
13. Treating epilepsy metaphorically distinguishes my work from a relatively recent and empirical investigation of epilepsy in Dostoevsky's novels. See Brian R. Johnson, *The Art of Dostoevsky's Falling Sickness* (Ann Arbor, MI: ProQuest, 2008).
14. See Temkin, *The Falling Sickness*, p. 366.
15. Cesare Lombroso, *The Man of Genius* (New York: Charles Scribner's Sons, 1895), pp. 337f.
16. Temkin, *The Falling Sickness*, p. 367.
17. Friedrich Nietzsche, *Twilight of the Idols, or How to Philosophize with a Hammer*, trans. by Duncan Large (New York: Oxford University Press, 2008), VII, par. 45.
18. See Eric V. D. Luft and Douglas G. Stenberg, 'Dostoevskii's Specific Influence on Nietzsche's Preface to *Daybreak*', *Journal of the History of Ideas*, 52 (1991), 441–61; see also C. A. Miller, 'Nietzsche's "Discovery" of Dostoevsky', *Nietzsche-Studien* (1973), 202–57.
19. In February 1887, Nietzsche wrote to his friend Overbeck:

    > I did not even know the name of Dostoevski just a few weeks ago — uneducated person that I am, not reading any journals. An accidental reach of an arm in a bookstore brought to my attention *L'esprit souterrain*, a work just translated into French [...] The instinct of kinship (or how should I name it?) spoke up immediately; my joy was extraordinary [...] (it is two novellas, the first really a piece of music, *very* strange, very *un*-German music; the second, a stroke of genius in psychology, a kind of self-derison of the *gnosi auto*).

    Quoted from *Selected Letters of Friedrich Nietzsche*, ed. and trans. by Christopher Middleton (Chicago: University of Chicago Press, 1969), p. 237. The French edition Nietzsche read was a combined edition of Dostoevsky's 'The Landlady' and *Notes from Underground.*
20. Friedrich Nietzsche, *Daybreak: Thoughts on the Prejudices of Morality*, trans. by R. J. Hollingdale (Cambridge: Cambridge University Press, 1982), par. 549, p. 550.
21. See Temkin, *The Falling Sickness*, p. 152. See Ibn Ishaq, *The Life of Muhammad*, trans. by A. Guillaume (Karachi: Oxford University Press, 1967), pp. 71–72.
22. The Byzantine historian Theophanes (d. *c.* 817) attributed Mohammed's vision of seeing the angel Gabriel and then falling down to the disease of epilepsy. See Temkin, *The Falling Sickness*, p. 153.
23. Mohammed, according to a German biographer Sprenger (1869), suffered from hysteria. See Temkin, *The Falling Sickness*, p. 372.

24. Temkin, p. 371.
25. Ibid.
26. On the subject of St Vitus and epilepsy, see E. R. Dodds, *The Greeks and the Irrational* (Berkeley, Los Angeles, and London: University of California Press, 1951), pp. 270–82; Temkin, *The Falling Sickness*, p. 109; Edward L. Murphy, 'The Saints of Epilepsy', *Medical History*, 3 (1959), 303–11.
27. See Walter Pagel, *Paracelsus: An Introduction to Philosophical Medicine in the Era of the Renaissance* (Basel and London: Karger, 1982). Also see Temkin, pp. 169–77.
28. See Sigmund Freud, 'The "Uncanny"' (1919), in *The Standard Edition of the Complete Psychological Works of Sigmund Freud*, trans. and ed. by James Strachey and others, XVII (London: Hogarth Press and the Institute of Psycho-Analysis, 1955), pp. 226–34.
29. Elizabeth Dalton, *Unconscious Structure in 'The Idiot': A Study in Literature and Psychoanalysis* (Princeton, NJ: Princeton University Press, 1979), p. 133.
30. Freud, *Writings on Art and Literature*, trans. by James Strachey (Stanford: Stanford University Press, 1997), p. 236.
31. See Marina Kanevskaya, *N. K. Mikhailovsky's Criticism of Dostoevsky: The Cruel Critic* (Lewiston, NY and Lampeter: Edwin Mellen Press, 2001).
32. Sigmund Freud, 'The Economic Problem of Masochism' (1924), in *On Metapsychology: Penguin Freud 11*, trans. by James Strachey (Harmondsworth: Penguin, 1984), p. 425.
33. '[The death drive] is the essence of the instinctual. [It] binds every wish, whether aggressive or sexual, to the wish for death'. Quoted in Nicholas Royle, *The Uncanny: An Introduction* (Manchester: Manchester University Press, 2003), p. 92.
34. Euripides, *Bacchae*, ed. by Philip Vellacott (Harmondsworth: Penguin, 1972), p. 196.
35. The name 'Bromius' is used to address Dionysus at least three times. Chorus: 'Take me O Bromius, take me and inspire Laughter and worship!' (205); Chorus: 'Bromius is with us, he shouts from prison the shout of victory!' (211); Dionysus: 'I and Bromius shall be Victors' (227).
36. Nietzsche compares the Apollonian with Schopenhauer's *principium individuationis* in the latter's *The World as Will and Representation*:

> As a sailor sits in a small boat in a boundless raging sea, surrounded on all sides by heaving mountainous waves, trusting to his frail vessel; so does the individual man sit calmly in the middle of the world of torment, trusting to the *principium individuationis*.

See *The Birth of Tragedy*, ed. by Douglas Smith (New York: Oxford University Press, 2008), p. 21.
37. See Douglas Smith's notes, ibid., pp. 133–34.
38. I have quoted from the King James Bible. Parallel versions are Matthew 17:14–20, Mark 9:14–29, and Luke 9:37–43.
39. Temkin, p. 91.
40. Cf. 'And as he was yet a coming, the devil threw him down, and tare *him*. And Jesus rebuked the unclean spirit, and healed the child, and delivered him again to his father' (Luke 9:42).
41. Nietzsche, *The Birth of Tragedy*, 4.31.
42. Temkin, *The Falling Sickness*, p. ix.
43. See Louis Breger's review of James Rice's *Dostoevsky and the Healing Art*, 'Dostoevskii and Medicine', *Slavic Review*, 45 (1986), 735–37. Also see Louis Breger, *Dostoevsky: The Author as Psychoanalyst* (New York: New York University Press, 1989). For Breger, Dostoevsky was trying to deal with his own neuroses through writing novels. Hence the writer is understood as a psychoanalyst. My argument diverges from this autobiographical approach.
44. Mikhail Bakhtin, *Problems of Dostoevsky's Poetics*, ed. and trans. by Caryl Emerson (Minneapolis and London: University of Minnesota Press, 1984), p. 36. Bakhtin's concept of polyphony has been compared to Nietzsche's Dionysus: see James M. Curtis, 'Michael Bakhtin, Nietzsche and Russian Pre-Revolutionary Thought', in *Nietzsche in Russia*, ed. by Bernice G. Rosenthal (Princeton: Princeton University Press, 1986), pp. 331–54.
45. Bakhtin, *Problems of Dostoevsky's Poetics*, p. 290. Bakhtin also discusses the representation of death in 'Author and Hero in Aesthetic Activity'. See *Art and Answerability: Early Philosophical Essays*, ed. by Michael Holquist and Vadim Liapunov, trans. by Vadim Liapunov (Austin: University of Texas Press, 1990), pp. 99–113.

46. Katerina Clark and Michael Holquist, *Mikhail Bakhtin* (Cambridge, MA and London: Harvard University Press, 1984), p. 247.
47. Bakhtin, *Problems of Dostoevsky's Poetics*, p. 61.
48. Catteau, *Dostoyevsky and the Process of Literary Creation*; Frank, *Dostoevsky*; James Rice, *Dostoevsky and the Healing Art: An Essay in Literary and Medical History* (Ann Arbor, MI: Ardis, 1985).
49. Rice, *Dostoevsky and the Healing Art*, p. 234.
50. Catteau, *Dostoyevsky and the Process of Literary Creation*, pp. 90–134.
51. Edward Wasiolek, 'Review of Jacques Catteau's *Dostoyevsky and the Process of Literary Creation*', *Modern Philology*, 89 (1992), 599.
52. Catteau writes:

> Certainly the feverish incandescence of the verb, the brutal discharge of the action in scenes of high tension is not merely a mimicry of the epileptic storm in writing, but their violent and convulsive tenor indicates that the writer had a secret inclination for the *noble* form of excess: aesthetic excess which is a metaphor for 'what goes beyond bounds' and so weighs heavier and penetrates more deeply. It is the *explosion* which reveals the truth. (131)

'What goes beyond bounds' echoes Nietzsche's discussion of 'flight from oneself' in *Daybreak*, par. 549, p. 550.

53. Quoted in Frank, *Dostoevsky: The Seeds of Revolt, 1821–1849* (Princeton: Princeton University Press, 1976), p. 167.
54. Quoted in Rice, *Dostoevsky and the Healing Art*, p. 158.
55. See James Rice, 'Dostoevsky's Medical History: Diagnosis and Dialectic', *Russian Review*, 42 (1983), 131–61 (p. 131). On what Dostoevsky could have read for his epilepsy, see Rice, *Dostoevsky and the Healing Art*, pp. 109–93.
56. Frank, *The Seeds of Revolt, 1821–1849*, p. 165.
57. Ibid.
58. Rice, 'Dostoevsky's Medical History', p. 135.
59. The last word is glossed in a marginal note: 'a stroke' [*udar*], James Rice, 'Dostoevsky's Medical History', p. 139.
60. Quoted in Catteau, *Dostoyevsky and the Process of Literary Creation*, p. 115.
61. See Frank, 'The Incident in Semenovsky Square', in *Dostoevsky: The Years of Ordeal, 1850–1859* (Princeton: Princeton University Press, 1983), pp. 49–66.
62. Quoted from *The Little Hero*, written when Dostoevsky was confined in Peter and Paul Fortress in 1849. See Frank, *The Years of Ordeal, 1850–1859*, pp. 49–65.
63. Maria Nemcova Banerjee, *Dostoevsky: The Scandal of Reason* (New York: Lindisfarne Books, 2006), p. 134.
64. Frank, *The Years of Ordeal, 1850–1859*, p. 58.
65. Fyodor Dostoyevsky, 'The Meek Girl', in *Uncle's Dream and Other Stories*, trans. by David McDuff (Harmondsworth: Penguin, 1989), p. 254. Also see Robert L. Jackson, *Dialogues with Dostoevsky: The Overwhelming Questions* (Stanford: Stanford University Press, 1993), p. 41.
66. Quoted in Liza Knapp, *The Annihilation of Inertia: Dostoevsky and Metaphysics* (Evanston, IL: Northwestern University Press, 1996), p. 70.
67. Quoted in Frank, *The Years of Ordeal, 1850–1859*, pp. 55–56.
68. Quoted in Rice, *Dostoevsky and the Healing Art*, pp. 83–84.
69. Ibid.
70. Quoted ibid., p. 233.
71. Catteau, *Dostoyevsky and the Process of Literary Creation*, pp. 124–25.
72. One of the very first fictional references to epilepsy appears in 'The Landlady', which was published serially in *Fatherland Notes* in 1847. The mystic old man Murin has a seizure when the Romantic hero Ordynov breaks in to save Katrina, a young woman who willingly subjects herself to the old man's custody. I shall document the passage that describes the seizure here:

> A shot rang out, followed by a wild, almost inhuman shriek, and when the smoke had cleared a strange spectacle met Ordynov's eye. Trembling all over, he bent down over the old man. Murin lay on the floor; he was being racked by convulsions, his face was distorted

> with agony, and foam was visible on his twisted lips. Ordynov realized that the unhappy man was suffering an acute fit of epilepsy. (*Poor Folk and Other Stories*, trans. by David McDuff (Harmondsworth: Penguin, 1988), p. 156)

For discussion, see Frank, *The Seeds of Revolt*, pp. 334–42; W. J. Leatherbarrow, 'The Sorcerer's Apprentice: Authorship and the Devil in Dostoevskii's *Poor Folk* and *The Landlady*', *The Slavonic and East European Review*, 83 (2005), 599–616.

CHAPTER 1

❖

'The Egoism of Suffering': Schiller with Sade

> I also read Mikhailovsky on Dostoevsky [...] He might have recalled that something similar occurred in French literature, namely the infamous Marquis de Sade. He even wrote a book entitled *Torments and Tortures*, where with particular pleasure he dwells upon the depraved voluptuousness to be derived from the inflicting of pain and suffering. In one of his novels Dostoevsky also describes in detail the satisfactions of one such person [...] And just to think that all the most important priests in the Russian Orthodox Church sang requiem masses for our de Sade and even read sermons on this universal man's love of all humanity! We really do live in strange times!
>
> IVAN TURGENEV, letter to M. Y. Saltykov-Shchedrin, 6 October 1882[1]

The Humiliated and Insulted

In January 1861, Dostoevsky was thirty-nine. He had returned from penal servitude at Omsk fortress and army service in Semipalatinsk (1850–59). Resettled in Petersburg, he was anxious to engage with literary circles again. Dostoevsky had started to write *Memoirs from the House of the Dead* (1860–62), in which he gives a portrait of his prison life in Omsk. One section of the novel depicts a hundred men packed into a small bathroom, a scene which is compared by the narrator to Hell, and which was also compared by Turgenev to Dante's *Inferno* (1.9.145). Van Gogh mentions the *Memoirs* in his letter, seeing the novel's title as the motto for his portraits of madmen.[2] In the same year, Dostoevsky had started a new journal, *Time* (*Время*, 1861–63), with his brother Mikhail and began to write *Humiliated and Insulted* (*Униженные и Оскорблённые*), which was published in serial form in the same journal.[3] Dostoevsky also published in *Time* an essay in response to the critic Dobroliubov's article on Marko Vovchok's short story *Masha*, discussing the critic's utilitarian view of literature.[4] Other publications in the journal include translations of Elizabeth Gaskell's *Mary Barton* and *Ruth*. The former addresses the social and economic conditions of 1840s Manchester workers. The publication of Gaskell's 'industrial novel' reflects the journal's concern with the future development of Russia. The editors of the journal, including Dostoevsky, are concerned with 'the great peasant question', suggesting that a transformation in Russia is needed and can be achieved through the reunion between the culture of the peasant and the educated class.[5] The emancipation of the serfs also took place in the same year, which *Time* describes as a 'sublime event', comparable to other historical moments such as the defeat of the Tartars and the reforms of Peter the Great. *Humiliated and Insulted* was written during this critical period of time.

The novel consists of four parts and an epilogue. It is the first Petersburg novel written since Dostoevsky's return from Siberia. The novel can be seen as a parody of a group of lower-class people who are anxious to fashion themselves as morally good even at the price of being humiliated and insulted.[6] The parody is presented in two stories which merge at the end of the novel. The critic Nikolai Dobroliubov wrote a review in 1861, entitled 'Downtrodden People', saying that the protagonists in the novel are successful in maintaining their humility, but fail to execute their bodily instincts. Such sacrifice of human desire means crime against the self, 'the inner suppression of one's human nature, the sincere admission that one was something far lower than a human being'.[7] The critic sees bodily instincts as more important than humility, suggesting that what defines a human being is the ability to execute his or her sensual desires. But Dobroliubov has overlooked the other side of the argument: first, the downtrodden people in *Humiliated and Insulted* have little interest in striving to execute their free will and satisfy their sensual desires. What occupies their concerns is whether their behaviour is morally good or not. These characters are marked by an anxiety at realizing their moral ideals. This anxiety is further complicated by pleasure that is attained when performing good deeds from an inferior social position. The motivation of being meek is no mere altruism but the fact that playing the role of the socially inferior person and at the same time being generous is actually pleasurable. The moral high ground is taken as a source of pleasure in satisfying bodily needs. We may even venture to say that the more downtrodden the people are, the more pleasure they feel. This phenomenon characterizes Turgenev's 'strange times' (as suggested in the epigraph), and it is the critical issue in *Humiliated and Insulted*.

To begin with, I will analyse the plot and highlight some of the key issues in the narrative. Part 1 begins with the introduction of the impoverished writer and narrator, Vanya (Ivan Petrovich), who is brought up as an orphan by Nikolai Ikhmenev, a small landowner, with Ikhmenev's daughter Natasha (13). The story is a recollection of what happened one year before. At that time Vanya is writing a long novel, which is later praised by a key literary critic (Belinsky, indicated as B. in the novel). Vanya associates his work with death: 'I was also working on a long novel — but as it happens, I've ended up in hospital, and shall probably soon be dead' (13). His large stuffy and low-ceilinged flat in Petersburg is ruining his health (50). He fantasizes about being sent to the asylum: 'At that time I was still given to daydreaming, hoping for a kind of rebirth. [...] Get them somehow to reset my brain in my head and make a new man of me!' (51). Vanya's affinity to death echoes the epileptic novella, 'The Landlady' (1847), in which the protagonist Ordynov becomes paralysed after failing to save Katrina, a young woman about whom he fantasizes, from a mystical old man's despotism. Strangely, '[Ordynov's] torments appeared sweet to him [...] For a moment he almost felt the presence of death, and was ready to greet it as a welcome guest'.[8] Vanya's affinity to death and madness is suggestive of typical themes in Romantic literature, and is subjected to parody by the Prince appearing in part 3.

Natasha has fallen in love with Alyosha, the son of Prince Valkovsky, and has recently eloped with him. Her elopement enrages her father Ikhmenev, who sees himself being humiliated and insulted. Vanya, in love with Natasha, has no intention of competing with the Prince's son. 'There is no need to leave home', he says, 'I will show you what to do, my darling Natasha. I'll see to everything for you, everything, your meetings too [...] I'll be your go-between. Why not?' (38). Vanya opts to play the role of an in-between for the forbidden relationship in order to encourage Natasha to stay. This is not so much because the romantic writer loves Natasha and wants to keep her to himself as he intends to protect the family structure of the Ikhmenevs. To maintain the moral order is much more important than personal impulses. He has a tendency to become a martyr-like figure. Such a masochistic tendency is also found in Natasha. After the elopement, Alyosha continues to visit 'a string of various *demi-monde* Josephines and Minnas' (73). For this, Natasha feels 'immediately doubly affectionate' to him. 'This wonderful creature', Vanya observes, 'seemed to derive endless delight from forgiveness and toleration, as though in the very act of forgiving she experienced some peculiar and subtle kind of pleasure' (73).

In part 1, Vanya also meets Jeremiah Smith, an old failed industrialist, to whom he is mysteriously attracted. He witnesses the old man's death on the street, and then occupies his empty flat. There Vanya meets Smith's granddaughter Elena, nicknamed Nelly, perhaps borrowed from Nellie Trent in Dickens's *The Old Curiosity Shop*.[9] It is also in part 1 that Vanya describes his experience of 'mystical terror', which he finds familiar as it attacks him almost every night as part of his illness (1.10.51). We are not told what that illness is, but the fact that Dostoevsky uses 'mystic terror' to describe his epileptic condition suggests that Vanya also suffers from epilepsy. He defines the terror as the fear of something which he 'cannot define, something unfathomable and non-existent in the normal course of events' (51). The mystic terror, as this chapter will show, points to an unrepresentable and incomprehensible moment that nullifies Vanya's desire for achieving moral ideals.

In part 2, Vanya follows Nelly and witnesses the girl being physically abused by her landlady. The girl has an epileptic fit on the spot (2.4.118). Later, from his detective friend Masloboev Vanya gathers that Nelly is being tricked into working as a prostitute. Nelly is used to beg on the streets, which attracts the attention of Arkhipov. Mrs Bubnova, who sells orphans to make money, arranges to sell Nelly to Arkhipov (135). Masloboev discovers Bubnova's plan. When he and Vanya arrive at the house,

> there was a terrible, piercing shriek from somewhere behind several sets of doors [...] This piteous cry was immediately followed by more screams, oaths, then a scuffle ending finally in a series of sharp, resounding, unmistakable slaps with the flat of a hand across a face. (2.7.138)

Nelly rushes out of the room, wearing 'a white, completely torn and rumpled cotton shift' (138). The description suggests that she is nearly raped and an epileptic fit might have taken place off-stage. After the abuse, Vanya takes her to live with him and looks after her welfare.

Back in Smith's flat, Nelly convulsively embraces Vanya, seeking a 'catharsis' of her 'strange passion' (164). It turns out that Nelly has a traumatic family history: Prince Valkovsky has seduced Nelly's mother and asked her to rob her wealthy father Jeremiah Smith. The mother follows the Prince's order. But the Prince abandons her after obtaining the money he wants. Smith is enraged and deserts Nelly's mother, who becomes terribly ill and eventually dies. Nelly's mother is a double of Natasha: they are both abandoned for going against the father's will and eloping with another man. In view of Nelly's sufferings and her mother being deserted by the Prince, Vanya summarizes his version of the novel:

> It is a melancholy story, one of those dismal, heart-rending stories which are so often played out unnoticed, almost shrouded in mystery, under the heavy St. Petersburg sky, in the dark hidden recesses of that huge city, amid the frenetic hustle and bustle of life with its unfeeling egoism, its conflicting interests, its sordid debauchery, clandestine crime, amidst all the infernally senseless and abnormal conditions of life. (2.11.169)

I said 'his version' because the phrases Vanya uses — dismal, heart-rending — are typical of his romanticization of experience. When he says the city is selfish and full of crime, he is mainly referring to the debauched Prince and his gang. The passage implies a distinction between the sad and humiliated 'us' and the happy and hedonistic 'them'. Just as Vanya gains pleasure from sacrificing his love for Natasha, he has his 'injured' identity reiterated by setting the sentimental tone of the story. Such language will be in contrast with the Prince's sober and pleasure-driven speech.

Schiller versus the Prince

In part 3, Masloboev, a friend of Vanya, gives a further account of what happens to Nelly's mother after she is deserted by the Prince. She has a German fiancé who is faithful to her and they spend their time reading Schiller and the like (3.6.219). Masloboev ironically describes him as 'an upstanding chap, a knight in shining armour, a veritable Schiller, a poet and a merchant to boot, a young dream — in a word, a German through and through, Pfefferkuchen or something like that' (217). Nelly's mother possesses the Prince's written promise of marriage and she can win back Jeremiah Smith's money from the Prince by legal means. And yet, as Masloboev says,

> [She and her husband are] so honourable they're asking to be duped, and secondly, rather than being brutally practical and, if possible, bringing the full force of the law to bear on the matter, they prefer to take refuge in virtuous and noble indignation. (219)

Vanya's 'dismal' and 'heart-rending' story actually is driven by his selfish insistence on maintaining a virtuous and noble image. And such self-importance is associated with the figure of a 'veritable Schiller'.

It is revealed that Masloboev is hired by the Prince to investigate his lost and illegitimate daughter Nelly. In order for the Prince to meet her, Masloboev arranges a meeting with Vanya so that he cannot stay with Nelly. During the meeting, the Prince meets Nelly alone, which takes place off-stage in the novel. Seeing the

Prince, Nelly has an epileptic fit. The Prince reports: 'Extraordinary girl! [...] she spoke to me normally at first, but later, having looked me over, rushed towards me crying out something, shaking all over, dug her fingers into me ... tried to say something, but couldn't' (223). Nelly has another fit when she is visited by the Prince again in part 3 (262). According to the Prince, Nelly seems to suffer from some kind of schizophrenic state: she shows her aggressiveness against him but retreats in the next moment. Nelly's consciousness is split in so far as she knows the Prince is her father but she cannot bear to acknowledge that fact. It seems that Nelly is also reminded of her mother's and grandfather's deaths, which are both indirectly caused by the Prince. It is at this moment of reminiscences that Nelly has the epileptic fit. The relationship between epilepsy and family history will be discussed at length in chapter 5.

The Prince criticizes the Schillerian self-importance in a dinner meeting with Vanya. The Prince says that he has a habit of engaging in the most eccentric debauchery with women (3.10.255). He is a 'veritable Pulcinella' and a 'snake or a huge spider' which Vanya would like to crush (246–47). The Prince was once passionate about a philanthropic society, but this 'romantic phase' is gone. The only principle he knows is 'love thy own self' (254). For him the moralist Vanya and other wronged characters — the Schillerian types — are no less selfish than himself. He teases Vanya for 'playing second fiddle', sacrificing his love for Natasha:

> Alyosha has stolen your bride-to-be, that much I do know, and like some kind of a Schiller you now torment yourself on the lovers' behalf, and offer them your assistance almost to the point of being their errand boy [...] this really is a rather nauseating travesty of magnanimity... (245)

The Prince then comes back to the issue of Nelly's mother, addressing her Schillerian pretentiousness. He says that the mother enjoys an 'ecstasy of hatred' by not asking for the money back:

> If I give her the money, I might even make her unhappy. I'd have deprived her of the pleasure of being totally miserable *on my account* and of cursing me for it for the rest of her life. Believe you me, my friend, there is supreme pleasure to be derived from the kind of misery where one knows oneself to be quite blameless and generous and totally justified in calling the wrongdoer a scoundrel. One comes across this ecstasy of hatred precisely in your Schillerian types. (257)

Although Nelly's mother is wronged and debased, she nonetheless takes pleasure from claiming a higher moral position by labelling those who do wrong to her as evil. Hence the Prince's key reading of the Schillerian types: 'the more pronounced and vociferous one's magnanimity, the more riddled it is with the worse kind of selfishness' (257).

The Prince's observation is Nietzschean. In *On the Genealogy of Morals*, the philosopher suggests that the morality of the slave is characterized by the affect of *ressentiment*. The slave lives in denial, negating all values of affirmation on the part of noble morality. To compensate for this negation, the slave imagines himself being assaulted and therefore has an excuse to take revenge on an imaginary wrongdoer. *Ressentiment* therefore is close to the English words 'bitterness', 'rancour', or 'resentment'. And the prefix of the word ('re-') points to the reactive nature of the affect. Nietzsche writes:

> While all noble morality grows from a triumphant affirmation of itself, slave morality from the outset says no to an 'outside', to an 'other', to a 'non-self' [...] In order to exist at all, slave morality from the outset always needs an opposing, outer world; in physiological terms, it needs external stimuli in order to act — its action is fundamentally reaction.[10]

While the Prince triumphantly affirms his egoistic interest, the Schillerian figures negate their selfishness and blame the other for being the wrongdoer, so creating the hateful 'outside' for the self to channel his bitterness. Vanya says, for instance:

> How often had I paced up and down my room with the unconscious desire that someone should hurry up and offend me or say something that could be interpreted as an offence and thus precipitate a crisis, an emotional catharsis. (266)

The emotional catharsis is what the Prince called the 'ecstasy of hatred' in the Schillerian types: in both cases the subject takes pleasure from the state of resentment, from reacting to the blameable 'outside'.

The ecstasy of hatred contaminates other characters. In part 4, Ikhmenev proposes to adopt Nelly to be his daughter in order to replace his daughter who has eloped with Alyosha. Nelly despises Ikhmenev as he resembles Jeremiah Smith who has abandoned her mother. Nelly rushes to Voznesensky Bridge and begs on the street, something she used to do before she is taken care of by Vanya. Vanya observes from afar:

> She was not begging out of need [...] It was as though she were trying to shock or frighten someone by her exploits; as though she were trying to impress someone [...] She had been wronged, her wound could not have healed, and it was as if she were deliberately trying to aggravate it by this air of mystery, this mistrust of us all; as if she were savouring her own pain and revelling in this *selfish orgy of suffering* [эгоизмом страдания], if I may put it that way. This rubbing of salt in the wound and taking pleasure in the act were familiar to me; it is the last refuge of the many who've been offended and humiliated [обиженных и оскорбленных], who've been oppressed by fate and are conscious of its unfairness. (4.4.281–82, 3:385–86)

Mischief cannot be reversed. The offended cannot will away the pain caused by the offences. As the pain cannot be undone, Nelly the masochist aggravates it, publicizes it, and takes pleasure from it, which is the 'last refuge' of the 'offended and humiliated'. The more humiliated Nelly feels, the more pleasure she can take from the begging. And perhaps the more pleasure she takes, the more humiliated she feels. Constance Garnett translates 'selfish orgy of suffering' as 'the egoism of suffering', a key phrase in this chapter and one which summarizes the idea that seeking suffering can be a selfish and pleasurable act.[11]

To restore the family order, Vanya persuades Nelly to relate her family history to Ikhmenev, so that he will be moved and decide to reconcile with his daughter Natasha. Nelly's story does change the father's mind and his family order is restored. But Nelly's account of her traumatic past triggers another epileptic fit (329). On her deathbed, Nelly shows that her mother has asked her to reconcile with the Prince.

But Nelly insists on concealing her identity as the Prince's daughter:

> Go and tell [the Prince] that I'm dead and I haven't forgiven *him*. Tell him also that I've been reading the Bible recently. It says there: forgive all thy enemies. Well, I read it, but I still haven't forgiven *him*. (355)

Vanya unconditionally does good to the other. He saves and takes charge of Nelly, volunteers to be the go-between in order to secure Natasha's happiness, criticizes Alyosha and yet helps him with the elopement. He sees the Prince as evil (he slaps his face for humiliating Natasha) and is inclined to disguise his intimate relationship with Nelly.[12] To this end, Konstantin Mochulsky says that Vanya's philanthropy recalls Kant's categorical imperative:

> There remains the writer Ivan Petrovich, the author of a philanthropic tale, the representative of conscious good. Alyosha has not yet matured as to the moral law; Ivan Petrovich is its convinced bearer. He is humanist and moralist. In him lives the Kantian imperative; he does good for the sake of good, sacrificing his own interests, placing himself at the service of others.[13]

Vanya does good deeds only for the sake of duty. Whether it is Natasha, Smith, or Nelly, he will serve their good by sacrificing his own interest. To be morally good becomes an imperative. In the Kantian sense, when the good deed is carried out, personal inclinations are excluded. For only by doing so can the moral maxim become universally valid.[14]

Dostoevsky possibly read Kant's philosophical writings or their commentaries.[15] But to say that Ivan Petrovich merely lives the Kantian imperative would give a definite close to the character's unfinalizability. *Humiliated and Insulted* suggests that the humiliated and insulted people enjoy no less pleasure than those who launch the assault. In fact, the wronged turn suffering into masochistic pleasure and sees themselves standing in a morally higher position. In this way, Mochulsky's proposition has to be reexamined. I will supplement it by giving a rereading of the categorical imperative, suggesting that this philosophical concept is apparently founded upon the exclusion of inclination, but is actually motivated by self-interest. By self-interest I refer to the egoism of suffering, the pursuit of pleasure by inflicting hatred and pain on the self. This point will be illustrated via two psychoanalytic essays: Sigmund Freud's 'The Economic Problem of Masochism' (1924) and Jacques Lacan's 'Kant with Sade' (1964). I show that Kant's seemingly impartial explanation for committing good is necessitated by the subject sadistically placing himself under the authority of the moral law. By juxtaposing Kant with Marquis de Sade (with whom the Prince is associated), this chapter will show that the Kantian project has repressed the sadistic/masochistic relationship between the subject and the law.[16]

After the discussion of the two essays, I will return to two particular 'moments' in the novel. First, in the dinner conversation, the Prince introduces to Vanya his female friend, who is so debauched that 'even the marquis de Sade himself could have learnt a thing or two from her' (253). The libertine couple likes to mock the Schillerian types and give them a shock. This habit of mockery exposes a repression: Vanya has sacrificed his own interest — particularly the interest of the body — in exchange for the creation of the humble, morally good man. I see the Prince's mockery as the moment which points to what is disavowed in Vanya and, in a larger context, the Kantian categorical imperative. I will elaborate on this mocking moment with a discussion of the 'mystic terror', a petrifying experience which haunts Vanya at nights. The mystic terror — which is also used by Dostoevsky to describe his epileptic condition — is translated into new significance in *Humiliated and Insulted*: the terror of the unknowable becomes a destructive force which punctuates the idealistic pursuit of universal goodness, loosening the moral structure Kant would like to build in his philosophy.

Vanya's compulsive philanthropy leads me to rethink the Schillerian character as Kantian. It is true that Schiller — a great admirer of Kant — disagrees with parts of his philosophy.[17] But to what extent the two German writers are intellectually similar is beyond the scope of this chapter. I am more interested in how Dostoevsky perceives the Schillerian type as Kantian. On the other hand, I want to rethink the Prince — who actually refers to Sade — as Sadean. I intend in this chapter to juxtapose Kant with Sade, hoping to illuminate a critique of not only Vanya's philanthropy but also Kantian moral philosophy.

Concerning the Prince's mockery of the Schillerian types, it should be noted that Dostoevsky's reception of the German thinker can be divided into three phases: 'fervent admiration, parody and satire, and creative assimilation'.[18] The first stage refers to the pre-Siberian Dostoevsky, who was passionate about pursuing social and moral ideals and engaged with the Petrashevsky Circle. Alyosha in *Humiliated and Insulted* refracts the voice of the young Dostoevsky: he joins an intellectual circle frequented by 'a young idealistic bunch, all ardent philanthropists', who fervently discuss topics such as freedom of speech, forthcoming reform, and love for humanity (182–83). The Prince, having heard of the group, replies with 'the most sarcastic smile' (184). That the Schillerian type is mocked as selfish, silly, and pretentious suggests that the novel belongs to the second stage, that of parody and satire. As for the third stage, Dmitri Karamazov in *The Brothers Karamazov* quotes Schiller's *Ode to Joy* (*An die Freude*, 1785) to define beauty as that which begins with the ideal of Madonna and ends with the ideal of Sodom. Dmitri's rereading of beauty as schismatic in Schiller's poem can be seen as the stage of 'creative assimilation'.

Freud and the Merciless Superego

I have demonstrated that the novel is a presentation of egoism of suffering. But how exactly does it work? And how does it characterize the epileptic mode of being? Part of the epileptic mode of being is distinguished by the need for some objective and permanent value in life and the realization that such a demand is fundamentally subjective and driven by the body. Kant, as Nietzsche puts it, is a philosopher who is 'building under the seduction of morality', and 'apparently aiming at certainty, at "truth", but in reality at "*majestic moral structure*"'.[19] For Kant, the categorical imperative is the objective principle of morality. It should be able to help us to decide what is morally good and what is not in all circumstances. Man is not only a means which he is driven by his inclination but an end in himself.[20] The Kantian imperative is based on the strict distinction between one's duty and inclination. Natural impulses and passions must be suppressed by the will in the name of imperatives as inferred by reason. A rational man must create an imperative for the self to follow; he is his own lawmaker.[21]

The categorical imperative is the psychic police for the psychoanalyst Sigmund Freud.[22] The superego functions in the role of self-criticism of the ego. The superego is the internalized voice of the parents or a mental representation of them. In 'The Economic Problem of Masochism' (1924), Freud writes that the superego is instituted at the point when the parents are internalized and removed from a tactile relationship with the child:

> [The super-ego] came into being through the introjection into the ego of the first objects of the id's libidinal impulses — namely, the two parents. In this process the relation to those objects was desexualized; it was diverted from its direct sexual aims. Only in this way was it possible for the Oedipus complex to be surmounted. (422)

The libidinal impulses for the parents are desexualized and diverted to a strict obedience to the moral law. Here the moral law is mainly derived from the father's law. In other words, the superego is characteristic of the father's order, that is, his power, severity, and the inclination to supervise and to punish (422). For in the Oedipus complex, the father is perceived as the obstacle to the realization of the Oedipal wishes (the unconscious desires for incest and parricide).[23] When the infantile ego is about to overcome the complex and fortifies itself, the child erects within himself the obstacle imposed on him before: that is, the law of the father. As a result, the more severe the father's education, the more rapidly the subject succumbs to repression, and the more dominant the superego will be over the ego later on. The overcoming of the Oedipus complex marks at the same time the moment of sexual repression and the establishment of the moral law.

Freud suggests that the ego is subservient to the superego in a 'compulsive' manner which is expressed in the form of a categorical imperative: 'As the child was once under a compulsion to obey its parents, so the ego submits to the categorical imperative of its super-ego' (389). He comes back to this Kantian connection later in the essay: 'The super-ego — the conscience at work in the ego — may then become harsh, cruel, and inexorable against the ego which is in its charge. Kant's Categorical Imperative is thus the direct heir of the Oedipus complex' (422). The ego and superego are capable of having emotions: the former is 'compulsive', the latter cruel and supervisory. It suggests that in the Freudian model, the categorical imperative is not always free of inclinations during its operation.

The Kantian imperative refers to obedience to the moral law as a duty and the negligence of inclination. But I have also shown that Vanya is strangely attracted to Jeremiah Smith and Nelly and feels compelled to show benevolence to them ('There was something besides pity in my feelings towards her. Whether it was the mysteriousness of the circumstances, or the impression that Smith had left on me, or my own whimsical mood — I just don't know, but something drew me irresistibly to her' (2.3.112)). If the Kantian imperative means absolute obedience without personal interest, why does Vanya's philanthropy appear to be integral to some kind of unidentified affectation?

Freud first says that the superego is established through desexualization. But then he observes that the subject unconsciously desires to be beaten by the father and to have a passive (feminine) sexual relation with him (424). This observation confirms what he calls the unconscious sense of guilt, that is, the subject is unconsciously guilty of bearing the Oedipal wishes and wants to be punished. In this way, the subject returns to the Oedipal complex, only this time in an unconscious and more binding manner, as Freud writes:

> Conscience and morality have arisen through the overcoming, the desexualization, of the Oedipus complex; but through moral masochism morality becomes sexualized once more, the Oedipus complex is revived and the way is open for a regression from morality to the Oedipus complex. (424)

The superego is sexualized again, which is expressed in the form of moral masochism and sadism. Resexualization of the self is the key to the egoism of suffering in *Humiliated and Insulted*. The more the subject intends to express aggression outwardly the more severely the superego will punish the ego: 'A person's conscience becomes more severe and more sensitive the more he refrains from aggression against others' (425). The aggression, which is instinctually renounced, is then taken up by the superego, which increases the aggressiveness against the self. And the tension between the severe superego and the subservient ego is expressed in the form of a sense of guilt. In this way, the sadism of the superego and the masochism of the ego form a circular system, which creates pleasures in pain and, more importantly, ensures the subject will not transgress the father's law (425).[24]

Conversely, the masochist tends to commit crimes simply in order to be punished, which Freud associates with the Russian types in literature: 'Masochism creates a temptation to perform "sinful" actions, which must then be expiated by the reproaches of the sadistic conscience (as is exemplified in so many Russian character types) or by chastisement from the great parental power of Destiny' (425).[25] In *A Writer's Diary* (1873), Dostoevsky thinks that the 'the principal and most basic spiritual need of the Russian People is the need for suffering, incessant and unslakeable suffering, everywhere and in everything' ('Vlas', 1.161). The claim that Russian people have a need for suffering leads the literary critic Rancour-Laferriere to write a book-length psychoanalytical study on moral masochism in Russian culture.[26] The passage from *A Writer's Diary* would be an apt description of the characters like Nelly and Vanya who unconsciously hope to be offended so that they can expect a rupture of masochistic pleasure.

Furthermore, Freud has shown that the subject cannot be 'naturally' subservient to the law, as Vanya appears to be; the subject becomes so only through the establishment of the superego, which relegates the ego through the condition of sadism and masochism, which is entirely sexual and painfully pleasurable. In this way, the common understanding of the formation of the ethical sense is reversed. Normally, it is understood that the moral law is established after one acquires the ethical sense. But Freud suggests the opposite: it is the imposition of the moral law which leads to the creation of the ethical sense. Ethics does not create law; law creates ethics.[27] The subject is unable to distinguish 'good' and 'bad' before the imposition of the moral law.

Lacan's *Kant with Sade*

Freud's analysis prompts the question: if the act of philanthropy is motivated by the pleasure principle, can we still be selflessly philanthropic? Freud would say yes, only if the superego undergoes desexualization once again and carries out the Kantian categorical imperative. In other words, the establishment of the universal moral law has to be conditioned by sexual repression.

Freud's point about repression is anticipated by Prince Valkovsky, who says to Vanya that morality is something based on the concealment of one's 'innermost secret'. This secret, as we can know from his overt confession of debauchery, would be referring to one's sexual impulses:

> If it could come about that each one of us were to describe his innermost secrets — secrets which one would hesitate and fear to tell not only to people at large, but even to one's closest friend, nay, fear to admit even to one's own self — the world would be filled with such a stench that each one of us would choke to death. That's why, speaking in parenthesis, all our social conventions and niceties are so beneficial. There is much profound wisdom in them, I won't say moral, but simply cautionary, comforting, which of course is all for the better, because in essence morality is comfort — that is, it has been devised solely for comfort [то есть изобретена единственно для комфорта]. (3.10.250, 3:362)

The passage envisages a world where the regulation of the moral law is taken away and the instinct of destruction finds its fullest expression. This world anticipates the apocalyptic world pictured in Raskolnikov's dream in the epilogue of *Crime and Punishment*. In that world, people who were infected with some mysterious virus

> did not know whom or how to judge, could not agree on what to regard as evil, what as good. They did not know whom to accuse, whom to vindicate. People killed each other in some sort of meaningless spite. (Epilogue, 547)

Raskolnikov's dream recalls the world envisaged by Sade, in which nature desires continuous destruction and the cessation of propagation. Robert Jackson suggests that Dostoevsky has taken the destructiveness from Sade's work: 'Dostoevsky found in Sade the archetypal ideologist of destruction and disintegration in society, and it is from this point of view that he approaches Sade and "sadism" in his work'.[28] The world in Raskolnikov's dream is driven by destructions and men are not bonded with morality anymore. And if the moral law is foundational to the constitution of a rational and humanistic subject, that world does not confirm any sort of subjectivity.[29] The Prince, through his view on morality, also envisages such a Sadean world, in which everyone 'would choke to death' as they unveil their 'innermost secrets'.

The Prince has pointed out that morality has been 'devised' (or invented, contrived), meaning that there is no such thing as natural good or evil. Moreover, he openly affirms his sexual impulses, which are always destructive to the moral order: 'You accuse me of vice, debauchery, immorality, whereas my only fault now perhaps is that I'm *more honest* than others, and nothing else; that I don't cover up what others conceal even from themselves' (250). Unlike the Prince, the Schillerian figures hardly acknowledge the pleasure they obtain from humiliation and insult. To push the point about 'honesty' further, we can say that the system of moral law is built upon a secret, and the disclosure of the secret — just like the Prince's honest confession — demolishes the foundation of the moral law.

Dostoevsky undoes the Schillerian kindness by juxtaposing it with the Prince's stark honesty. Later in the field of psychoanalysis, Jacques Lacan further interrogates the importance of keeping a secret by juxtaposing two 'extremes'. In 'Kant with Sade', an essay intended to be published as a preface to Sade's *Philosophy in the Bedroom* (*La Philosophie dans le boudoir*, 1795), he unveils the underside of the Enlightenment, showing that the rational subject has to repress his desire in exchange for the universal moral law.[30] Lacan comments on his pairing up of Kant and Sade:

> [Kant's] theory of consciousness, when he writes of practical reason, is sustained only by giving a specification of the moral law which, looked at more closely, is simply desire in its pure state, that very desire that culminates in the sacrifice, strictly speaking, of everything that is the object of love in one's human tenderness — I would say, not only in the rejection of the pathological object, but also in its sacrifice and murder. That is why I wrote *Kant avec Sade*.[31]

The passage distinguishes desire 'proper' from 'pure' desire. The former refers to the desire for enjoyment. It has to be sacrificed, repressed, and substituted by the 'pure' desire, that is the desire for reason, to obey the moral law as an absolute duty. Lacan says that 'pure' desire is obtained through the 'sacrifice and murder' of desire 'proper', suggesting that the desire for enjoyment is being violently rejected. This process of rejection has a ritualistic undertone. Indeed, Lacan uses the phrase 'commandments' to describe the moment when we abandon our desire for enjoyment. He argues that the pursuit of good is transformed into an abstract ideal, the Good, that is the object of the moral law: 'It is indicated to us by our experience of listening within ourselves to commandments, whose imperative presents itself as categorical, that is, unconditional'.[32] Lacan continues by comparing the Good as a heavy weight:

> This good is only supposed as the Good by proposing itself, as has just been said, over and against any object which would set a condition to it [...] in an *a priori* equivalence, in order to impose itself as superior by virtue of its universal value. Thus its weight only appears by excluding anything — drive or sentiment — which the subject might suffer in his interest for an object, what Kant therefore qualifies as 'pathological'. (56)

The establishment of the Good must be based on the elimination of personal inclination. The Good has a weight. Lacan however, did not invent the metaphor. Kant consciously used it to introduce his imperative theory:

> Since the idea of the moral law deprives self-love of its influence and self-conceit of its delusion, it lessens the obstacle to pure practical reason and produces the idea of the superiority of its objective law to the impulses of sensibility; it increases the weight of the moral law by removing, in the judgement of reason, the counterweight to the moral law which bears on a will affected by sensibility. Thus respect for the law is not the incentive to morality; it is morality itself, regarded subjectively as an incentive [...][33]

Morality as such and nothing else is the incentive for carrying out a good deed. This sounds tautological, but that is the way the categorical imperative keeps away impurities like 'respect for the law'. It should be noticed that Kant uses 'weight' as a metaphor to explain the effectiveness of the moral law, suggesting a sense of suppressive force of the law. And he writes that by removing the 'counterweight', that is, personal impulses, the 'weight' of the law will be stronger and more powerful. Since Kant uses the language of metaphor, it is not unreasonable then to ask with respect to the above quotation: who is 'moving' the weight of law?

For Lacan, the object of the Kantian moral law is the supreme good, which is universally true and valid. Such an object of the good does not exist in the phenomenal world: it can only exist in the noumenal world, which is beyond the conceptions of time, space, and mortality.[34] Lacan writes: 'in order to assure [the object] to the will in the fulfilment of the Law, [Kant] is constrained to send [it] off into the unthinkability of the Thing-in-itself'.[35] Kant constructs the object, the thing-in-itself, for the subject to rationalize the possibility of a universal moral law. But on the other hand, as for the question 'who is "moving" the weight of law?', Lacan asks: who enunciates the object? Using the concept developed by the linguist Émile Benveniste, he points out that the way in which Kant formulates the categorical imperative has repressed the difference between the subject of statement (*sujet de l'énonciation*) and the subject of enunciation (*sujet de l'énoncé*) (59). For instance, in the statement 'one should not kill', the subject of enunciation is unmentioned. We are asked to obey the moral law but we are not told the origin of the law; the 'voice' of reason has been silenced. For Lacan, this silencing of the subject of enunciation necessitates a split subject:

> The bipolarity by which the moral Law institutes itself is nothing other than this splitting of the subject which occurs in any intervention of the signifier: namely that of the subject of the enunciation from the subject of the statement. (59)[36]

The implication of the split subject is that the 'I' is the agent which both imposes the law and obeys the law, recalling Jeremy Bentham's design of the Panopticon, where the prisoner becomes both a criminal and (internalized) police.[37] The splitting of the subject is comparable to the sado-masochistic structure of the ego. The 'I' is the 'tormenting agent' which creates the object of the supreme good, sending it to unthinkability (Thing-in-itself) and back to the self as the law: 'This object, isn't it there in Sadian experience, descended from its inaccessibility, and unveiled as Dasein of the agent of torment?' (60). In fact, Lacan quotes a passage from Kant showing that the philosopher himself recognized the moral law as tormenting. Kant writes: 'We can see *a priori* that the moral law as the determining principle of will, by reason of the fact that it sets itself against our inclinations, must produce a feeling that one could call pain'.[38] But the pain, as demonstrated in an earlier quotation from Kant as the 'counterweight' to the moral law, must be suppressed or, in Lacan's comparison with Stoicism, has to be despised (60).

For Sade, perpetual torture of the body is desirable and is the condition for entering enjoyment (*jouissance*). But in Kant, this desire for pain is immediately concealed with the affect of contempt. The moral law is founded upon the universally supreme good, which transcends time. This can only be achieved by repressing the experience of pain before the injunction of the law. Slavoj Žižek argues that Kant's thesis is not about the immortality of the soul but that of the body: 'Is not the phantasmic "truth" of the immortality of the soul its exact opposite, the immortality of the body, its ability to sustain endless pain and humiliation?'[39] The Kantian subject has repressed the body, recalling Freud's discussion of the superego, according to which the subject is desexualized and diverted from their Oedipal wishes in exchange for dutiful obedience to the moral law. Only when the subject is sexualized will sadism/masochism be at work once again. But that is beyond Kant's thoughts.

Mystic Terror and the Prince

Now I return to show how Vanya's philanthropy is mocked and suspended by Prince Valkovsky's libertinism. For Lacan, Sade is more honest than Kant, as he writes:

> The Sadian maxim, by pronouncing itself from the mouth of the Other [i.e. the authoritative 'voice' of the moral law], is more honest than appealing to the voice within, since it unmasks the splitting, usually conjured away, of the subject. (59)[40]

Similarly, disclosing his obscene habits, the Prince says that his only fault is that he is more honest with his sensual impulses (250). Kant needs Sade's idea of perpetual torture to spell out the sadism in the institution of the moral law, just as Vanya needs the Prince's honest confession of his debauchery in order to illuminate the repression in Vanya's philanthropy.

The Prince says that, apart from fame, money, and gambling, his ultimate pleasure is derived from women:

> the main, the most important thing is women ... women in all their shapes and forms. I even go for debauchery that's covert, secretive, and the more eccentric and depraved the better, even with a whiff of sordidness for extra delectation ... (255)

The Prince is not simply a 'womanizer' but a Sadean libertine who enjoys all kinds of perverted sexual acts. His debauchedness marks an absolute break with morality and sexuality. Such heterogeneity in the Prince terrifies Vanya.

It should be remembered that the Prince is a 'snake or a huge spider' which Vanya would like to crush. The image of the spider is often associated with mystery in Dostoevsky. Svidrigailov in *Crime and Punishment* pictures eternity as a bathhouse with spiders forever lurking at the blackened corners (4.1.289). Ippolit in *The Idiot* describes the mysterious power that attracts himself to death as the impossible shape of a tarantula (3.6.409). Stavrogin in *Demons* observes a red little spider crawling while waiting for the girl he has raped to hang herself ('At Tikhon's', 699). That Prince Valkovsky is thought of as a spider suggests a mysterious power inside him which ambivalently attracts and repels the Schillerian types.[41]

The mysterious and perhaps destructive force in the Prince is well captured in the characterization of the 'mystic terror' that haunts Vanya every night when he is working on his novel. Vanya describes this terrifying moment in a long paragraph:

> Whether it was because of my nervous disorder, or the impressions my new dwelling made on me, or my recent dejection, at the first approach of dusk I would gradually, almost imperceptibly, enter that spiritual state (so familiar to me now at night-time in my illness), which I call *mystical terror* [я называю мистическим ужасом]. It is a most dreadful, agonizing fear of something I cannot define, something unfathomable and non-existent in the normal course of events, but which may at any given moment materialize and confront me as an unquestionable, terrible, ghastly and implacable reality, making a mockery of all evidence of reason. (1.10.52, 3:208)

This mystic terror has at least two traits and the first one leads to the latter. It is an extreme fear of something unknown, something 'non-existent', imperceptible, or beyond language. But the 'unknown' suddenly materializes and confronts the subject as an 'implacable reality'. The mystic terror therefore is the fear of something which is both unknown and known, just as the fearful anticipation of epilepsy is always cut off by the sudden attack of a seizure. The sudden materialization of the unknown 'something', as the passage continues, '[makes] a mockery of all evidence of reason'. The terror of it, 'totally confounding all rationalization, normally increases inexorably, so that in the end the mind — which oddly enough on such occasions can function with particular lucidity — nevertheless loses all capacity to counteract the sense' (51). The passage conveys the image of the terrified subject who becomes 'deaf and dumb' — losing the faculty of reason — and at the same time is highly conscious of his own being. The subject is placed in a fearfully passive position where the mind becomes 'unresponsive and impotent'. All the subject can do is to witness the powerlessness of reason or, to put it in Sadean terms, to witness how reason is tortured with fear.

Vanya compares the mystic terror to necrophobia ('It seems to me that something similar must be experienced by those who suffer from necrophobia' (52)). Similarly, Dostoevsky is anxious that he will be buried after having a seizure, as his body will look like a corpse. It is not coincidental that the above passage refers to necrophobia: the fear of the corpse implies the fear of the self, who is always subject to the epileptic seizure, which turns the self into a 'corpse'. Although Vanya does not literally suffer from an epileptic seizure in the novel, the fact that he is haunted by the mystic terror every night suggests that he is subject to the power of seizure. In contrast with the categorical imperative which has repressed the body, the mystic terror refers to this epileptic moment during which the subject loses the ability to reason and the body is about to have a fit. During the mystic terror, the repressed Kantian subject has to cope with its own convulsive body, which can be seen as a radical revolt against the bodily repression that is instituted throughout the subject's dutiful obedience to the moral law.

Another source of mystic terror comes from the Prince's performance of mockery. Speaking of the egoism of suffering, he introduces his ingenious method of dealing with his 'hatred of all this banal, utterly pointless show of innocence and sentimentality':

> One of my most sporting amusements [is] to pretend I am that way inclined myself and, as I enter into the spirit of it, to befriend and string along some everlastingly juvenile Schiller, only suddenly and unexpectedly to give him the shock of his life — lift up my mask, pull a face, poke my tongue out at him just at the moment when he's least expecting it. (247)

The alternation of the Prince's performance pluralizes his identity. Perhaps it is the fluidity in his utterance which Vanya, imposing on himself a single philanthropic identity, cannot bear. Besides, this 'sporting amusement' of the Prince is sadistic in nature as it takes pleasure from mocking the juvenile Schiller and giving him a shock. The Prince elaborates: 'There's a peculiar gratification to be derived from the sudden tearing-down of a mask, from the cynicism of not even deigning to betray any sense of shame in suddenly exposing oneself to another indecently' (251). The moment of sudden disclosure of obscenity is also the moment when the moral order is mocked and suspended. The Prince tells another story of a clerk in Paris who, during his 'bouts of madness', wraps his naked body with a large cloak and strolls along the street. Stopping in front of a person, the clerk 'fling[s] his cloak open and expose[s] himself in all his ... glory' (251). The exhibitionist enjoys the moment of 'suddenly knocking some kind of jumped-up Schiller into the middle of next week by poking one's tongue out at him when he's least expecting it' (251).

The Prince has a female friend whose debauchery 'skill' is even more 'professional'. She is the Prince's 'secret and mysterious paramour', who is 'so lascivious that even the Marquis de Sade himself could have learnt a thing or two from her' (253). On the surface, the woman is 'stern', 'severe', 'daunting', as 'frigid as an iceberg', and engages in 'contemplative mysticism'. On the other hand, 'there was no harlot who was more debauched than she' (253). It is suggested that the female libertine is an allusion to Marquise de Merteuil in Laclos's *Les Liaisons Dangereuses* (1782), who also has multiple sexual relationships with men without moral restraints.[42] In the case of the Sadean woman, she not only commits debauchery shamelessly but also performs the role of Schiller, only in order to tear the mask off with indecency. 'The strongest, the most exciting and thrilling aspect of this sport', the Prince says, 'was its air of mystery and the sheer effrontery of the deception' (253). The Sadean woman unmasks her indecency at the most unexpected moment. The Prince continues:

> This mockery of everything [Эта насмешка над всем] that the Countess preached in society as being elevated, sublime and inviolate, no less than her inner satanic laughter and premeditated flouting of everything that ought not to be flouted — all this without restraint, taken to its utmost limit, beyond the reaches of even the wildest imagination — was that which constituted the principal and most vivid feature of the gratification. (2.10.253, 3:364)

What Sade could 'learn' from this woman is her way of finding pleasure: she takes pleasure from mocking all kinds of moral virtues and suddenly shifting from frigid iceberg to excessive debauchery. Her 'inner satanic laughter' recalls Goethe's Mephistopheles, who is also a figure of mockery. The laughter also anticipates the scene in *Crime and Punishment* where Raskolnikov dreams of the pawnbroker. He tries to murder her again with an axe, but the pawnbroker 'heave[s] all over with laughter' and she does not stir or bleed 'as though she were made of wood' (3.6.277). The pawnbroker's laughter is 'inaudible', hinting at its undecided nature (277). The laughter mocks any attempts to rationalize the murder. Likewise, the Sadean woman's laughter, her excessive debauchery, and the subversion of moral order — all these are mockery of the elevated and sublime virtues which she pretends to preach.

Mockery is carried out in a sudden revelation of the Sadean indecency, which gives a terrifying shock to the Schillerian figure, dismantling the Kantian wish to postulate immortality of the body. It is this sudden moment of switch that punctuates the idea of an inviolable moral law. And it should be remembered that the mystic terror is the phrase derived from Dostoevsky's description of epilepsy. The phrase in *Humiliated and Insulted* has been translated into the shocking fear of the moment when the fantasy of 'natural goodness' shatters and Kant's 'majestic moral structure' collapses.[43] And because epilepsy implies the convulsive body, the mystic terror has also been understood as the reaction against the subject who has repressed the body in exchange for the attainment of the Good, an ideal which does not exist in the phenomenal world.

One of the few things Sade could learn from Dostoevsky's libertine couple would be their destructive interest in mockery. Mockery refers to the moment of sudden change in which the Schillerian figure is horrified by the unmasking of the most indecent behaviour. This mockery is destructive in tendency in so far as it puts the Schillerian figure in terror and confounds his reason. In the mockery, the position of the Prince and his female friend turns upside down or, in Bakhtin's words, is carnivalized. It is through this carnivalization of the character that the perversity of the Schillerian figure is exposed. The mockery — which terrifies, turning the Schillerian hero 'deaf and dumb' — is the power of the moment.

The Russian Sade

When Turgenev disapprovingly says that Dostoevsky is the Russian Sade, he seems to have missed the point. He is critical of Dostoevsky portraying characters like Prince Valkovsky, who triumphantly admit their obscene debauchery. But, unlike the writings of Marquis de Sade, to portray obscenity is not an end in itself. When Pushkin's unfinished story 'Egyptian Nights' — specifically the section involving Cleopatra and her lovers — was compared to the work of Sade, Dostoevsky rejected this view by saying that the story, instead of being scabrous, provides 'a point of view (and just this point of view is the main thing)' for the reader to witness the 'corruption of human nature that has attained frightful proportions'.[44] Similarly, *Humiliated and Insulted*, through the Prince's point of view, has made the stark observation that the impoverished and wronged are no less egoistic and perverted than the Sadean characters.

The characterization of the humiliated and insulted in this novel (such as Vanya, Nelly, Natasha, and Ikhmenev) is in distinct contrast with the Prince and his female friend, which has enabled this chapter to present a critique of the Schillerian type through the Sadean type. In the next four novels, however, Dostoevsky's heroes are increasingly complicated and schismatic: the pursuit of moral ideals, for instance, will be discovered in a single character who manifests his desire for sensual pleasure. This tendency in creating the split subject will bring us closer to the epileptic mode of being. With this in mind, we now move on to *Crime and Punishment*.

Notes to Chapter 1

1. *Turgenev's Letters*, trans. by A. V. Knowles (London: Athlone Press, 1983), p. 285. Turgenev mentions a 'Sadean' passage which 'describes in great detail the pleasure of a lover'. Turgenev might be thinking of Svidrigailov in *Crime and Punishment*, Stavrogin in *Demons*, or the Underground Man in *Notes from Underground*, whose indulgences in obscene debauchery are well known. An earlier and more relevant reference would be Prince Valkovsky in *Humiliated and Insulted*. For Sade's influence on Dostoevsky, see William C. Brumfield, '*Thérèse philosophe* and Dostoevsky's Great Sinner', *Comparative Literature*, 32 (1980), 238–52; Robert L. Jackson, 'Dostoevsky and the Marquis de Sade: The Final Encounter', in *Dialogues with Dostoevsky* (Stanford: Stanford University Press, 1993), pp. 144–61.
2. See Sander Gilman, *Disease and Representation: Images of Illness from Madness to AIDS* (Ithaca, NY and London: Cornell University Press, 1988), pp. 120–21. He quotes a letter Van Gogh wrote to his brother:

   > Some days ago I was reading in the *Figaro* the story of a Russian writer who suffered all his life from a nervous disease which he finally died of, and which brought on terrible attacks from time to time. And what's to be done? There is no cure, or if there is one, it is working zealously. (121)

   Van Gogh seems to identify himself with Dostoevsky in so far as they both suffered from incurable illnesses, which can be dealt with through creative work (121).
3. The novel's title has been translated into different English versions: *Insult and Injury* (Frederick Whishaw, 1887); *The Insulted and Injured* (Constance Garnett, 1915); *The Insulted and Humiliated* (Olga Shartse, Soviet Union, 1957); *Humiliated and Insulted* (Ignat Avsey, 2008).
4. 'Mr. -bov and the Question of Art', in *Dostoevsky's Occasional Writings*, trans. by David Magarshack (Evanston, IL: Northwestern University Press, 1997), pp. 86–137.
5. *Time* as a literary journal represented the voice of the 1860s social-cultural tendency called *pochvennichestvo* (roughly 'return to the soil'; Joseph Frank points out that the word *pochva* has the accessory sense of 'foundation' or 'support'), which advocated a new Russian cultural union between the people and the educated class. See Joseph Frank, *Dostoevsky: The Stir of Liberation, 1860–1865* (Princeton: Princeton University Press, 1986), pp. 34–47.
6. For discussion of this novel, see Frank, *Dostoevsky: The Stir of Liberation, 1860–1865*, pp. 110–32; Ronald Hingley, *The Undiscovered Dostoyevsky* (Westport, CT: Greenwood Press, 1962), pp. 41–59; Konstantin Mochulsky, *Dostoevsky: His Life and Work*, trans. by Michael A. Minihan (Princeton: Princeton University Press, 1973), pp. 198–218; Susanne Fusso, *Discovering Sexuality in Dostoevsky* (Evanston, IL: Northwestern University Press, 2006), pp. 17–41. Also see Donald Fanger, *Dostoevsky and Romantic Realism: A Study of Dostoevsky in Relation to Balzac, Dickens and Gogol* (Cambridge, MA: Harvard University Press, 1965), pp. 152–83; Ignat Avsey's introduction to the novel, <http://www.litencyc.com/php/sworks.php?rec=true&UID=11266>.
7. Quoted in Victoria S. Frede, 'Materialism and the Radical Intelligentsia: The 1860s', in *A History of Russian Philosophy 1830–1930: Faith, Reason, and the Defense of Human Dignity*, ed. by G. M. Hamburg and Randall A. Poole (Cambridge: Cambridge University Press, 2010), p. 81.
8. Dostoevsky, 'The Landlady', in *Poor Folk and Other Stories*, trans. by David McDuff (Harmondsworth: Penguin, 1988), p. 187. The whole passage is epileptic by nature since the subject, like Ivan Petrovich, meditates intensively on a mystical moment:

   > It was strange — his torment even appeared sweet to him, though he had an obscure sense throughout the whole of his being that he would not be able to withstand another such onslaught. For a moment he almost felt the presence of death, and was ready to greet it as a welcome guest: so strained was his imagination, with such an overwhelming rush had his passion re-erupted on his awakening, by such a wave

> of ecstasy had his soul been washed that his life, accelerated by this intense activity, seemed on the point of breaking, of being destroyed, of dying away in a single flash and of being extinguished for ever. (187)

9. While Dickens's Little Nell is portrayed as predominantly good and innocent, Dostoevsky's epileptic Nelly is an illegitimate beggar who bears a traumatic past in relation to her mother. Little Nell dies before she has sexually matured, while Nelly is sexually abused and she manifests her affection for the protagonist Vanya. For further comparison, see N. M. Lary, *Dostoevsky and Dickens: A Study of Literary Influence* (London: Routledge and Kegan Paul, 1973), pp. 46–49; Loralee MacPike, *Dostoevsky's Dickens: A Study of Literary Influence* (London: Barnes & Noble, 1981), pp. 19–121; Michael H. Futrell, 'Dostoevskii and Dickens', in *Dostoevskii and Britain*, ed. by William J. Leatherbarrow (Oxford: Berg, 1995), pp. 83–121.
10. Friedrich Nietzsche, *On the Genealogy of Morals: A Polemic*, trans. by Douglas Smith (New York: Oxford University Press, 1996), 1.10.22.
11. See Fyodor Dostoevsky, *The Insulted and Injured*, trans. by Constance Garnett (London: Heinemann, 1915), 4.4.
12. See Fusso, *Discovering Sexuality in Dostoevsky*, p. 22.
13. Mochulsky, *Dostoevsky*, p. 214.
14. Stephan Körner, *Kant* (Harmondsworth: Penguin, 1990), p. 136.
15. One of the sources would be Karamzin's *Letters of a Russian Traveller*, which records the author's private conversation with Kant on the subjects of moral conscience and immortality. Karamzin was read aloud in the Dostoevsky family circle. See Joseph Frank, *Dostoevsky: The Seeds of Revolt, 1821–1849* (Princeton: Princeton University Press, 1976), p. 57. During his exile in Siberia, Dostoevsky requested a copy of Kant's *Critique of Pure Reason* in a letter saying that his whole future depended on that book. See Evgenia Cherkasova, *Dostoevsky and Kant: Dialogues on Ethics* (Amsterdam: Rodopi, 2009), p. 1.
16. The critique of the sadism in Kant through Sade was first carried out by Theodor Adorno and Max Horkheimer in *Dialectic of Enlightenment* (1944), trans. by John Cumming (London: Verso, 1979), pp. 81–119.
17. Henry Garland, *Schiller* (London: Harrap, 1949), pp. 157–66.
18. Alexandra Lyngstad, *Dostoevskij and Schiller* (The Hague: Mouton, 1975), p. 110. Also see Malcolm V. Jones, 'Dostoevsky and An Aspect of Schiller's Psychology', *The Slavonic and East European Review*, 52 (1974), 337–54; John D. Simons, 'The Myth of Progress in Schiller and Dostoevsky', *Comparative Literature*, 24 (1972), 328–37; John D. Simons, 'The Nature of Suffering in Schiller and Dostoevsky', *Comparative Literature*, 19 (1967), 160–73.
19. Friedrich Nietzsche, *Daybreak: Thoughts on the Prejudices of Morality*, trans. by R. J. Hollingdale (Cambridge: Cambridge University Press, 1982), p. 3.
20. Kant writes: 'Act always so that you treat humanity whether in your person or in that of another always as an end, but never as a means only'. Quoted in *Kant: Political Writings*, ed. by Hans S. Reiss (Cambridge: Cambridge University Press, 1991), p. 18.
21. Kant writes: 'Act always in such a way as if you were through your maxims a law-making member of a universal kingdom of ends' (Reiss, p. 19).
22. Freud, 'The Ego and the Id' and 'The Economic Problem of Masochism', in *On Metapsychology, Penguin Freud 11*, trans. by James Strachey (Harmondsworth: Penguin, 1984), pp. 374, 389, 422.
23. Freud, 'The Ego and the Id', p. 374.
24. Freud in *Civilization and its Discontents* (1930) declares his 'intention to represent the sense of guilt as the most important problem in the development of civilization' (*Penguin Freud 12*, trans. by James Strachey (Harmondsworth: Penguin, 1964), p. 327).
25. The moral masochism recalls Freud's early paper, 'Some Character-Types Met with in Psycho-analytic Work' (1916), in which he suggests a character-type which he calls the 'criminal from a sense of guilt'. Freud suggests that in this case the act of crime is preceded by (not followed by) a sense of guilt which is unconscious. The Oedipal subject commits crimes to seek punishment only to expiate the greater crime he desires, i.e. parricide and incest. See *Art and Literature, Penguin Freud 14*, trans. by James Strachey (London: Penguin, 1990), pp. 291–333.
26. Daniel Rancour-Laferriere, *The Slave Soul of Russia: Moral Masochism and the Cult of Suffering* (New York and London: New York University Press, 1995). The psychoanalytical study tends to

identify moral masochism as a national trait of the Russian people. Such an essentialist approach to masochism would be in opposition to Freud, who would not make connections between the patient's neuroses and his nationality.

27. At the end of 'The Economic Problem of Masochism', Freud writes:

> The situation is usually presented as though ethical requirements were the primary thing and the renunciation of instinct followed from them. This leaves the origin of the ethical sense unexplained. Actually, it seems to be the other way about. The first instinctual renunciation is enforced by external powers and it is only this which creates the ethical sense, which expresses itself in conscience and demands a further renunciation of instinct. (425)

28. Jackson, *Dialogues with Dostoevsky*, p. 145. There are plenty of passages which evoke the image of destruction in Sade's works; here I shall quote the one quoted by Lacan. Sade writes:

> Without destruction the earth would receive no nourishment and, as a result there would be no possibility for man to reproduce his species. It is no doubt a fateful truth [...] Crime is necessary in the world. But the most useful crimes are no doubt those that disrupt the most, such as the *refusal of propagation or destruction* [...] Murder only takes the first life of the individual whom we strike down; we should also seek to take his second life, if we are to be even more useful to nature. For nature wants annihilation; it is beyond our capacity to achieve the scale of destruction it desires.

See Jacques Lacan, *The Ethics of Psychoanalysis 1959–1960: The Seminar of Jacques Lacan*, ed. by Jacques-Alain Miller, trans. by Dennis Porter (London: Routledge, 1992), pp. 210–11.

29. See Pierre Klossowski, 'A Destructive Philosophy', *Yale French Studies*, 35 (1965), 61–80 (p. 74).

30. The essay instead appeared in the journal *Critique*, no. 191, April 1963, which was edited by Georges Bataille. For the primary text, I use two translations for comparison: 'Kant with Sade', trans. by James Swenson, *October*, 51 (1989), 55–75; *Écrits*, trans. by Bruce Fink (New York: W. W. Norton, 2006), pp. 645–68. Quotations are from Swenson's translation. His annotations of the essay are very helpful: James B. Swenson, Jr., 'Annotations to "Kant with Sade"', *October*, 51 (1989), 76–104. For discussions on Lacan's essay, see Gilbert D. Chaitin, *Rhetoric and Culture in Lacan* (Cambridge: Cambridge University Press, 1996), p. 193; David Martyn, *Sublime Failures: The Ethics of Kant and Sade* (Detroit: Wayne State University Press, 2003), pp. 171–216; Kenneth Reinhard, 'Kant with Sade, Lacan with Levinas', *Modern Language Notes*, 110 (1995), 785–808. Reinhard points out the importance of the use of 'with' in Lacan's essay. It is through looking at two disparate thinkers (Kant and Sade) can we reveal the uncanny proximity of their ethical systems.

31. Jacques Lacan, *The Four Fundamental Concepts of Psychoanalysis: The Seminar of Jacques Lacan, Book XI*, ed. by Jacques Alain-Miller, trans. by Alan Sheridan (New York: W. W. Norton, 1977), pp. 275–76.

32. Lacan, 'Kant with Sade', p. 56.

33. Immanuel Kant, *Critique of Practical Reason*, trans. by Lewis White Beck (Indianapolis: Bobbs-Merrill, 1957), p. 78. Cited in Swenson's annotations, p. 79.

34. See Martyn, *Sublime Failures*, p. 187.

35. Lacan, 'Kant with Sade', p. 60.

36. Fink's translation is: 'The bipolarity upon which the moral law is founded is nothing but the split in the subject brought about by any and every intervention of the signifier: the split between the enunciating subject and the subject of the statement' (650).

37. Louis Sass, *Madness and Modernism: Insanity in the Light of Modern Art, Literature, and Thought* (New York: Basic Books, 1992), p. 252.

38. Lacan, *The Ethics of Psychoanalysis 1959–1960*, p. 80. See Immanuel Kant, *Critique of Practical Reason*, trans. by Werner S. Pluhar (Indianapolis: Hackett, 2002), pp. 95–96.

39. 'Kant and Sade: The Ideal Couple', *lacanian ink*, 13 (1998), 12–25. Quoted from part I of the online version: <http://www.lacan.com/zizlacan4.htm#_ftnref9>.

40. The Sadean maxim is summarized by Lacan with a quote from Sade's *Juilette*. Lacan rephrases the quote: 'I have the right of enjoyment over your body, anyone can say to me, and I will exercise this right, without any limit stopping me in the capriciousness of the exactions that I

might have the taste to satiate' ('Kant with Sade', p. 58). If we take Sass's argument that what makes a subject modern is its split subjectivity, we can say that Kant's dishonesty is what makes him a 'modern' thinker.

41. In psychoanalysis, the shape of a spider in dreams suggests the images of castration and erection at the same time. The ambivalence of the spider image can be seen as constitutive of the mystical terror. See Karl Abraham, 'The Spider as a Dream Symbol' (1922), in *Selected Papers of Karl Abraham*, trans. by Douglas Bryan and Alix Strachey (London: Maresfield Library, 1988), pp. 326–32.
42. See Frank, *Dostoevsky: The Stir of Liberation, 1860–1865*, pp. 110–32.
43. Nietzsche, *Daybreak*, p. 3.
44. Quoted in Jackson, *Dialogues with Dostoevsky*, p. 145.

CHAPTER 2

❖

Petersburg and the Deaf and Dumb Spirit

> Some strange thought suddenly stirred within me. I shuddered and at that moment my heart seemed to be flooded with a warm rush of blood that boiled up suddenly from the surge of a powerful, previously unknown sensation. It was as if at that moment I came to understand something that until then had only been stirring vaguely within me, and had yet to be comprehended; it was as if my eyes were opened to something new, to a completely new world, unfamiliar to me and known only from obscure rumors and some mysterious signs. I suppose it was precisely at that moment that my existence began ...
>
> DOSTOEVSKY, 'Petersburg Visions in Prose and Verse', 1861[1]

Reading Raskolnikov: Reading the City

Crime and Punishment (*Преступление и Наказание*), in six parts and an epilogue, was published in instalments in the literary journal *Russian Messenger* in 1866. In the summer of 1865, Dostoevsky was writing a short novel about the low life of Petersburg called *The Drunkards*. It was rejected and later turned into a subplot of *Crime and Punishment* concerned with the jobless alcoholic Marmeladov. To alleviate his financial situation, the writer signed an agreement with the publisher Stellovsky, agreeing to finish a new novel by November 1866. The novel turned out to be *The Gambler*, published while Dostoevsky was writing *Crime and Punishment*.

Dostoevsky started writing *Crime and Punishment* in September 1865 from a first-person point of view. He changed the idea and rewrote the novel as a third-person narrative.[2] Parts 1 and 2 were published in January and February 1866. Part 3 was delayed because a Petersburg student Dmitri Karakozov attempted to shoot the Tsar in March (Alyosha in *The Brothers Karamazov* is based on the assassin, which I will return to in chapter 5). Katkov, the editor of the journal, delayed the publication, fearing that the novel would be seen as an incitement of the assassination, after which two left-wing journals were closed down. Chapter 4 of part 4, which describes the young prostitute Sonia reading the Gospel, was considered inappropriate and rejected. The chapter was amended and then published in June and July. Nothing came out in September and October as Dostoevsky needed to write *The Gambler* for the contract he had signed. The remaining parts came out in the November and December issues.

Crime and Punishment centres on the murder of a female pawnbroker and her sister that takes place in the most crowded area in Petersburg. Dostoevsky describes the early stage of writing the novel:

> The action is contemporary, in the present year. A young man, expelled from the university, petty-bourgeois in origin and living in extreme poverty, as a result of levity and unsound ideas, gives himself to certain strange half-baked notions, which are in the air, and decides at once to break out of his wretched situation. He has decided to kill an old woman, the wife of a titular councillor, who lends money at interest.[3]

Rodion Romanovich Raskolnikov, formerly a law student, is driven by his philosophical ideas to commit a crime, a word which literally means 'stepping over' in Russian (преступление). In the opening page, the 23-year-old articulates a raw notion of stepping-over: 'Hm ... yes ... man has it all in his hands, and it all slips through his fingers from sheer cowardice ...This is an axiom ... I wonder, what are people most afraid of? A new step, their own new word [Нового шага, нового собственного слова], that's what they're most afraid of' (1.1.4, 6:6). The desire to speak the 'new word', to break through some internal restrictions, will form the basis of the 'Napoleonic theory' in part 3 of the novel.

The name 'Raskolnikov' is derived from the word 'schismatic' (*raskolnik*), the Old Believers, who split off from the Russian Orthodox Church in the mid-seventeenth century, in disagreement with the patriarch Nikon's religious reforms. If Raskolnikov wants to speak the 'new word', he is just as 'old' in so far as his name signifies the radically conservative sect.[4] 'Raskolnikov' also comes from the word 'split' (раскол). His friend Razumikhin describes him:

> There really were two opposite characters in him, changing places with each other. At times he's terribly taciturn! He's always in a hurry, always too busy, yet he lies there doing nothing. Not given to mockery, and not because he lacks sharpness but as if he had not time for such trifle. [... He] sets a terribly high value on himself and, it seems, not without a certain justification. (2.2.215)

This chapter will further explore the splits of character suggested by Raskolnikov's name. Schizophrenia is at the core of the epileptic mode of being, and such unstable and contradictory interiority will spread over the entire design of the nineteenth-century city.[5]

As described in chapter 5 of part 3, six months before the story opens, Raskolnikov has written an article on the subject of crime. Speaking to the examining magistrate Porfiry, he gives an interpretation of his own work, which mainly draws on the ideas in *The Life of Julius Caesar* (1865) by Napoleon III. The idea put forth in *The Life*, as Joseph Frank points out, recalls Hegel's characterization of 'the-world-historical-individual'. It aims at 'defending the right of great historical figures to accomplish their world-transforming role unhampered by the narrow standards of conventional social morality'.[6] Similarly, Raskolnikov identifies himself with 'the-world-historical-individual' in order to justify his right to murder. His 'Napoleonic theory' divides humankind into two categories: a majority of ordinary people and a minority of extraordinary ones. The extraordinary men, including Napoleon I, have the self-given right to allow their conscience to 'step over certain obstacles' (259). These exceptional men break an old law and found a new one, even at the price of sacrificing other people's lives. These men, who are able to speak the 'new

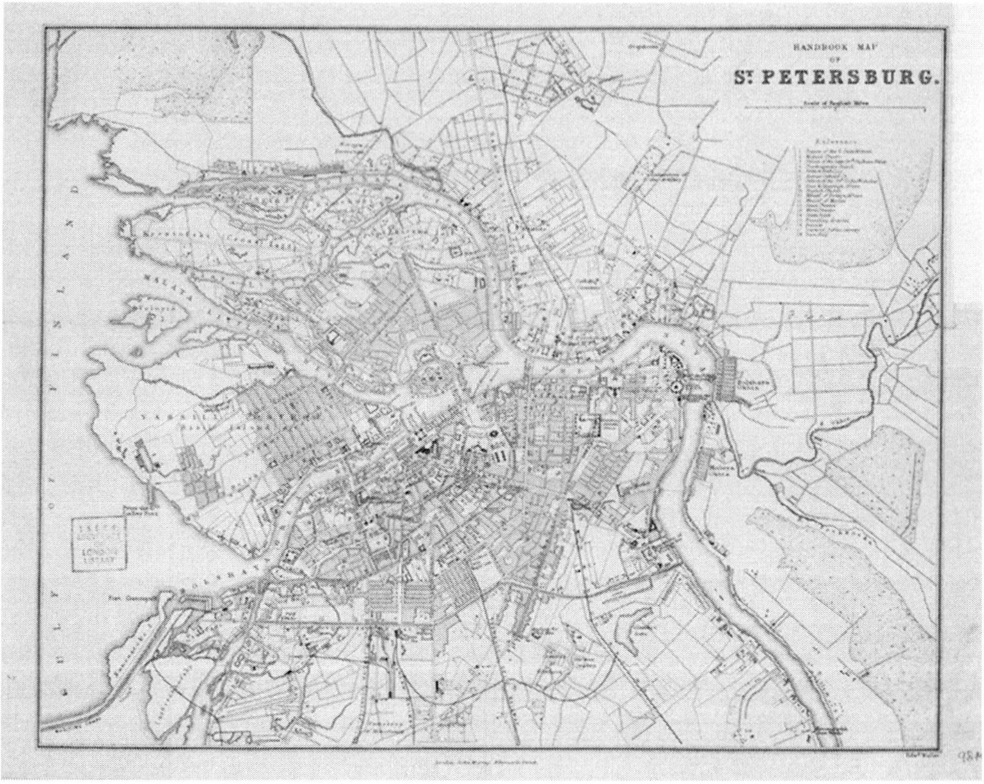

FIG. 2. Map of St Petersburg published by John Murray in 1888

word', must inevitably be criminals. On the other hand, the ordinary men are by nature 'conservative, staid, live in obedience, and like being obedient' (260).[7]

In part 5, Raskolnikov struggles to confess his crime to Sonia. He invents multiple reasons to justify his crime, but the next minute he negates them all. He explains his crime with causes like philanthropy, the need for money, his 'evil', his 'madness'; at the end he cites the Napoleonic theory by saying that he wants to become a Napoleon, and that is why he killed (415). But earlier he doubts whether he has actualized the Napoleonic theory:

> I was in a hurry to step over ... it wasn't a human being I killed, it was a principle! So I killed the principle, but I didn't step over, I stayed on this side ... All I managed to do was kill. (3.6.274)

Raskolnikov is anxious to find an ultimate cause to explain everything about his murder. The failure of doing so implies that the cause of the murder is overdetermined. He unconvincingly, perhaps also uncontrollably, insists on justifying a single doer behind the deed, presenting the murder case as being logical and reasonable. In response, the magistrate Porfiry calls the murder a 'fantastic, gloomy and modern case [Тут дело фантастическое, мрачное, дело современное]' (6.2.456, 6:348):

> There are bookish dreams here, sir, there is a heart chafed by theories; we see

> here a resolve to take the first step, but a resolve of a certain kind — he resolved on it, but as if he were falling off a mountain or plunging down from a bell-tower, and then arrived at the crime as if he weren't using his own legs. He forgot to lock the door behind him, but killed, killed two people, according to a theory. (456)

Raskolnikov's crime is not motivated by any manifest conflicts with the two women he kills. What drives him to kill is a theory derived from a book written by Napoleon III, who wanted to justify himself as the rightful and powerful heir to the throne by comparing himself to Julius Caesar. The theory is referential itself and has no concrete material ground.

Raskolnikov's unrealistic desire to fashion himself as a Napoleon continues after the murder. In part 2, he meets the police clerk Zamyotov in a tavern and virtually confesses to him of having committed the murder (2.6). Later, in a detour, he compulsively returns to the crime scene: 'An irresistible and inexplicable desire drew him on' (2.6.170). He walks up to the pawnbroker's flat and rings the bell in order to experience the moment of transgression once again: 'The former painfully horrible, hideous sensation began to come back to him more clearly, more vividly; he shuddered with each ring, and enjoyed the feeling more and more' (2.6.172). Raskolnikov takes pleasures from seeing himself 'stepping-over' again.

Raskolnikov's anxiety to kill the old woman to prove his ability to transgress marks what I will call the 'intentional' or 'premeditated' side of the novel. In gender terms, his wish to become a Napoleon is symptomatic of his desire for the fantasy of a masculine self.[8] The thirst to step over or to speak the 'new word', I suggest, is likewise integral to the Tsar's intention to rebuild the city of Petersburg in a grandiose style. In chapter 6 of part 1, just before the murder, Raskolnikov, walking in the Haymarket, fantasizes about constructing tall fountains in the market area in order to freshen the air:

> He arrived at the conviction that if the Summer Garden were expanded across the entire Field of Mars and even joined with the Garden of the Mikhailovsky Palace, it would be a wonderful and most useful thing for the city. (1.6.73)

Adele Lindenmeyr points out that Raskolnikov's fantasy to rebuild Petersburg corresponds to his desire to prove his Napoleonic theory.[9] She supports the case by discussing how Napoleon III, in order to establish legitimacy by his link with his illustrious predecessor, hired the city planner Georges Haussmann in 1852 to rebuild Paris from a medieval city into a modern city, in which areas like the Haymarket were all removed.

On the other hand, Raskolnikov is absorbed by a contradictory thought:

> he suddenly became interested in precisely why the people of all big cities are somehow especially inclined, not really out of necessity alone, to live and settle in precisely those parts of the city where there are neither gardens nor fountains, where there is filth and stench and all sorts of squalor. (1.6.73)

The place referred to here is best illustrated by the Haymarket, which was one of the oldest, largest, and busiest retail trade centres of Petersburg. The problem of overcrowding intensified after the emancipation of the serfs in 1861, which caused peasants to migrate to the city to seek jobs. Each house in the market neighbourhood could accommodate up to 250 people. About eighteen taverns were located just outside the area where Raskolnikov lives.[10] The conditions of the Haymarket, as described in the opening pages of the novel, cause 'a feeling of the deepest revulsion [that] flashed for a moment in [Raskolnikov's] fine features' (4).

During his walk in Petersburg, Raskolnikov carries multiple thoughts in his mind. He compares such a state of mind with that of the condemned man: 'It must be the same for men being led out to execution — their thoughts must cling to every object they meet on the way' (73). Just like the condemned man who indulges virtually every desire just before his death, Raskolnikov has the same inclination to reflect on every object he sees during his walk in the city. The moment after he fancies rebuilding the city according to the grandiose city plan, he is distracted by the stench and crowd in the Haymarket district. Petersburg's topology is like that of consciousness: both are rhizomic in nature. Raskolnikov's vision is constantly distracted by other images. Seeing one thing means 'seeing' the others. The group of political buildings in the Admiralty district, for instance, can be seen as an allegory of the Haymarket area, and vice versa.[11]

In Dostoevsky's *Notes from Underground* (1864), the Underground Man says that 'St. Petersburg [is] the most abstract and intentional city in the whole world'. He qualifies his statement in a bracket: '(Cities can be either intentional or unintentional)' (1.2).[12] The Field of Mars, as Raskolnikov refers to, is located in the Admiralty district of Petersburg, in which all the political and military buildings or monuments were built. As in modern Paris, roads are straight and wide and the buildings are all built with tidy, symmetrical, classical façades. Buildings in this district — such as the Admiralty, Alexander Column, Bronze Horsemen statue (monument of Peter the Great) — are the intentional display of tsarist power. They represent, as the Underground Man would say, the intentional city.

Where is the unintentional city? Less than one kilometre away from the centre of this district is the Haymarket square, a crowded and disease-brewing slum in the city. This is the place where all the major characters live and the murder takes place. This is also the most mysterious part of the city, infected by chances, accidents, randomness, and all kinds of carnivalesque activities.

Living in this slum area, Raskolnikov planned the murder six weeks before the action of the novel begins. The distance, as he calculates, between his room and the pawnbroker's flat is exactly 730 steps (1.1.5). Yet, the murder is committed largely by chance. For instance, Raskolnikov decides to execute his plan only after hearing from afar a conversation that the pawnbroker will be alone in her flat on the night (1.5). In a tavern he hears another conversation between two young men mentioning the idea that killing the pawnbroker will benefit common good (1.6). Another accident is that the pawnbroker's sister Lizaveta enters the flat during the murder, which causes Raskolnikov to kill her as well. Lizaveta is described as quiet, gentle, mild, and 'will consent to anything' (1.6). She is continually abused by her sister and arguably by many men who are attracted to her. In fact, she is pregnant when she is killed. So, Raskolnikov meant to kill one woman but accidentally kills two; and actually he destroys three lives altogether. The action of attacking the pawnbroker with an axe is like the movement of a machine (1.6.76).[13] That so many accidents happen in leading to the murder redefines the case as unpremeditated. It is

> as if someone had taken him by the hand and pulled him along irresistibly, blindly, with unnatural force, without objections. As if a piece of his clothing had been caught in the cogs of a machine and he were being dragged into it. (1.6.70)

The element of chance outwits Raskolnikov's meticulous plan, exposing the futility of trying to make himself a Napoleon by following a theory.

The master plan for the city is to build rigid and uniform architecture. But it turns out to be eclectic and disorienting in the eyes of the Petersburgers. The meaning of the city is always excessive and therefore cannot be fully comprehended. The dark streets and corners, the underground activities, the hidden aggressiveness of Raskolnikov, the chance effect of the murder — all these point to the unintentional side of the city, which destabilizes the intentional side, creating a disorienting space.

The formation of disorienting space is integral to that of Raskolnikov's schismatic consciousness. The novel is decentred at the level of urban space as well as Raskolnikov's interiority. These two aspects of the text are allegorical of each other. In this chapter, the writing of Petersburg will be read as commentaries on the writing of Raskolnikov. Conversely, the schism in Raskolnikov helps us understand the Underground Man's riddling statement on the most 'abstract and intentional' city. I will further investigate two 'moments' in the novel. First, I will explore the way in which Petersburg, particularly St Isaac's Cathedral, is represented in the novel. Significantly, the Petersburg panorama, which includes the Cathedral, is described as filled with a 'mute and deaf spirit', which implies the city itself is 'epileptic' by nature (2.2.114). I will look at the Cathedral's eclectic architectural style to show how the Petersburgers' experience of seeing is disoriented with respect to the eclectic cityscape.

The second part will move on to discuss Raskolnikov's dreams, particularly the mare-beating dream, showing how they overthrow the logic of the Napoleonic theory. The dream depicts the image of 'crime' and 'punishment' at the same time, suggesting the impossibility of transgression. This section shows that the eclectic quality of the dreams is integral to the eclectic setting of Petersburg's geography. That is, the experience of seeing in the dreams is split, just as the visual experience of walking in the city is always schismatic. The dominance of eclecticism will demonstrate that the relationship between 'crime' and 'punishment' is not consequential; they occupy Dostoevsky's hero at the same time and necessitate a split and unfinalized subject, which marks the epileptic mode of being.

The Vision on the Neva

When Raskolnikov justifies his crime to his sister Dunya, he has Julius Caesar in mind as he names the place where the general was crowned: 'men spill [blood just] like champagne, and for which they're crowned on the Capitoline and afterwards called benefactors of mankind' (6.7.518). The concept of Tsar derives from Caesar, implying the status of a Roman emperor. It should be remembered that Raskolnikov's Napoleonic theory is based on Napoleon III's reading of Julius Caesar. In a metonymical shift, Raskolnikov's wish to kill like a Napoleon is equivalent to that of wanting to be a Caesar as well as a Tsar.

After the murder, Raskolnikov has to dispose of the property he has stolen. Roaming on Voznesensky Prospect towards the river Neva, he says to himself: 'Why the Neva? Why in the water? Wouldn't it be better to go somewhere very far away [...] in some solitary place [...] to bury it all, and maybe also make note of the tree?' (2.2.108). Raskolnikov could hide the property in a much more desolate area. Yet, he decides to hide it under a stone in a deserted courtyard along Voznesensky Prospect, an artery to Haymarket, recalling his affinity with the lower part of life.

After hiding the property, Raskolnikov turns down to Konnogvardeisky Boulevard and crosses Nikolaevsky Bridge to reach Vasilevsky Island, where his friend Razumikhin lives: 'Well, well, I seem to have brought myself to Razumikhin! The same story all over again ... It's very curious, however: did I mean to come, or did I simply walk and end up here?' (2.2.110). Razumikhin offers Raskolnikov a translation job, which he first accepts and then rejects. Leaving the flat, he crosses the bridge again to return to the Haymarket area.

Walking in the middle of Nikolaevsky Bridge, Raskolnikov is whipped by a driver for falling under the horses' hooves. An elderly woman, taking the young man for a beggar, thrusts a twenty-copeck coin into his hand. Continuing to walk, he stands at the centre of the bridge, turns his head towards the Admiralty district and fixes his gaze on the golden dome of the highest building in Petersburg: St Isaac's Cathedral. Fascinated and terrified by the panorama before him, Raskolnikov's gaze is fixed:

> He clutched the twenty kopecks in his hand, walked about ten steps, and turned his face to the Neva, in the direction of the palace [Tsar's Winter Palace]. There was not the least cloud in the sky, and the water was almost blue, which rarely happens with the Neva. The dome of the cathedral, which is not outlined so well from any other spot as when looked at from here, on the bridge, about twenty paces from the chapel, was simply shining, and through the clear air one could even make out each of its ornaments distinctly. The pain from the whip subsided, and Raskolnikov forgot about the blow; one troublesome and not entirely clear thought now occupied him exclusively. He stood and looked long and intently into the distance; this place was especially familiar to him. While he was attending the university, he often used to stop, mostly on his way home, at precisely this spot (he had done it perhaps a hundred times), and gaze intently at the indeed splendid panorama, and to be surprised almost every time by a certain unclear and unresolved impression. An inexplicable chill always breathed on him from this splendid panorama; for him the magnificent picture was filled with a *mute and deaf spirit* ... [Необъяснимым холодом веяло на него всегда от этой великолепной панорамы; духом немым и глухим полна была для него эта пышная картина ...] (2.2.114, emphasis mine, 6:90)[14]

The mute and deaf spirit, as the Introduction has discussed, is a reference to the Bible, where Christ speaks to an epileptic child who is possessed by an unclean spirit: 'Thou dumb and deaf spirit, I charge thee, come out of him, and enter no more into him' (Mark 9:18). The deaf and dumb spirit recalls Nietzsche's discussion of the Dionysian force in Raphael's *Transfiguration*, which has to do with chaos, contradictions, violence, and dissolution of identity.[15] Regarding the 'inexplicable chill' which breathes on Raskolnikov, the deaf and dumb spirit suggests a state of shock and terror, recalling the mystic terror which attacks Vanya in *Humiliated and Insulted*. The spirit here also anticipates the epigraph of *Demons*, which includes a quote from the Bible about a man being possessed by demons and later cured by Christ (Luke 8:27).[16] The writer's notebook uses a first-person perspective to describe Raskolnikov's deaf and dumb experience:

> The view has a [complete] coldness and [deadness] about it. This is a quality that destroys everything [kills everything], turns everything into nothing. An inexplicable cold blows from it. The spirit of muteness [every time] [and a certain negation] and silence, the spirit — 'mute and dumb' is poured over all this panorama [oppressing my heart]. I can't express myself but I know that my impression was not at all what is known as abstract, intellectual, and reasoned out, but completely immediate.[17]

The cityscape is muting, negative, and murderous, throwing the viewer into a state of annihilation to which the self can give no reason or expression. This is not like the Kantian sublime in which the faculty of reason is awed but still functional. This epileptic 'magnificent picture' is more radical. Another variation of the notebook entries reads: 'it was impossible for me to have [any thoughts] about this or about other things; that everything was a matter of indifference to me, that everything for me was (...) that it was no longer my thoughts, but someone else's, alien' (138). The gaze is compelled to fix on a view that is completely foreign and alienating. The source of alienation is presumably the officialdom and bureaucracy that the state architecture represents. But, if this is the case, why would Raskolnikov pause to take in such view every day he goes to the University?

A possible answer can be found in the historical development of Petersburg's landscape painting from the eighteenth to the twentieth century. The architectural historian Grigory Kaganov shows that the popularity of depicting a panoramic Petersburg in art declined after the 1840s. The focus changed from a macroscopic view to a quotidian one. The Haymarket, for instance, became a popular subject in the post-1840s cityscape paintings. Kaganov cites Raskolnikov's vision on the Neva to illuminate this change:

> What we have here is no longer a simple touch of comedy or a slight irritation, but full and irreparable alienation. In the inner world of the *raznochinets* of the 1860s [Russian intellectuals of non-aristocratic descent], there is no longer a place for any 'splendid panoramas', solemnly open and easily surveyable space. His imagination is entirely absorbed by the narrow corners and dark depth of the city. And Raskolnikov especially keeps pondering this curious fact.[18]

Instead of the lofty and beautiful buildings, Raskolnikov is absorbed by the much-unseen space scattered in the Haymarket area. Kaganov seems to suggest that Raskolnikov is a prime example of the decline of panoramic painting, as the young man represents the slum, the underground, the illegal. But the historian has not yet explained why Raskolnikov is strangely attracted to fix his gaze on such self-destructive view. It should be remembered that the young man who wants to kill like a Napoleon is also the one who wants to identify himself with the Tsar. Since the vision on the Neva is filled with the most important state buildings, such as the Winter Palace and St Isaac's Cathedral, it is not surprising that Raskolnikov is fascinated by this cold and stiffening view.

In 'Petersburg Visions in Verse and Prose' (1861), an article published by Dostoevsky in the journal *Time*, the narrator remembers a 'fantastic, magic vision' from his youth, when he stood on the bank of the Neva on a January evening. The narrator, like Raskolnikov, is confounded by 'some strange thought', which makes him shudder.[19] The cityscape reveals to him 'a completely new world that was unfamiliar to [him] and known only by some murky rumours or secret signs'. The strangeness creates a sense of alienation, which leads the narrator to say: 'I suppose that my existence began at that precise moment'.[20] For Dostoevsky, the Petersburger's existence is deeply marked by the continuous influxes of strange and unfamiliar thoughts. In this way, the Petersburger is not far away from falling into madness, as Svidrigailov, who comes to Petersburg to propose to Raskolnikov's sister, says:

> I am convinced that many people in Petersburg talk to themselves as they walk. This is a city of half-crazy people. [...] One seldom finds a place where there are so many gloomy, sharp, and strange influences on the soul of man as in Petersburg. (6.3.466)

Not crazy, but half-crazy. The Petersburgers are on the verge of nervous breakdown. This is exemplified by Raskolnikov, who is torn between the desire to become a Napoleon and the compulsion to return to his slum area. Svidrigailov goes on to say to Raskolnikov:

> I've already observed you several times from the side. You walk out of the house with your head still high. After twenty steps you lower it and put your hands behind your back. You look but apparently no longer see anything either in front of you or to the sides. Finally you begin moving your lips and talking to yourself, sometimes freeing one hand and declaiming, and finally you stop in the middle of the street for a long time. (466)

Svidrigailov is a non-Petersburger who stays in the city for a short period of time. He shows that Raskolnikov, like many other Petersburgers, is troubled by some contradictory thoughts: he wishes to become a Napoleon, fashion himself as the exceptional man, and take charge of the intentional city. But at the same time, another part of him belongs to the dark corners and hidden streets, the carnivalesque Haymarket, the unintentional city. The half-crazy Petersburger is distinguished by a radical schism between the two sides of the city.

Eclectic Architecture and Cinematic Montage

The bifurcation discussed above takes place not only in Raskolnikov's inclination but also in the perception of architecture. In the vision on the Neva, Raskolnikov is able to see at least two important buildings: the Winter Palace, which was the Tsar's home, and St Isaac's Cathedral, originally commissioned by Peter the Great. If we plot two lines from where Raskolnikov stands to these two buildings on a

FIG. 3. St. Isaac's Cathedral, St Petersburg.
Photograph © Evgeny Gerashchenko 2006 (source: Wikimedia Commons)

map, his field of vision can be schematized in the shape of a triangular cone, inside which most of the political and social buildings are located. They include: the Bronze Horseman statue, Admiralty, the Senate house, the Alexander Column. The Palace and the Cathedral are set up as two anchor points of the field of vision, within which are other state buildings. The Neva vision enables Raskolnikov to contemplate these grandiose buildings with classical style, which are symbolic of tsarist power. But as I will show, the eclectic style of these buildings contaminates the purity of the classical style, making it impossible to identify these buildings with a pure, monological expression of tsarist power. I would like to illuminate this point by examining the Cathedral.

St. Isaac's is the tallest Cathedral in Petersburg (101.5 metres), which explains why Raskolnikov can even see the ornamentation of the Cathedral's dome from approximately 800 metres away. The Cathedral is square in shape, with four facades surrounded by grandiose Corinthian porticoes. It is distinguished by its gilded dome, which punctuates the city skyline, and it has been compared with St Peter's Basilica in the Vatican City and St Paul's Cathedral in London. The dome is surrounded by a colonnade and topped with an octagonal lantern. Around the gilded dome, there are four smaller turrets, which serve as bell-towers. Enormous reliefs cover each side of the facades. There are angel statues standing on the corners and around the gilded dome.[21] Peter the Great named it after St Isaac the Dalmatian because the legendary

Byzantine monk was his patron saint (their birthday is 30 May). But the name Isaac also recalls the son of Abraham, who nearly kills and sacrifices Isaac under God's request (Genesis 22:1–19). That the panorama makes Raskolnikov deaf and dumb suggests that St Isaac's Cathedral bears a castrating force. But the Abraham reference also suggests that the Cathedral is subject to castration. St Isaac's can therefore be understood as representing the father and the son at the same time. Besides, 'Isaac' in Hebrew implies laughter ('he will laugh'), recalling the pawnbroker's laughter in Raskolnikov's dream (3.6.227) and Porfiry's winks. These references suggest an eclectic reading of the Cathedral, which resists the intention to see the building as a pure expression of tsarist power.

Prior to the nineteenth-century building of St Isaac's, three earlier versions — much smaller and less sophisticated in style — were built in the same district. That St Isaac's was demolished and rebuilt three times in a hundred years suggests the importance of the Cathedral as a symbolic display of tsarist power. The first version was commissioned by Peter the Great in 1703, the year that he founded Petersburg. In 1712, Peter and Catherine held their public wedding in that Cathedral — a small wooden church built in the Admiralty district. To suit the grand scale of the developing city, Peter commissioned the second St Isaac's on the bank of the Neva, where the Bronze Horseman statue now stands. The ground in that location was not firm enough and it was decided that the structure be destroyed in 1735. The third version was commissioned by Catherine II, the Empress who gained her autocracy through a palace *coup d'état* in 1762, during which her husband Peter III was assassinated. One of the strategies she used to consolidate her legitimacy as the rightful heir was the pulling down of baroque-style architecture left by Empress Elizabeth who came before her, and subsequently building a series of classical constructions such as St Isaac's. The insistence on displaying power through classical buildings is suggestive of a desire for the fantasy of a pure and universal form.[22]

Catherine, whose governance is often described as enlightened absolutism, approved the reconstruction of St Isaac's in the name of Peter the Great. She entrusted the project to Antonio Rinaldi, the 'master of marble facades', to invigorate the classical style. Catherine also commissioned the French sculptor Etienne-Maurice Falconet, a friend of her favourite *philosophe* Diderot, to build the Bronze Horseman statue that captures Peter the Great on a galloping horse. On the stone plinth supporting this monument was inscribed the phrase 'Catherine the Second to Peter the First, 1782', in both Russian and Latin. During the consecration of the fourth St Isaac's, it was proposed that a walk around the Bronze Horseman should be followed by the traditional procession around the Cathedral.[23] St Isaac's and the Bronze Horseman statue were inseparable for symbolizing the power of the Tsar. One of the paintings of Vasily Surikov actually places the statue and the Cathedral together.[24] An aura is suggested when the icon of tsarist power (the statue) is sanctified by the icon of transcendental power (the Cathedral) in the artistic representation of the city. Dostoevsky also comments on how the statue is perceived to possess an aura, without which Petersburg will 'disappear'. In *The Adolescent* (1875), he writes:

> And what if this fog dissipates and goes away? Won't this whole rotting and slimy city disappear also, float up with the fog, and vanish into thin air like

FIG. 4. The Bronze Horseman statue
photograph © Heiko Dassow 2005 (source: Wikimedia Commons)

> smoke, leaving behind the old Finnish bog and, in the middle, for decoration perhaps, the Bronze Horseman on his feverish, weary horse?[25]

The Cathedral commissioned by Catherine did not work out well. Her successor Paul was unhappy with the slow progress, and instructed the architect to finish the project more quickly, resulting in a one-domed church which was felt to be out of keeping with the capital's 'majestic image'.[26] In 1816, Alexander I decided to rebuild the Cathedral and commissioned the project from the French architect Auguste Montferrand (1786–1858), who also built the monolithic Alexander Column.[27] The Tsar asserted that the new design must preserve the Cathedral's 'rich marble facing' and lend 'grandeur and beauty to so famous a building'.[28] The project took

FIG. 5. Vasily Surikov (1848–1916),
View of the Monument to Peter I on the Sanate Square (1870)

more than forty years to accomplish. During those years, hundreds of thousands of craftsmen, who lived in barracks by the construction site, died of ill health, epidemic disease and accidents, such as mercury poisoning when fire-gilding the dome.

The reconstructions of the Cathedral express the autocrats' anxiety to confirm their power since Peter the Great. Similarly, if we zoom out from the picture of St Isaac's, Petersburg itself was built because of the intention to display the autocrat's power. In 1703, Peter the Great decided to build Petersburg out of a maze of islands which he had conquered from the Swedes. The site chosen was a marshy river delta in the Gulf of Finland and subject to frequent flooding. The extreme northern location causes the city to have prolonged darkness in the winter and extended daylight — the 'white nights' — in the summer. It was estimated that Peter ordered between 10,000 and 30,000 serfs, prisoners of war, and common criminal to be sent to the delta to build the city. Thousands died under the poor working conditions.[29]

The intentional city, however, is inseparable from its unintentional quality. For instance, Petersburg has experienced about 270 major floods since its erection on the marshy ground. Alexander Pushkin's narrative poem *The Bronze Horseman* (1833) is based on one of the most severe floods in 1824. The poem expresses ambivalence towards Peter's creation of the city. On the one hand, it glorifies the aesthetics of uniformity and grandiosity of the intentional city. But on the other hand, the city built by violence induces the flood which causes the low-ranked civil servant Evgeny to become mad and eventually be drowned in the Neva. The first part of the poem expresses the narrator's admiration for Peter's creation, for instance:

> Mysterious water, now there rise
> Great palaces and towers; a maze

Of sails and mastheads crowd the harbour;
[...]
I love thee, Peter's proud creation,
The princely stateliness of line,
The regal Neva coursing, patient,
'Twixt sober walls of massive stone;
The iron lacework of thy fences,
Thy wistful, moonless, lustrous nights,
Dusk-clothed but limpid ...[30]

The second part opens with the signs that the city is about to flood. As the flood destroys the city, Evgeny sits in Peter's square, surrounded by the flood with the Bronze Horseman statue looking down on himself ('And high above him, all undaunted | By foaming stream and flooded shores, | Deaf to the storm's rebellious roars, | With hand outstretched, the Idol, mounted | On steed of bronze, majestic, soars'). The flood destroys the life of Parasha, a woman whom Evgeny admires. He falls into a delirium and roams the city like a mentally deranged man. A year later he curses the Bronze Horseman statue when passing by, which causes it to come to life and start pursuing Evgeny:

For there,
Behind him, to the darkness wedded,
Lit by the moon's pale ray and slight,
One hand in warning raised, the dreaded
Bronze Horseman galloped through the night.
Till morn, where'er Evgeny, frightened,
Did bend his steps and wander, mute,
The fell Bronze Horseman rode, benighted,
In mad, in thunderous pursuit. (96)

The poem finishes with the city returning to the glamorous image portrayed in the opening. We see Evgeny's corpse floating on the river.

Pushkin's reading of Petersburg through the Bronze Horseman is analogous to Dostoevsky's reading of the city through St Isaac's Cathedral. The intentional side of the city is integral to its unintentional side. Peter's will to speak the new word — to build a city out of a swamp — is inseparable from the advent of flood and the production of madness. St Isaac's can also be seen as the utmost expression of tsarist power. But on the other hand, the Cathedral's architectural style is eclectic, which contrasts with the Tsar's intention to impose uniformity on the city.

Georghy Butikov, writing on the Cathedral, points out that by the middle of the nineteenth century, classicism in Russian architecture had begun to decline. This was followed by a trend of eclectic architectural style, which is characterized by 'a loss of stylistic purity, a departure from the principle of architectural and decorative unity, and a tendency to indulge in ornamental elements which had no structural meaning'.[31] Eclecticism tends to combine elements from two or more historical styles in architecture. The construction of the last St Isaac's was very much influenced by this trend.

The exterior of the Cathedral is decorated with excessive sculptures on the pediments. The Cathedral's interior is equally over-decorated. Building materials such as coloured marble were transported from the Caucasus, Finland, France, and Italy (Genoa and Siena). Count Francesco Aglarotti, who famously said Petersburg is 'the great window to the west', described the buildings in the city as 'bastard architecture'.[32] A century later, the nineteenth-century French aristocrat Marquis de Custine elaborates on the same point in his travel writing: 'A taste for edifices without taste has presided over the buildings of St Petersburg' (32). The writer Théophile Gautier devotes a lengthy chapter to the Cathedral in his *Voyage en Russie* (1866), in which he says that the Cathedral is 'unquestionably the most beautiful and modern church' located in Petersburg, 'the youngest and newest of the European capitals'. He likes the 'absolute unity' of the Cathedral. He adds: 'What a symphony of marble, of granite, bronze and gold!' Gautier appraises the church's adherence to classical form and also its infusion with other historical styles, especially Eastern styles. Julie Buckler, who argues that eclecticism was the dominant aesthetic of nineteenth-century Petersburg, elaborates: 'St. Isaac's is more than slightly eclectic in its fusion of neoclassical pediments, columns, and porticoes with Italian Renaissance-style paintings, Greek-Orthodox crosses, Church Slavonic lettering, and Byzantine architectural features, in a grand marriage of West and East'.[33]

The word 'eclecticism', as Buckler points out, comes from the Greek *eklektikos* ('selective') and *eklegein* ('to select'). But in the nineteenth century, eclecticism was associated with randomness, unintentionality, and the absence of hierarchy. While classical style gives the impression of a form which transcends time, the rather random aggregation of various styles moves away from the traditional attempt to historicize a particular period or style.[34] Eclecticism, as Buckler puts it, 'asserted that a new reality could be constructed from fragments of the past, since invoking the past in fragmented form pays tribute to history, while denying its power to determine the future — a particularly potent notion for Russia' (53). It should be noted that eclecticism does not break with the past. Rather, it comes from 'fragments of the past'. These fragments are arranged almost randomly on the surface of the building, opening up a sense of heterogeneity in the building design. Seeing St Isaac's is seeing various fragments of the past at the same time, creating an eclecticism of time.

In the essay 'Little Picture' (1873), published in *A Writer's Diary*, Dostoevsky comments on the lack of expression in Petersburg's architecture: 'All of Petersburg's architecture is remarkably characteristic and distinct and always impresses me specifically by the fact that it expresses all the lack of character and personality typical of the city over the entire period of its existence' (1.255). The writer further characterizes the idea of eclecticism without referring to the term:

> There is no such city as Petersburg; from the point of view of architecture, it is a reflection of all architectural styles of the world and of all periods and fashions; everything has been, bit by bit, borrowed and distorted in its own way. In these buildings you can read as in a book all the currents of all great and trivial ideas that, appropriately or accidentally, have landed here from Europe and that gradually overcame and captured us. (1.255)

Seeing the eclectic architecture is like seeing an unfamiliar object agglomerated of different styles, which is constitutive to the indefinite and enigmatic nature of the

Petersburg panorama. Dostoevsky's observation is a critique of the ways in which the influx of European cultures creates the characterless man. He calls the men who absorb European cultures without a critical distance and who despise their own native origins 'the general, universal man (*obshchechelovek*), the homunculus'.[35] Having said that, the writer here is not so much trying to restore a pure Russian architectural style as characterizing an urban experience that will change our understanding of the modern men.

The new architectural trend allows the juxtaposition of multiple historical styles, which anticipates Sergei Eisenstein's formulation of the cinematic montage. In his discussion of the Italian artist Piranesi, Eisenstein calls the dissonance and disjunction between different styles in classical architecture an 'ecstatic transfiguration'.[36] Referring to the etymology of the word 'ecstasy' (that is, 'standing outside oneself'), he says that the relationship between different architectural styles in a building is not static. They are juxtaposed, 'dissolved', and reconfigured from within. Commenting on the interior of classical architecture, he says: 'these arches can undergo an "explosion" within their own form'.[37] An internal 'split' happens in the classical architecture, in which the multiple historical styles enact a dialectical relationship within moments of explosion.

The explosion of architectural forms inspires the theory of montage, as Eisenstein continues:

> Montage is the stage of explosion of the movie frame. [...] When the tension within a movie frame reaches a climax and cannot increase any further, then the frame itself explodes, fragmenting itself into two pieces of montage.[38]

St Isaac's can be understood as montage: the image of the Cathedral is filled with a tension created by the oppositions of styles. When this tension reaches a climax, which would be the moment when the intention to impose uniformity is the strongest, the image explodes and forms montages which come to an active and unstable relationship with each other. When the narrator says that Raskolnikov is confounded by the Petersburg panorama, all the former impressions reappear before him:

> It was as if he now saw all his former past, and former thoughts, and former tasks, and former themes, and former impressions, and this whole panorama, and himself, and everything, everything, somewhere far down below, barely visible under his feet ... (2.2.114–15)

The return of the impressions is like pieces of montage in Raskolnikov's imagination. This imagination is evoked from looking at the eclectic cityscape.

Dostoevsky's Petersburg is a series of montages. In fact, the opening page marks the dominance of this form for representing the city. In the Haymarket,

> it was terribly hot out, and moreover it was close, crowded; lime, scaffolding, bricks, dust everywhere, and that special summer stench known so well to every Petersburger who cannot afford to rent a summer house — all at once these things unpleasantly shook the young man's already overwrought nerves. (1.1.4)

Various images of the hot Petersburg are pushed together in Raskolnikov's consciousness, giving the young man a shock. Then another set of images follows, forming a cinematic montage: 'The intolerable stench from the taverns, especially numerous in that part of the city, and the drunkards he kept running into even though it was a weekday, completed the loathsome and melancholy colouring of the picture' (1.1.4). The above passage is synaesthetic: the market is visualized with stench. One image is juxtaposed with another, forming a sensually repulsive picture. Petersburg here is presented through a piling up of images. They resemble the way in which cinema is created by piecing numbers of shots together. This incessant jumping from one 'shot' to another in Raskolnikov's imagination evokes a sense of shock: 'A feeling of the deepest revulsion flashed for a moment in the young man's fine features' (4).

Another moment of montage is when Raskolnikov stands on Voznesensky Bridge:

> Leaning over the water, he gazed mechanically at the last pink gleams of the sunset, at the row of houses, dark in the thickening dusk, at one distant window, somewhere in a garret on the left bank blazing as if aflame when the last ray of sunlight struck it for a moment, at the dark water of the canal — he stood as if peering intently into the water. Finally red circles began spinning in his eyes, the houses began to sway, the passers-by, the embankments, the carriages — all began spinning and dancing around him. (169)

Raskolnikov's gaze fixes on one spot and then moves on to another, jumping from one image to another like a montage ('the last pink gleams of the sunset', 'the row of houses', 'one distant window', 'the dark water of the canal'). In the next moment, all the images he perceives piece together and spin before him, just like a film shown to him in twenty-four frames per second. Raskolnikov has just murdered two women; he wants to sit or lie down somewhere in the street (168). But Petersburg is so full of maddening images that the young man has no time to take rest. Consciousness is bombarded with shock. The novel continues:

> Suddenly he gave a start, perhaps saved from fainting again by a wild and ugly sight. He sensed that someone was standing next to him, to his right, close by; he looked — and saw a woman, tall, wearing a kerchief, with a long yellow, wasted face and reddish, sunken eyes. She was looking straight at him, but obviously saw nothing and recognized no one. Suddenly she leaned her right forearm on the parapet, raised her right leg, swung it over the railing, then her left leg, and threw herself into the canal. (2.6.169)

The passage, which reads like a film script, begins with a shock that 'saves' Raskolnikov from fainting and then it moves on to study closely the woman who commits suicide. Dostoevsky's segmented sentences that describe the suicide break the woman's actions into multiple parts. Each part focuses on one segment of the body, resembling a series of cinematic close-up shots.

The Petersburger is under constant attack of shock in so far as he, through his 'camera-eye', sees images from multiple locations in various distances within an infinitely brief period of time. Walter Benjamin's discussion of the film camera can be read as an anachronistic commentary:

> Our taverns and our metropolitan streets, our offices and furnished rooms, our railroad stations and our factories appeared to have us locked up hopelessly.

> Then came the film and burst this prison-world asunder by the dynamite of the tenth of a second, so that now, in the midst of its far flung ruins and debris, we calmly and adventurously go travelling.[39]

The film camera has the capacity to illuminate the minimal changes taking place in fractions of a second that make up actions which we only know as wholes (Benjamin uses the example of the way people walk and a hand reaching a spoon). If we take Raskolnikov's vision as that of a film camera, the concept of a stable viewing subject has to be challenged: what he sees are fragments of images pieced together in the form of montage. A series of 'splittings' takes place in Raskolnikov's vision, which makes the formation of a stable viewing subject impossible. Benjamin writes: 'With the close-up, space expands; with slow motion, movement is extended. [...] The enlargement of a snapshot [...] reveals entirely new structural formations of the subject' (230). What cinema does to the viewer is comparable to what Petersburg does to Dostoevsky's urban hero: both engender an unstable and unfinalized subject.

The Mare-beating Dream

I will conclude by examining Raskolnikov's mare-beating dream. I want to show that his vision is split not only during his detour in the city, but also in his dream. There are at least six of Raskolnikov's dreams scattered in the seven parts of the novel and more than half of them involve beating.[40] In part 2, he walks in the middle of the road, which enrages a coach driver, who whips him heavily on his back. After that he dreams of his landlady being beaten by Porfiry's assistant 'the Squib' (2.2.115–16). In the same part of the novel, Raskolnikov wanders into a building where virtually everyone is drunk. From the singing and dancing crowd, he hears a song from a singer with a thin voice: 'My soldier-boy so fine and free, | What cause have you for beating me!' (2.6.157). At the end of part 3, he dreams of returning to the crime scene, where he frantically axes the pawnbroker who appears to be made of wood (3.6.277). In part 1, just before the murder happens, Raskolnikov has the mare-beating dream (1.5.54).

Raskolnikov is about seven in the dream and he is strolling with his father towards the cemetery to commemorate his grandmother and young brother whom he has never seen. On the way to the cemetery, the little boy witnesses 'some sort of festivity' happening near a huge tavern, where a crowd of drunken people are singing. One of them, named Mikolka, asks everyone to get into his huge cart tied to a 'small, skinny, grayish peasant nag' (55). He whips the nag to make her gallop. The mare remains silent, whereupon Mikolka beats her with a long and stout shaft. With other peasants joining the torture, he beats her with an iron crowbar until she dies. It should be noted that Mikolka is also the name of the innocent painter who insists on confessing to the pawnbroker's murder (6.2).

The entire beating scene is witnessed by the young Raskolnikov. In the beginning, the son is curious about what is happening: 'Papa, what are they doing? Papa, they're beating the poor horse!' (56). The boy has often seen peasants whipping a horse on the muzzle and eyes, and he would feel 'so sorry, so sorry as he watched it that he almost wept' (55). In the past his mother has usually taken him away from the window. This time in the dream, the father becomes the authority. The curiosity to see and know what is going on is suppressed by the father: ' "Come along, come along!" says his father. "they're drunk, they're playing pranks, the fools — come along, don't look!" ' What is forbidden to be looked at by the father is the carnivalesque and violent scene taking place near the tavern. 'Six men pile in [the cart], and there is still room for more' (56). A 'fat and ruddy' woman who cracks nuts and giggles also gets in, contrasting with the skinniness of the mare. The violence inflicted on the mare is intensified by the instruments Mikolka uses to beat her. The father dismisses the beating as pranks and foolishness, and seems to have neglected the violence involved. The father disavows the violence in his description and forbids the son from looking into the scene.

The young Raskolnikov disobeys the father's order, he 'tears himself from his father's hands and, beside himself, runs to the horse' (56). Two fellows start whipping the mare from the side and then Mikolka shouts: 'On the muzzle, on the eyes, lash her on the eyes!' (57). Other participants continue to sing drunken songs. Running past the mare, the boy has a closer view of the beaten horse: '[He] sees how they are lashing her on the eyes, right on the eyes!' This causes the boy to be beaten, suggesting that his eyes are also wounded: 'One of the whips grazes his face, he does not feel it, he wrings his hands, he shouts, he rushes to the gray-bearded old man, who is shaking his head in disapproval of it all' (57). A peasant woman takes the boy away, but he breaks free and rushes back to the mare and he is beaten again. One of the peasants suggests killing the mare with an axe. At the end, the mare is surrounded by a group of drunken peasants who hasten to destroy her with all kinds of instruments.

'It's my goods!' says Mikolka after the mare heaves a deep sigh and dies (57). The boy shouts and dashes again to the mare. He 'throws his arms around her dead, bleeding muzzle, and kisses it, kisses her eyes and mouth' (58). He throws himself at Mikolka with his little fists. But at the same time, the father returns to the scene and snatches the boy away from the crowd. The young Raskolnikov asks: 'Papa! What did they ... kill ... the poor horse for!' And the father replies with the same answer: 'They're drunk, they're playing pranks, it's none of our business, come along!' (59).

Raskolnikov wakes up just after being pulled away by the father:

> God [...] but can it be, can it be that I will really take an axe and hit her on the head and smash her skull ... slip in the sticky, warm blood, break the lock, steal, and tremble, and hide, all covered with blood ... with the axe ... Lord can it be? (59)

Raskolnikov appears to think that the beating of the mare in the dream prefigures the murder of the pawnbroker in reality. Mikolka strikes the female mare on her back continuously and could have used an axe to do so — these details tally with what happens during the actual murder. It can be said that Raskolnikov is sympathetic to the pawnbroker as the young Raskolnikov sheds tears for the beaten mare.

And yet the dream is more unusual than that. It has, for instance, a strange repetition of the image of the eye. First, the father forbids Raskolnikov to look at the beating. Second, the beating of the mare involves the beating of the eye. Third, when Raskolnikov embraces the mare, his face is being beaten, which suggests that his eyes are injured as well. Lastly, Raskolnikov the dreamer has been looking at himself experiencing the mare-beating scene.

In view of the father's prohibition of looking, the fact that the son breaks free and looks can be understood as stepping over the father's order. That Mikolka beats Raskolnikov's eyes is a form of punishment for transgressing the father's order 'Do Not Look'.

The mare's eyes and the boy's eyes have a metonymical resemblance in the dream.[41] When the boy witnesses the mare's wounded eyes, he cries and feels terribly sorry. If the theory about transgressing the father's law is valid, when the boy sees the mare's injured eyes, he is actually seeing his own injury. In this way, uncannily speaking, Raskolnikov is stepping over the father's law by looking at the beating and seeing himself being punished for transgressing that law at the same time. Crime and punishment are not to be understood either sequentially or causally; they take place at the same time. Equally uncanny is the name Mikolka, which represents both a criminal (who beats the mare to death in the dream) and a remorseful sinner (who confesses to the police even though he has committed no crime).

The mare-beating dream has demonstrated the limit of Raskolnikov's Napoleonic theory. The attempt to step over, to transgress the law, is always inseparable from the punishment imposed by the law itself. If that is the case, the idea of speaking the 'new word' becomes an impossible act, a stepping over which only reinstates the father's law.

This chapter has shown how Dostoevsky's Petersburg is eclectic in nature, which in the first place produces alienation in Raskolnikov. A further analysis has suggested this alienated position confounds the subject. Hence the deaf and dumb spirit which haunts the Petersburg cityscape: the viewer at the particular moment is shocked and loses the ability to reason. Yet, this alienated position has created a different mode of existence, which I have illuminated through the experience of montage. Eisenstein's phrase 'ecstatic transfiguration' can be used to describe the 'splendid panorama' of Petersburg: a series of urban images are pieced together dialectically, which creates a polyphonic merging and diverging of meanings. A single viewing subject can hardly survive in the city. Vision is bifurcated, just as Petersburg is schismatic by nature.

Raskolnikov's desire for becoming a Napoleon expresses the thirst for an ideal in many of Dostoevsky's heroes. Sonia reads the passage of Lazarus' resurrection to Raskolnikov. At the end of the novel, he is just about to turn to the passage in his Bible. But the question of whether the young man will experience a renewal of life, as the narrator puts it, is the subject of a new story (551). The ending of the novel anticipates a question concerning a person's transformation into something uncertain. If *Crime and Punishment* is about how the hero deals with his ineradicable past, the next novel will be about how he makes sense of the unknown future. With this in mind I shall move on to *The Idiot*.

Notes to Chapter 2

1. Michael R. Katz, 'Petersburg Visions in Prose and Verse', *New England Review*, 24 (2003), 99–116 (p. 101).
2. See Gary Rosenshield, *Crime and Punishment: The Techniques of the Omniscient Author* (Lisse: The Peter de Ridder Press, 1978), pp. 14–25.
3. Quoted ibid., pp. 14–15.
4. The 'old' and the 'new' in this case are not necessarily contradictory. Dostoevsky, arguing that both the Westernizers and Slavophiles have misunderstood the Old Believers by just focusing on their ritualism and betrayal of Orthodoxy, saw the Old Belief as 'the most significant phenomenon in Russian life and the best pledge of hope for a better future in Russian life'. Quoted from William J. Comer, 'Rogozhin and the "Castrates": Russian Religious Traditions in Dostoevsky's *The Idiot*', *The Slavic and East European Journal*, 40 (1996), 85–99 (p. 87).
5. On the novel, see Donald Fanger, *Dostoevsky and Romantic Realism: A Study of Dostoevsky in Relation to Balzac, Dickens and Gogol* (Cambridge, MA: Harvard University Press, 1965); Gary Cox, *Crime and Punishment: A Mind to Murder* (Boston: Twayne Publishers, 1990); Robert L. Jackson, *Twentieth Century Interpretations of Crime and Punishment* (Englewood Cliffs, NJ: Prentice-Hall, 1974); *Fyodor Dostoevsky's 'Crime and Punishment': A Casebook*, ed. by Richard Peace (Oxford: Oxford University Press, 2006).
6. Joseph Frank, *Dostoevsky: The Miraculous Years 1865–1871* (Princeton: Princeton University Press, 1995), p. 74.
7. Frank, pp. 74–75. For a further discussion of Raskolnikov's article, see Cox, *Crime and Punishment: A Mind to Murder*, pp. 56, 75–79. On this novel's connection to the subject of law, see William Burnham's review, 'The Legal Context and Contributions of Dostoevsky's *Crime and Punishment*', *Michigan Law Review*, 100 (2002), 1227–48; Gary Rosenshield, *Western Law, Russian Justice: Dostoevsky, the Jury Trial, and the Law* (Madison: University of Wisconsin Press, 2005).
8. The critic Nina P. Straus writes: 'Female images (nag, pawnbroker, landlady, sister, mother) are sources of uncontrollable misery which [Raskolnikov] longs to transcend through the "fascinating audacity" of a violent, manly act'. See Nina P. Straus, '"Why Did I say 'Women!'"? Raskolnikov Reimagined', *Diacritics*, 23 (1993), 54–65 (p. 55).
9. Adele Lindenmeyr, 'Raskolnikov's City and the Napoleonic Plan', in *Fyodor Dostoevsky's Crime and Punishment: A Casebook*, ed. by Peace, pp. 37–50.
10. I have cited the statistics of the Haymarket from Adele Lindenmeyr's essay.
11. A study on the topography of *Crime and Punishment* was done by Nikolai Antsiferov's 1923 book, *Dostoevsky's Petersburg* (Leningrad: Lenizdat, 1991; in Russian). See the discussion of the book in Julie A. Buckler, *Mapping St. Petersburg: Imperial Text and Cityshape* (Princeton and Oxford: Princeton University Press, 2007), pp. 110–12.
12. Dostoevsky comments on the experience of travelling in Europe in February 1862: 'Everything ordered and made to order from Europe at that time fit in very comfortably with us, beginning with Petersburg — the most fantastic city with the most fantastic history of all the cities on the face of the earth'. 'And a Completely Superfluous One', in *Winter Notes on Summer Impressions*, trans. by David Patterson (Evanston, IL: Northwestern University Press, 1997), pp. 13–17 (p. 19).
13. 'He took the axe all the way out, swung it with both hands, scarcely aware of himself, and almost without effort, almost mechanically, brought the butt-end down on her head. His own strength seemed to have no part in it. But the moment he brought the axe down, strength was born in him.' (1.6.76)
14. On Raskolnikov's experience on the bank of the Neva, see George A. Panichas, *Dostoevsky's Spiritual Art: The Burden of Vision* (Brunswick, NJ: Transaction Publishers, 2004), pp. 23–46; Henry Buchanan, *Dostoevsky's Crime and Punishment: An Aesthetic Interpretation* (Nottingham: Astra Press, 1996), pp. 2–15; Donald Fanger, 'Apogee: *Crime and Punishment*', in *Fyodor Dostoevsky's Crime and Punishment: A Casebook*, ed. by Peace, pp. 17–34; Konstantin Mochulsky, *Dostoevsky: His Life and Work*, trans. by Michael M. Minihan (Princeton: Princeton University Press, 1973), pp. 290–91.

15. Friedrich Nietzsche, *The Birth of Tragedy: From the Spirit of Music*, ed. by Douglas Smith (New York: Oxford University Press, 2008), p. 31.
16. It should be noticed that the demons in *Demons* are allegorical of the European ideas which 'possess' the Russian educated class. This is not far away from what is depicted in the vision on the Neva, where Raskolnikov is seized upon by the glamour of the Cathedral built in an eclectic mixture of European styles.
17. *The Notebooks for 'Crime and Punishment'*, ed. and trans. by Edward Wasiolek (Chicago and London: University of Chicago Press, 1967), p. 138. Following Wasiolek's edition, brackets represent additions to the text. Ellipses which appear in parentheses (...) indicate words that were undecipherable in the notebooks themselves.
18. Grigory Kaganov, *Images of Space: St. Petersburg in the Visual and Verbal Arts*, trans. by Sidney Monas (Stanford: Stanford University Press, 1997), p. 130.
19. Quoted in Buckler, *Mapping St. Petersburg*, p. 22. For discussion, see Joseph Frank, *The Stir of Liberation, 1860–1865* (Princeton: Princeton University Press, 1986), pp. 64–75.
20. Buckler, *Mapping St. Petersburg*, p. 22.
21. For further discussion of the Cathedral's design, see Georghy Butikov, *St. Isaac's Cathedral Museum* (Leningrad: SMART, 1990).
22. The discussion of Catherine's reform is quoted from Buckler, *Mapping St. Petersburg*, p. 259, originally discussed by Grigory Kaganov, *Peterburg v kontekste barokko* (Saint-Petersburg: Stella, 2001). Buckler discusses the crisis of classicism in the age of urban modernization: 'City dwellers grew weary of relentlessly classical facades that seemed no longer to proclaim eternal civic precepts or embody Johann Joachim Winckelmann's ideal of "noble simplicity and calm grandeur", but rather suggested an oppressive ever-present state power'. Buckler, *Mapping St. Petersburg*, p. 29.
23. Alexander M. Schenker, *The Bronze Horseman: Falconet's Monument to Peter the Great* (New Haven and London: Yale University Press, 2003), p. 296.
24. See Kaganov's discussion of the painting, in *Images of Space*, p. 136.
25. Quoted in Schenker, *The Bronze Horseman*, p. 296.
26. Butikov, *St. Isaac's Cathedral Museum*, p. 7.
27. The Column is erected in commemoration of the Russian victory over Napoleon in 1812.
28. Butikov, *St. Isaac's Cathedral Museum*, p. 7
29. For the history of the establishment of Petersburg, see Alekseevich Egorov, *The Architectural Planning of St. Petersburg* (Athens, OH: Ohio University Press, 1969); *Peter the Great Transforms Russia*, ed. by James Cracraft (Lexington, MA.: D. C. Heath, 1991), pp. 37–76; W. Bruce Lincoln, *Sunlight at Midnight: St. Petersburg and the Rise of Modern Russia* (New York: Basic Books, 2000), p. 20; Solomon Volkov, *St. Petersburg: A Cultural History*, trans. by Antonina W. Bouis (New York: Simon and Schuster, 1997), pp. 1–56.
30. Alexander Pushkin, *The Bronze Horseman*, in *Selected Works in Two Volumes*, trans. by Irina Zheleznova, I (Moscow: Progress Publisher, 1974), p. 85.
31. Butikov, *St. Isaac's Cathedral Museum*, p. 16.
32. Quoted in Buckler, *Mapping St. Petersburg*, p. 32.
33. Ibid., p. 47.
34. The Italian artist Piranesi explores how the pure style of classicism is always already contaminated, an idea which is picked up by Eisenstein in his discussion of the cinematic montage. See Stanley Allen, 'Piranesi's "Campo Marzio": An Experimental Design', *Assemblage*, 10 (1989), 70–109.
35. 'There is no native soil, no people; nationality is merely a system of taxation; the soul is a *tabula rasa*, a piece of wax from which the real man can be immediately molded, the general, universal man, the homunculus — you need only apply the fruits of European civilization and read two or three books.' (*Winter Notes on Summer Impressions*, p. 21)
36. Quoted in Allen, p. 90. The phrase is originally from Sergei Eisenstein, 'Piranesi, or the Fluidity of Forms', trans. by Roberta Reeder, *Oppositions*, 11 (1977), 84–110 (p. 85).
37. Ibid., p. 90.
38. Ibid., p. 92.
39. Walter Benjamin, 'The Work of Art in the Age of Mechanical Reproduction', in *Illuminations*, trans. by Harry Zorn (London: Pimlico, 1999), p. 229.

40. For discussion of the dreams in *Crime and Punishment*, see Mikhail Bakhtin, *Problems of Dostoevsky's Poetics*, ed. and trans. by Caryl Emerson (Minneapolis and London: University of Minnesota Press, 1984), pp. 167–70; Edward Wasiolek, 'Raskolnikov's Motives: Love and Murder', *American Imago*, 31 (1974), 252–69. Wasiolek's essay is a response to Snodgrass's essay. See W. D. Snodgrass, 'Crime for Punishment: The Tenor of Part One', *The Hudson Review*, 13 (1960), 202–53.
41. Commenting on the interpretation of dreams, Freud writes: 'As a result of condensation, one element in the manifest dream may correspond to numerous elements in the latent dream-thoughts; but, conversely too, one element in the dream-thoughts may be represented by several images in the dream'. See Sigmund Freud, 'Revision of the Theory of Dreams', in *New Introductory Lectures on Psychoanalysis* (1933), *The Standard Edition*, trans. and ed. by James Strachey, XXII (London: Vintage, 2001), pp. 7–30 (p. 20).

CHAPTER 3

The Image without an Image: The Guillotine and Holbein's *Dead Christ*

I will begin this chapter with a summary of *The Idiot* (*Идиот*), and then I will focus on the novel's morbid denouement, which Dostoevsky deemed as the most important part of this text.[1] By doing so I intend to situate the novel in the context of the corpse-image, which is exemplified by the German artist Hans Holbein's depiction of the dead Christ.

After four years of medical treatment in Switzerland for a nervous condition which has the symptoms of idiocy, Prince Lev Nikolaevich Myshkin, born to a declined noble line, returns to Petersburg in order to find his distant relative Princess Epanchin. On the train he meets Parfyon Rogozhin, a merchant's son, who is obsessed with the remarkable woman Nastasya Filippovna Barashkov. Nastasya's mother died when their family estate was burnt down. Her father went mad and died in delirium after the event. Nastasya survives and is brought up by Afanasy Ivanovich Totsky. The master plans to get rid of Nastasya by marrying her to Ganya Ivolgin, the secretary of General Epanchin. During the party where Nastasya is to show her preference concerning Totsky's arrangement, Rogozhin suddenly turns up with a pile of rouble notes, intending to take her away. The first part of the novel finishes with her eloping with Rogozhin.

The Prince, who is attracted to Nastasya, has secret meetings with her after the elopement. Rogozhin, feeling jealous, attacks the Prince and later murders the woman. In part 4, the Prince is asked to choose either Nastasya or Aglaya, the daughter of General Epanchin. The Prince remains silent. Later, Nastasya marries the Prince, but only elopes again with Rogozhin during the wedding. Finally, Rogozhin stalks the Prince and tells him that he has killed Nastasya. They keep vigil over her corpse. Eventually, the police arrive while the Prince is stroking Rogozhin like a child. Rogozhin is sentenced to hard labour and the Prince is sent back to Switzerland for medical treatment again.

The last part of the novel, which Dostoevsky valued the most, ends with a remarkable depiction of Nastasya's dead body. Rogozhin attempts to hide the corpse in his bed. A silk curtain stretches across his dark and stuffy study, separating the alcove where the bed is set up from the remaining area. The interior resembles the architecture of a church in which the iconostasis divides the chancel and the nave. A garden knife has been plunged into the woman's left breast causing little bleeding. The corpse is covered with white oiled clothes and surrounded by four

FIG. 6. Hans Holbein the Younger, *The Body of the Dead Christ in the Tomb* (1521), photographed by Martin P. Bühler (© Kunstmuseum Basel)

uncorked bottles of Zhdanov liquid for preserving the dead. Rogozhin leads the Prince towards the alcove to have a closer view of the corpse:

> Someone was sleeping there, a completely motionless sleep; not the slightest rustle, not the slightest breath could be heard. The sleeper was covered from head to foot with a white sheet, but the limbs were somehow vaguely outlined; one could only see by the raised form that a person lay stretched out there. Scattered in disorder on the bed, at its foot, on the chair next to the bed, even on the floor, were the taken-off clothes, a costly white silk dress, flowers, ribbons. On the little table by the head of the bed, the taken-off and scattered diamonds sparkled. At the foot of the bed some lace lay crumpled in a heap, and against this white lace, peeping from under the sheet, the tip of a bare foot was outlined; it seemed carved from marble and was terribly still. The prince looked and felt that the more he looked, the more dead and quiet the room became. Suddenly an awakened fly buzzed, flew over the bed, and alighted by its head. The prince gave a start. (606)

The passage describes in great detail the material aspect of death. The heap of white lace contrasts with the buzzing fly that marks the deterioration. The room is in the dark despite the white night in a Petersburg summer. The flesh is completely covered and its identity is veiled. What remains is a vague outline of a body. The corpse, particularly the tip of the foot, is as stiff as marble, suggesting the image of a sculpture rather than that of human flesh. The more the Prince looks, the less can he identify the body. Figuratively, the cadaver has substituted the re-enactment of Christ's sacrificial death conducted in the chancel. The idea of the Resurrection is denied and replaced by the deadliness of the corpse.[2] The non-identity of Nastasya's corpse renders Rogozhin's attempt to preserve her body, his desire for amassing his 'property', futile.[3]

The denouement captures one of the many corpse-images and its hindrance to cognitive activity. In the following I will examine three more such images: Holbein's Dead Christ, the guillotine and the Prince's epilepsy. These images constitute a constellation of disfigured bodies. They will be understood as different forms of 'death sentence' which put the Dostoevsky's heroes in a tantalizing situation where the boundaries between life and death, the transcendent and the mundane, become uncertain. Such ambiguity problematizes the heroes' relationship with their own death and therefore destabilizes their sense of subjectivity. It is this unfinalizable state in the heroes that I want to explore.

Dostoevsky's Corpses

In August 1867, on their way from Baden-Baden to Geneva, Dostoevsky and his wife Anna Grigorievna decided to change trains and spend a day visiting the town museum in Basel, where the *Dead Christ* is kept. This painting, depicting Christ taken down from the cross, fascinated Nikolai Karamzin, who writes in *Letters of a Russian Traveller* (1801), which was read aloud and discussed in the Dostoevsky family circle: '[In this painting] one doesn't see anything of God. As a dead man he is portrayed quite naturally. According to legend, Holbein painted it from a drowned Jew'.[4] The painting had an enormous impact on Dostoevsky, as his wife wrote in her diary:

> A remarkable work but it simply horrified me. Yet it impressed Fedya so much that he proclaimed Holbein a wonderful artist and poet. Contrary to tradition, Christ is depicted in this painting, with an emaciated body, the bones and ribs showing, the hands and feet pierced by wounds, swollen and very blue, as in a corpse that is beginning to rot. The face is agonized and the eyes are half open but unseeing and expressionless. The nose, mouth and chin have turned blue. In general, this so closely resembles a real corpse that, truly, I don't think I would dare to remain in the same room with the painting. Perhaps it is amazingly exact, but, truly, it is not in the least aesthetic and in me it aroused nothing but revulsion and a sort of horror. But Fedya is full of admiration for this painting.[5]

The painting has different effects on the writer and his wife. While the wife finds the image of the dead Christ obscene, Dostoevsky is absorbed by its enormously detailed depiction. The dead Christ, with such vivid depiction of a decomposing body, represents the loosening of bodily boundaries. The distinction between what is alive and dead, inside and outside becomes ambiguous. This is the source of abjection and it could be the reason why Dostoevsky was electrified. Julia Kristeva writes:

> Corpses *show me* what I permanently thrust aside in order to live. [...] There, I am at the border of my condition as a living being. [...] The corpse, the most sickening of wastes, is a border that has encroached upon everything, it is no longer I who expel, 'I' is expelled.[6]

In front of the *Dead Christ*, the viewer's subjectivity is threatened as the bodily boundary is intruded upon and becomes unstable. Rather, that the viewer fixes his gaze upon the obscene image suggests that he has transgressed the norm, or, in the vocabulary of *Crime and Punishment*, he has committed a 'crime' (преступление), or stepped over. It is at this ambivalent moment of boundary-crossing and the threat of its dissolution that Dostoevsky almost has an epileptic seizure on the spot:

> The painting overwhelmed Fyodor Mikhailovich, and he stopped in front of it as if stricken. For my part, I was unable to keep my eyes on it. It was too painful, especially in my delicate condition, and I went into another room. When I returned about fifteen or twenty minutes later I found Fyodor Mikhailovich still standing there as if rooted to the spot. On his agitated face was the sort of frightened expression I had often noticed during the first moments of an epileptic seizure. I quietly took my husband's arm, led him to another room and

> made him sit down on a bench, expecting him to have a seizure any minute. Fortunately, it did not come. Little by little, Fyodor Mikhailovich calmed down, and when we were leaving he insisted on going to take another look at the painting that had made such an impression on him.[7]

Karamzin claims that nothing is akin to God in Holbein's *Dead Christ*. Anna Grigorievna says that the dead Christ in the painting resembles closely a human corpse. Dostoevsky appeared to be deeply attracted by the enormously detailed depiction of the cadaver. But what made the writer stand in front of it for so long, even climbing on a chair to have a closer look at it, was not only the stark realism which does violence to a stable viewing subject, but also the horrifying idea that Christ is but a human corpse and is not going to rise again.

Holbein's *Dead Christ* is a painting contained within a wooden frame bearing the inscription *Jesus Nazarenus Rex Judaeorum* ('Jesus of Nazareth, King of the Jews'). The upper and thicker part of the frame resembles a tombstone suppressing the painting, which is only thirty centimetres high and two metres long. The painting represents a life-sized human corpse lying on a slab covered with a cloth. The corpse fully occupies the space in the tomb; Christ's chest almost touches the upper frame, intensifying the impression that Christ will not rise again. The only details which distinguish the dead Christ from a human corpse are the wounds on his side, his feet, and right hand. This painting differs from most medieval and early modern paintings, in which the dead Christ is depicted in a more 'humane' manner: 'his body slumps in agony, his facial expression is pained, and his followers mourn'.[8] But Holbein's *Dead Christ* analyses just a dead body, creating a break between the image and the narrative of the Resurrection.[9]

In January 1868, less than six months after he saw the *Dead Christ*, Dostoevsky wrote to his poet friend Apollon Maikov that he was tormented by a certain idea out of which he wants to create a novel. The idea is to portray a 'perfectly beautiful man'. In another letter to his niece Sofya Ivanova written on the next day, the writer says that the perfectly beautiful is an ideal: 'There is only one perfectly beautiful person — Christ — so that the appearance of this immeasurably, infinitely beautiful person is, of course, already an infinite miracle'.[10] He then compares the beautiful man to Cervantes's Don Quixote, Dickens's Pickwick, and Victor Hugo's Jean Valjean. These figures however, are beautiful only because they are at the same time ridiculous (Don Quixote and Pickwick) or pitiable as being treated unjustly by society (Valjean). Dostoevsky wants to test his idea by creating the childish, saintly, and epileptic Prince Myshkin.[11] The idea is also implied in the poem by Aglaya, which is about a 'poor knight', 'an image of pure beauty', who is 'more serious' than Don Quixote, and is 'capable of having an ideal and, second, once he has the ideal, of believing in it and, believing in it, of blindly devoting his whole life to it' (2.6.249). In this poem is the 'extraordinary image' of the 'whole immense concept of the medieval chivalrous platonic love of some pure and lofty knight' (249). Don Quixote is interpreted in isolation from Sancho Panza, hence the removal of the carnivalesque quality of the character. The old knight is taken too seriously. The comical element in the knight is removed and his idealism and seriousness are emphasized. Aglaya's 'poor knight', in which the feeling of platonic love 'reached the ultimate degree — asceticism', forms a stark contrast with Holbein's *Dead Christ*, where all attempts of idealization are denied.

On the other hand, Prince Myshkin suffers two epileptic seizures in public. After keeping vigil over the corpse of Nastasya together with Rogozhin, he returns to the state of idiocy and is sent back to Switzerland. The writer's pursuit of the perfectly beautiful, which is Christ himself, seems futile. Ippolit's comment on the *Dead Christ* also shows that the perfectly beautiful is hardly seen in the novel. In traditional paintings of the crucifixion, 'a shade of extraordinary beauty' is still found in the image of Christ (3.6.407). But there is 'not a word about beauty' in the *Dead Christ*. Ippolit continues:

> In the picture [Christ's] face is horribly hurt by blows, swollen, with horrible, swollen, and bloody bruises, the eyelids are open, the eyes crossed; the large, open whites have a sort of deathly, glassy shine. [...] Here the notion involuntarily occurs to you that if death is so terrible and the laws of nature are so powerful, how can they be overcome? (408)

How could the idea of the perfectly beautiful man be possibly realized with respect to this image of the dead Christ? And why would Dostoevsky bring in the *Dead Christ* when he wants to portray Christ as positively beautiful? Even Christ who exclaims '*Talitha cumi*' and raises Lazarus alive from the dead is subject to the laws of nature and struck so deadly in the tomb (408). The *Dead Christ* is opposite to classical paintings in style, where Christ's beauty is often preserved 'even in his most horrible suffering' (407). For the writer the latter kind of paintings would be kitsch. Kitsch, as Milan Kundera puts it, is an aesthetic ideal 'in which shit is denied and everyone acts as though it did not exist'.[12] Holbein's *Dead Christ* on the other hand, exposes the violent, disgusting, and depressing sides of the scene. It disconfirms expected reactions, evoking revulsion and a sense of horror. If classical paintings of Christ confirm religious faith, the *Dead Christ* does the opposite, as the Prince responds to Rogozhin's replica of the painting: 'Look at that painting! A man could even lose his faith from that painting!' (218). Similarly, Ippolit the empiricist believes only in what he literally sees. He continues to describe the painting, comparing nature to some kind of destructive force to which every individual, including Christ, is submitted:

> Nature appears to the viewer of this painting in the shape of some enormous, implacable, and dumb beast, or, to put it more correctly, much more correctly, strange though it is — in the shape of some huge machine [громадной машины] of the most modern construction, which has senselessly seized, crushed, and swallowed up, blankly and unfeelingly, a great and priceless being — such a being as by himself was worth the whole of nature and all its laws, the whole earth, which was perhaps created solely for the appearance of this being alone! (3.6.408, 8:339)

Ippolit compares nature to a beast and a modern machine. At the end he sums up all these images, seeing nature as an infinitely mystical power. He does not refer to the cross or the injustice done to Christ as related in the Bible, but emphasizes how nature forbids the corpse from rising up again. The phrase 'enormous, implacable dumb beast' points to the deaf and dumb spirit in the Bible and it is hinted again in the Prince's second seizure: the 'spirit that convulsed and dashed down' (554).[13]

Ippolit uses the metaphors for epilepsy to describe nature's destructive power in producing the corpse.

Here nature is also compared to an enormous machine of modern design which crushes the body of Christ. The modern machine ('громадной машины') could imply the railway system, which started to operate in Russia in the early nineteenth century. Lebedev, who says that he has been interpreting the Apocalypse, has the reputation of calling the network of railways spread over Europe the star of Wormwood (243, 372). The passage in the Bible referred to reads: 'And the name of the star is called Wormwood: and the third part of the waters became wormwood; and many men died of the waters, because they were made bitter' (Rev. 8:10–11). Lebedev is critical of the development of science and utilitarianism, which he sees as a curse of the 'wellspring of life': 'Hurrying, clanging, banging, and speeding, they say, for the happiness of mankind! "It's getting much too noisy and industrial in mankind, there is too little spiritual peace", complains a secluded thinker' (375).[14]

Ippolit's comment also evokes the guillotine, which the Prince describes earlier as a 'heavy, powerful and special machine' (22). Both the image of epilepsy and the 'modern machine' aptly express the abruptness and violence of nature. As Ippolit says, nature has 'seized', 'crushed', and 'swallowed up' Christ. Each verb points to a specific power which destroys the body — the epileptic spirit that seizes, the guillotine that crushes, and possibly the web of railways that 'swallows'. The image of the dead Christ, the guillotine, and epilepsy — all represent a definite, quick and violent death, which interrupts the narrative of the Resurrection.

It should be remembered that the idea of losing faith in the Resurrection is based on the visual experience of Holbein's *Dead Christ*. Also, Ippolit is not seeing the actual painting: his observations are based on the memory of Rogozhin's replica. The question of whether death can be overcome is mediated by the experience of looking, to which Ippolit raises a fundamental question concerning the subject of imagery: 'Can something that has no image come as an image? [Может ли мерещиться в образе то, что не имеет образа?]' (409, 8:340). The question can be examined from two levels: what is the 'something' which has no image? And how does that 'something' appear to the viewer as an image? The guillotine and epilepsy, as implied in Ippolit's tirade on nature, interrupt all kinds of attempts to create idealized images such as the Resurrection. The guillotine and epilepsy produce the corpse, or a corpse-like body, where the very materiality resists the viewer's contemplation of an afterlife. If there can be something which has no image, it would be the dead body of Christ. It has no image in so far as it denies idealism and resembles nothing but itself.[15]

Robert Jackson positions Ippolit's question as a central question in modern aesthetics. Dwelling on the word 'formless' (that which has no image) as 'ugliness' (*bezobrazie*), he said that the question points to a moral contradiction of the *Dead Christ*: 'Can one realize in an image that which is ugly? Can that which is monstrous and evil, full of disharmony and discord, be depicted in an aesthetically attractive way?'[16] In other words, can there be ugliness in an image? If so, can that ugliness be depicted attractively?

Jackson connects morality to art, giving value to art according to whether it is morally good or not. Holbein's painting would therefore be bad art as it 'deeply disturbs man's moral and religious tranquility' (67). In a chapter called 'Two Kinds of Beauty', the critic argues that most of Dostoevsky's heroes are attracted to sensual beauty but at the same time struggle to achieve moral beauty, which is considered more important (40–70). Jackson argues that

> one might enjoy the lacerating beauty and poetry of Holbein's disfigured Christ (as one might enjoy beauty in Sodom), but in principle, in the sphere of aesthetic theory and religious convictions, one had to deny this kind of beauty all along the way. (68)

This statement is valid in terms of Dostoevsky's 'philosophy' indicated in his letters and diaries, that is, the necessity to overcome the earthly delights with suffering and pursue a higher religious ideal.[17] However, in *The Idiot* we do not see a clear hierarchy between moral and sensual beauty. At the heart of the novel is not so much the attainment of ideals as the impossibility of attaining them. Jackson seems to have overlooked Dostoevsky's fascination of the *Dead Christ*, the fact that he could not stay away from it. With so many instances of attraction of the morbid images in *The Idiot*, what is called beautiful in the world of Dostoevsky is more likely to be, or at least consists of, that which is inharmonious, fragmented, cadaverous. This is not because such an image is morally debased. Rather, it is beautiful because it destabilizes the concept of the proper. Beauty sides with the Castrates, who represent the marginalized in the novel. Dostoevsky said he failed to create a 'perfectly beautiful individual' in *The Idiot*. Paradoxically, that is the reason for Myshkin to remain 'beautiful', as we consider his compulsive and morbid attraction to epilepsy, the guillotine, the *Dead Christ*, and Nastasya's corpse.

Ippolit's ekphrasis (the activity which renders the visual objects into words) summarizes the Prince's intensive engagement with images. One side of the epileptic mode of being refers to a continual wish to produce images akin to beauty, ideal, eternity. But that wish is always annihilated at its most intense existence. I would like to elaborate on 'something which has no image' by exploring the significance of the dead body. In his essay 'Two Versions of the Imaginary', Maurice Blanchot writes that 'the strangeness of a cadaver is also the strangeness of the image', suggesting that the study of the cadaver can illuminate our understanding of imagery.[18] He discusses the image from two perspectives: first, the image pacifies as it feeds the desire to look and confirms a stable viewing subject. The image veils certain 'nothingness' and appropriates it into art. The cleaning up of that 'nothingness' keeps the viewer satisfied, powerful, and active. On the other hand, the image can also make the viewer powerless, strangely mute, and passive (418). Blanchot uses examples of the image of a face or a corner of a room. But the ultimate example is the dead body, which unreservedly exposes its nothingness to the field of vision:

> The cadaver is its own image. He no longer has any relation with this world, in which he still appears, except those of an image, an obscure possibility, a shadow which is constantly present behind the living form and which now, far from separating itself from that form, completely transforms itself into a shadow. (421)

There is a temptation to imagine the dead body as the person who lived. But an unbridgeable gap emerges between the living form and the dead body, which resembles nothing but itself. Normally, a shadow is an index of an object, just as a body part is an index of a person's identity. Here, the dead body is analogous of the shadow, which completely cuts itself off from the object. The dead body becomes an index of nothing, suggesting an image without content, and 'imageless' image. What remains in the dead body is the 'elemental strangeness' and the 'shapeless heaviness of the being that is present in absence' (421). The dead body exists contradictorily in the field of vision; it exists as something both meaningful and meaningless: 'it can be elsewhere than where it is, where we are without it, where there is nothing, an invading presence, an obscure and vain fullness' (422). This is not to say that the dead body revisits the living like a spectre or anything akin to a metaphysical presence. Rather, the dead body points to the very density of absence itself. What haunts the living is the 'inaccessible which one cannot rid oneself of, what one does not find and what, because of that, does not allow one to avoid it. The ungraspable is what one does not escape' (422).

Blanchot uses oxymoronic phrases — 'shapeless heaviness', 'obscure and vain fullness', 'that [which] is present in absence' — to draw attention to the mass of nothingness of the dead body. The dead Christ represents that 'something which has no image' since the materiality of the corpse denies all kinds of idealization of death. That explains why one can lose faith by just looking at the painting. On the other hand, the dead Christ is an image on the canvas. The image of the dead Christ is 'nothing' but becomes 'something' within the frame.

Imagining the Guillotine

I now move on to the Prince's visit to the Epanchins, during which he recalls a story of a decapitated man. The Prince is intensely interested in reading and rereading images. To demonstrate his calligraphy, he writes variations on the signature of the fourteenth-century monk Pafnuty: 'Here is a simple, ordinary English script of the purest sort: elegance can go no further, everything here is lovely, a jewel, a pearl; this is perfection' (1.3.34). The Prince is then fascinated by Nastasya's portrait photo: 'Remarkably good-looking!' (31). He comments later:

> An astonishing face! [...] And I'm convinced that her fate is no ordinary one. It's a gay face, but she has suffered terribly eh? It speaks in her eyes, these two little bones, the two points under her eyes where the cheeks begin. It's a proud face, terribly proud, and I don't know whether she's kind or not. Ah, if only she were kind! Everything would be saved! (36)

The picture captures an instant, and yet the Prince imagines what happened before ('she has suffered terribly, eh?'), which is symptomatic of his deep interest in developing theories or narratives out of images.

To Mrs Epanchin and her daughters the Prince relates his experience in Switzerland. He says he often had severe seizures, lapsed into stupor, and lost his memory. He then remembers a day in Basel — the same city where Holbein's *Dead Christ* is kept — where he saw the braying of an ass in the town market: 'The ass struck me terribly and for some reason I took an extraordinary liking to it, and at the same time it was as if everything cleared up in my head' (56). The natural scenery in Lucerne made him feel 'terribly oppressed' (58). He dreams of himself as a foreigner suffering 'blankly and mutely' in view of the 'shining sky' and 'the bright and infinite horizon' (3.7.423). Swiss immense landscape contrasts with the crowded cityscape of Petersburg. Whereas Raskolnikov is struck deaf and dumb by the hybrid panorama and proximity with others, Myshkin is suppressed by the vastness of space and a sense of foreignness. The traditional beauty of natural landscape does not quite accommodate him.

The second sister Adelaida asks the Prince to find her a subject to paint, saying that she does not know how to look (58). He then enters into a lengthy reflection on 'how to live'. For him, to look refers not only to a physical vision but also a metaphysical reflection:

> There would come a call to go somewhere, and it always seemed to me that if I walked [...] the whole answer would be there, and at once I'd see a new life [...] I dreamed about all kinds of thing! And then it seemed to me that in prison, too, you could find an immense life. (59)

The Prince recommends painting a condemned man's face just before the guillotine falls. The sister, who mainly paints landscapes, does not quite understand: 'What? Just the face? [...] How should the face be portrayed? As just a face? What sort of face?' (63). In the museum of Basel, there is Hans Fries's *The Beheading of John the Baptist* (1514), which depicts the face of St John just before his head is cut off with the sword. The Prince, who saw the braying of the ass in Basel, may have Fries's painting in mind.[19] The face being sought here should express what is felt in the critical moment before the guillotine strikes. That moment will be a compression of all the events that took place throughout the execution: 'I thought then that it would be a useful painting. You know, here you have to imagine everything that went before, everything, everything' (64).[20]

Earlier on, the Prince meets the valet of the Epanchins and relates his experience of witnessing an execution in Lyons. The event stays in his mind and he dreams of it five times (1.2.22). He comments on the moment when the criminal's head is cut off: 'It's instantaneous. The man is laid down, and a broad knife drops, it's a special machine called the guillotine, heavy, powerful ... The head bounces off before you can blink an eye' (22). The special machine which cuts people's heads off will later become for Ippolit 'some huge machine of the most modern construction' which crushes Christ's body (408). Seventy years later, the special machine will reappear as a modern tram-car that runs over the literary journal editor Berlioz and severs his head in Bulgakov's *The Master and Margarita*.[21]

Bakhtin once said: 'Dostoevsky thought socially, but uses psychological wrought images'.[22] The Prince's observation of the convict's psychology can be read as a social critique. No screaming is heard from the convict as he or she dies instantaneously when the guillotine strikes.[23] This was made possible by the advancement of mechanics in eighteenth-century France when the number of executions was increasing. Decapitation done by the sword wielded by the hand became more difficult and inhuman. Dr Guillotin proposed in the Constituent Assembly in

1789 that the method of punishment should be the same for all people sentenced to death and should be carried out effectively by a simple mechanism.[24] The idea behind the invention of the guillotine was to treat massive numbers of human lives systematically, just as Hegel comments on the meaninglessness of deaths created by the guillotine during Robespierre's Reign of Terror:

> The sole work and deed of universal freedom is therefore *death*, a death which has no inner significance or filling, for what is negated is the empty point of the absolutely free self. It is thus the coldest and meanest of all deaths, with no more significance than cutting off a head of cabbage or swallowing a mouthful of water.[25]

Hegel's description is not far away from that of Holbein's *Dead Christ*, in which death is depicted as without inner depth or fulfilment. Both the guillotine and the *Dead Christ* point to the banality of death produced under injustice. In fact, the Prince is no less critical of capital punishment: 'To kill for killing is an immeasurably greater punishment than the crime itself. To be killed by legal sentence is immeasurably more terrible than to be killed by robbers' (23).

The Prince is fascinated by the inevitability of death in an execution: 'There have been examples when a man's throat has already been cut, and he still hopes, or flees, or pleads. But here all this last hope, which makes it ten times easier to die, is taken away *for certain*' (23). The loss of hope in life is more sufferable than physical pain. The convict is already 'dead' before the guillotine strikes. On another level, the convict's mind is infinitely active and undetermined. In the last twenty minutes before the guillotine strikes the Prince claims the convict has this in mind: 'It's still long, there are still three streets left to live; I'll get to the end of this one, then there's still that one [...] It's still a long way to the bakery!' (64). Then the Prince emphasizes the convict's ability to know 'everything' before the guillotine strikes, just as he speculates 'everything' about the convict:

> It's strange that people rarely faint in those last seconds! On the contrary, the head is terribly alive and must be working hard, hard, hard, like an engine running; I imagine various thoughts throbbing in it, all of them incomplete, maybe even ridiculous, quite irrelevant thoughts [...] There is this one point that can never be forgotten, and you can't faint, and around it, around that point, everything goes and turns. (65)

The guillotine metaphor returns. The brain works like an overloaded and senseless automaton. The intensification of consciousness reaches such a level that it resembles an engine. Seeking infinity in life ends up becoming a mechanical activity. Death, in other words, is prefigured in life. Previously, the Prince envisages a life after death ('Imagine, to this day they still argue that, as the head is being cut off, it may know for a second that it has been cut off — quite a notion!' (65)). Here, death announces its power in life. Death has already taken place before the much-anticipated decapitation; the execution becomes a 'non-event' because the event has already taken place in life.

For the Prince, the convict desperately demands more time to live. This recalls the Prince's civil servant friend Lebedev's reference to the execution of the Countess du Barry during the French Revolution:

> This former ruling lady was dragged guiltless to the guillotine by the executioner [...] She saw that he was bending her neck down under the knife and kicking her from behind — with the rest all laughing — and she began to cry out: '*Encore un moment, monsieur le bourreau, encore un moment!*' which means "Wait one more little minute, mister boorow (executioner), just one!' (197, 8:165)

The countess would like to live longer. But what are the implications if such a thought intensifies to the extent that the mind becomes numb and mechanical? Dostoevsky comments on the same event later in the entry called 'Vlas' in *A Writer's Diary* (1873). First of all, he evokes a story from real life about a peasant who accepts a dare from another to do the most shocking thing ever. The first time he steals the Eucharist; the second time he is asked to shoot the stolen Eucharist. Pulling the trigger, he hallucinates and sees Christ on the cross and then falls into unconsciousness.

The writer proceeds to explore the psychological state of the peasant. He suggests that the last moments express the peasant's ability to detach himself from the horror of the shooting itself:

> The young lad carefully loaded the gun, and he remembered doing it; he remembered taking aim, and remembered everything, right to the very last moment. It is also possible that the process of loading the gun was a relief, a release for his suffering soul, and he was happy to concentrate but for a brief moment on some external objects that provided this release. This is what happens at the guillotine to those about to be decapitated. Mme. Dubarry cried to the executioner: '*Encore un moment, monsieur le bourreau, encore un moment*!' (1.167)

When the convict's head is working hard like an engine, it is not only a way to contemplate an eternal life, but it can also be seen as a self-detachment which postpones the arrival of death. A similar analysis is found in *Crime and Punishment*, in which the murder of the pawnbroker is carried out 'mechanically', suggesting that Raskolnikov is in a state of blankness when committing the crime (1.7.76).

The Prince tells the story of the execution to the valet and the Epanchins. In between the two narrations he relates another story about 'a certain man' and his comrades being reprieved at the last moment of an execution by firing squad (60). The 'certain man' turns out to be Dostoevsky himself, who was sent to a mock execution in 1849 for being a member of the Petrashevsky Circle. The Prince virtually speaks of execution three times in succession, suggesting a compulsion to repeat the experience of witnessing death. Like the guillotine execution he sees in Lyons, the Prince emphasizes the clarity of the mind of that 'certain man' and his desperation to think and know about 'everything'. This time the Prince is more specific in terms of what 'everything' is. After bidding farewell to his comrades and processing all the external objects in his mind, he spends the last two minutes in '*thinking about himself*' (60). He is anxious to have a clear 'picture' of what will happen after death: 'now he exists and lives, and in three minutes there would be something, some person or thing — but who? And where?' (61). Aglaya says the Prince must know how to look as he knew how to live happily when he was in Switzerland (58). From his reading of the execution, we can see the Prince tends to look for things that are invisible and even non-existent. To look suggests a vision of something beyond what appears in the field of vision. The convict fixes his gaze on the rays reflected from the dome of a cathedral on his way to the execution site, imagining that in the next minute he will merge with them (61). He is petrified by the unknowable: 'The ignorance of and loathing for this new thing that would be and would come presently were terrible' (61). The convict detaches himself from the terrifying 'new thing' by contemplating infinity through the dome: 'What if life were given back to me — what infinity! And it would all be mine! Then I'd turn each minute into a whole age, I'd lose nothing, I'd reckon up every minute separately, I'd let nothing be wasted!' (61).

But what happens to the convict at these last moments can by no means be confined to escapism. It might be true that the convict wants more time to live. But the convict contradictorily rebukes his thirst for life: 'In the end this thought turned into such anger in him that he wished they would hurry up and shoot him!' (61). Perhaps the convict is angry with himself because he realizes that he will not be able to seize hold of each minute if he is reprieved. In fact, the convict did not keep the promise he made to himself. The Prince says: 'I asked him about it — he didn't live that way at all and lost many, many minutes' (61). Similarly, Mrs Epanchin and her daughters are sceptical of what happens to the convict in the last minutes as he is released at the end. Aglaya is ambivalent about the Prince's passion to philosophize the executions: 'With your quietism one could fill a hundred years of life with happiness. Show you an execution or show you a little finger, you'll draw an equally praiseworthy idea from both and be left feeling pleased besides. It's a way to live' (62). Aglaya's comment recalls her poem about the 'poor knight', who is capable of an ideal and is devoted to it for his whole life (248–49). 'Quietism', as Aglaya refers to it, is a religious mysticism that consists of passive contemplation and a withdrawal from experience of the senses. Are we supposed to agree with Aglaya's comment, which seems to relegate the Prince to some secluded hedonist who obtains happiness by pure meditation? Later we will see that the Prince's mode of thinking is more vigorous and compulsive than what Aglaya thinks. His thinking is epileptic: it involves tremendous movements and disruptions. The happiness he gains from such thinking can hardly be described as simple or tranquil.

The Prince's eagerness to know the unknowable is comparable to Dostoevsky's theory of seeing, as indicated in his criticism of Turgenev. In the article 'The Execution of Tropmann' (1870), Turgenev describes himself following the entire process of the execution — the convict's conversations with notables, the setting up of the guillotine, the rehearsal of the event on the square. But when Tropmann is about to be decapitated, he turns his head away. Dostoevsky is very critical of Turgenev's turning away. He writes in a letter to the critic Nikolai Strakhov:

> This pompous and finicky article exasperated me [...] Man on the surface of the earth does not have the right to turn away and ignore what is taking place on earth, and there are lofty moral reasons for this: *homo sum et nihil humanum*, etc. The most comic thing of all is that in the end he turns away and doesn't see how [Tropmann] is finally executed [...]. Moreover, he gives himself away: the chief impression one gets from the article is a frightful concern — fussy to the nth degree — about himself, his integrity, his composure — and all this over a decapitated head![26]

Dostoevsky quotes from the Roman dramatist Terence's *Self-Tormentor*: 'Homo sum: humani nil a me alienum puto' (I am a man: nothing human is alien to me). The same quote is spoken by Svidrigailov in *Crime and Punishment* and the devil-figure in *The Brothers Karamazov*.[27] That Dostoevsky is concerned with all activities akin to men is not much different from the convict, projected by the Prince, wanting to know everything about the world and the self at the last moments of the execution. That is reflected in Dostoevsky's insistence on witnessing the entire process including the head being cut off, just as the Prince says he would definitely hear the screech if he was on the plank of the guillotine. But here, to look not only means to envisage a metaphysical presence but also to witness the actual dismemberment of the convict's body. The two aspects of looking are integral to each other. Activities akin to human beings are not confined to those of the soul but also the body including its mutilation. In fact, the body and soul are inseparable entities because the question of the afterlife only arises when Ippolit sees the body of the dead Christ. Turgenev is deeply interested in the psychology of the convict. He depicts in detail the events prior to and after the guillotine. He claims he has no right to watch the last moment, saying that he would be an accomplice in the killing of the convict.[28] The writer is anxious to maintain his stable bourgeois subject, or what Robert Jackson called 'a vision of equilibrium'.[29] He keeps himself away from the most bodily moment of death, closes his eyes, and contemplates the convict's death. Regarding Aglaya's comment on quietism, the Prince could have disagreed with her that he can say 'equally praiseworthy idea' from both an execution and a little finger. This is because his intense reflection — his epileptic mode of being — is not merely metaphysical but is always dependent on physical conditions, such as the dismemberment of the body by the guillotine, and the senseless convulsion and spasm during the epileptic seizure, to which I now move.

Epilepsy and Death

The Prince has two epileptic seizures. The first one takes place on the spiral staircase of a hotel just before Rogozhin stabs him; the second one happens in the party at the Epanchins' house, after he has compulsively broken a valuable Chinese vase and given a speech about the importance of his identity as a prince (4.7.553). I would like to focus on the first seizure, on which the Prince reflects extensively.

In part 2, Rogozhin relates how he is humiliated by Nastasya who turns away from him. He physically abuses her and hints that he will kill her: 'But that's why she's marrying me, because she probably expects to get the knife from me! But can it be, Prince, that you still haven't grasped what the whole thing is about?' (2.3.215). It is in the same meeting that Rogozhin shows the Prince his replica of Holbein's *Dead Christ*. Leaving the house, the Prince roams the streets and enters into a state of intense self-reflection. He sees himself responsible for Rogozhin's jealousy, wanting 'to be alone and give himself over to all this suffering tension completely passively' (224). Meanwhile he is aware that he is stalked by a 'burning gaze'. Often mentioned in this long reflection is Rogozhin's garden knife. Earlier in Rogozhin's house, the Prince spots a brand new six-inch garden knife and picks it up 'absentmindedly' twice (217). Later he remembers looking for a similar knife in a shop and wants to make 'absolutely sure' that the knife still exists in the window case (227). Both images of the knives and Rogozhin's eyes are integral to the Prince's reflection on his own death:

> He insistently wanted to see 'today's eyes,' [...] Yes, they were *those same eyes* (and there was no longer any doubt that they were the same) that had flashed at him that morning [...] The prince had wanted terribly to go up to Rogozhin and tell him 'whose eyes they were!' (231)

Rogozhin's eyes finally meet the Prince's at the hotel's staircase. For a second the two faces almost touch each other. The Prince seizes Rogozhin closer to the light in order to confirm his identity. The Prince shouts 'Parfyon, I don't believe it!' and then has his seizure, which paralyses Rogozhin and saves himself from being killed (234). He has an 'irrepressible desire' to see Rogozhin's eyes (233), suggesting a kind of machine-like compulsion for a particular moment of encounter, where his mind, to quote from the Prince on the convict, 'is terribly alive and must be working hard, hard, hard, like an engine running' (65). If Myshkin proves the eyes are Rogozhin's — which he does — he will be 'crushed and astounded' (231). The Prince is not so much concerned with his own life as with whether the stalker is Rogozhin or not. The Prince's desire to look at the eyes, the knife, and finally Rogozhin's face expresses his 'blind devotion' to the ideal that Rogozhin is innocent. But that vision of the ideal is refuted by the face-to-face encounter with the merchant's son whose 'castrating' power destroys the Prince's idealization.

The Prince's convulsive desire to meet Rogozhin's eyes parallels his compulsion to reflect on his seizures. He perceives his epilepsy as contradictory owing to the coexistence of 'eternal harmony' and banal idiocy. In the condition of 'sadness', 'the darkness of soul', 'the pressure', his brain would 'momentarily catch fire' (225). The 'sense of life' suddenly increases in exponential scale. Along with this elation is the sense of 'harmonious joy and hope, filled with reason and ultimate cause' (226). These moments are infinitely minimal. But during these moments he would say to himself: '"Yes, for this moment one could give one's whole life!"' (226). The ecstatic moments are so immeasurably pleasurable that the Prince thinks that he will sacrifice his life for it. The way in which he sees infinity in these minimal seconds before the seizure is virtually the same as the way he describes the convict's thirst for infinite time. He then remembers saying to Rogozhin in Moscow that during those ecstatic moments he was somehow able to understand the phrase '*time shall be no more*' ('*времени больше не будет*' (8:189)) from the Book of Revelation (227).[30] In 'The Angel with the Little Scroll', the seventh angel speaks to St John:

> And sware by him that liveth for ever and ever, who created heaven, and the things that therein are, and the earth, and the things that therein are, and the sea, and the things which are therein, that there should be time no longer. (Rev. 10:6)

The Prince does not elaborate on how he understands the phrase. But then he compares it with another moment of timelessness. He evokes the legend of Mohammed, who manages to travel across heaven within the time when a jug spills. The earthly time (the spilling) bursts open into the heavenly time (travelling across heaven). The phrase 'time shall be no more' suggests not only the cancellation of the concept of time, but also a replacement of the earthly time with the heavenly one. The Prince, retrospectively, treats those few seconds of ecstatic moment as apocalyptic and eternal.

On the other hand, the Prince sees the eternal harmony attained in those epileptic moments as a sign of physical illness, 'a violation of the normal state', which turns the 'harmonious' moments from the expression of 'highest being' to the very lowest (226). Yet he believes in these ecstatic moments even if they are merely symptoms of an illness:

> He finally arrived at an extremely paradoxical conclusion: 'So what if it is an illness?' he finally decided. 'Who cares that it's an abnormal strain, if the result itself, if the moment of the sensation, remembered and examined in a healthy state, turns out to be the highest degree of harmony, beauty, gives a hitherto unheard-of and unknown feeling of fullness, measure, reconciliation, and an ecstatic, prayerful merging with the highest synthesis of life? [и восторженного молитвенного слития с самым высшим синтезом жизни?]' (226, 8:188)

The paradox lies in the way in which the Prince looks retrospectively — do the last moments in epilepsy represent eternal harmony or mere illness? The state of sadness, the darkness of soul and pressure — all these 'abnormal strains' are worth having if they are the conditions of eternal harmony. The Prince wants to seek a resolution between the two incompatible images, constructing a synthesis between the ecstatic moments and the physical symptoms of the illness. His reflection on his epileptic condition echoes Hegelian dialectic, which, to over-summarize, generates a synthesis out of the alternations between a thesis and antithesis in the course of historical time.[31] The Prince puts his paradoxical conclusion in a question form, opening up the plurality of his thinking. In the next moment, he seems to refute the dialectic he has formulated:

> However, he did not insist on the dialectical part [диалектическую часть] of his reasoning: dullness, darkness of soul, idiocy stood before him as the clear consequence of these 'highest moments'. Naturally, he was not about to argue in earnest. His reasoning, that is, his evaluation of this moment, undoubtedly contained an error, but all the same he was somewhat perplexed by the actuality of the sensation. What, in fact, was he to do with this actuality? (226, 8:188)

A dialectical framework fails to capture the irreducible plurality of the epileptic condition. Unlike Hegel's idea of the Absolute Spirit, which eventually abolishes all contradictions, epilepsy ends each time with an abrupt annihilation of consciousness. The 'dullness', 'darkness of soul', and 'idiocy' are not in a synthetic relationship with those 'highest moments'; they are mutually exclusive. Here we should recall that the Prince confesses to Ippolit that he has 'always been a materialist' (387). Perhaps the Prince realizes he is brought back to reality every time he attempts to idealize experience. Alexander Herzen, from whom Dostoevsky learned about Hegel, comments on the philosopher in relation to the death sentence:

> Hegel, with perfect logic, makes the discovery that the absolute is the confirmation of the unity of being and thought. But when it comes to the

> point, this same Hegel, like Leibniz before him, sacrifices everything temporal and existent to thought and spirit; idealism, in which he was reared, which he drank at the breast with his milk, draws him into that one-sidedness upon which he himself has read the death sentence — and he tries to suppress nature by the spirit of logic; he is ready to regard every individual product of nature as a phantom, he observes every appearance from aloft.[32]

Things which are transient and contagious are sacrificed in a dialectical logic which seeks the unity of being and thought. The actual beheading and the epileptic seizure are overlooked and appropriated into this logic of the spirit. Herzen's critique of Hegel's reading of the death sentence resembles Dostoevsky's critique of Turgenev turning away from the beheading.[33] Both Hegel and Turgenev tend to dismiss — even suppress, as Herzen puts it — the dismemberment of the body, the material base of the death sentence.

Thinking retrospectively, the Prince is aware of the 'trap' of dialectical thinking, but all the same: 'Because [the seizure] *had happened*, he *had succeeded* in saying to himself in that very second, that this second, in its boundless happiness, which he fully experienced, might perhaps be worth his whole life' (226, italics mine). The Prince wills those ecstatic moments, just as he wants to see the convicts desiring infinity in the last moments of execution, even though he is well aware of the absence of a material foundation.[34]

Ippolit's Explanation

This chapter has shown that there is an irreducible conflict between the Prince's wish for the ideal and the force that refuses that wish. This conflict is mainly expressed in the Prince's reflection on the execution and his epilepsy. I have examined these conflicts through his enthusiasm for reflecting on images such as the photographic portrait, the guillotine, the knife, Rogozhin's eyes, the spilling jug, the Chinese vase, and the corpse. His vision is pluralistic: on the one hand, under the guillotine death takes place instantaneously. On the other hand, the powerful machine evokes the wish for infinite time. Similarly, the epileptic seizure cuts off consciousness abruptly. But it is preceded by the ecstatic moments for which the Prince says he would sacrifice his life. In both cases, there is the tendency to seek an infinite existence in vision, which is later annihilated.

This conflicting state of existence also illuminates the meaning of eventuality. The commonsensical reading of the execution or seizure as an experienced event does not stand in the world of Dostoevsky. Death does not take place at a particular time but continually announces its traumatic power in the Prince's intensive and repetitive meditation. Put another way, the moment is the 'non-event'. It is the absence of the event that makes the Prince's reflection traumatic. That is why Hegelian dialectic does not work for the Prince. There is no eventual synthesis in contemplation for it is always destroyed by the seizure. In the realm of experience, there is only the will to epilepsy but not epilepsy as such. Its singularity is only anticipated but not experienced.

While the Prince struggles to overcome nature and attain ideals from his reflections, the consumptive Ippolit decides to overcome nature by committing suicide to prove his self-will. In his 'Explanation', Ippolit more than once emphasizes that, because his consumption will take his life in no more than a month, he is condemned to death (387, 389, 394, 412). He speaks of being scared by a seven-inch-long reptile in a dream whose secretion can kill. His dog Norma, confronting the reptile, seems to feel 'mystical fear' and is eventually killed by it. Ippolit then says he wants to accomplish a 'good deed' before he dies. At the end he says he has reached the 'ultimate conviction', which is to commit suicide before consumption takes his life:

> Nature has so greatly limited my activity by her three-week sentence that suicide may be the only thing I still have time to begin and end of my own will. So, maybe I want to use my last opportunity of *doing* something? (415)

Ippolit sees nature as sentencing him to death. This understanding of nature recalls his ekphrasis of Holbein's *Dead Christ*, comparing nature to some senseless dumb beast, which crushes and reduces Christ to nothing but a corpse. Previously, the eighteen-year-old raises the question of whether death can be overcome by viewing the dead Christ. Here he decides to overcome his consumption and prove his mastery over nature by committing suicide.

Apparently, Ippolit's resolution is a logical conviction derived from his intention to overcome the laws of nature, that is, his natural death. Yet, he emphasizes that his decision to commit suicide is not according to logic but revulsion: Ippolit does not consciously choose to commit suicide. Rather, he is subject to a certain force, which leads him to reach such a decision, as he says: 'It is impossible to remain in a life that assumes such strange, offensive forms. This apparition humiliated me. I am unable to submit to a dark power that assumes the shape of a tarantula' (411). He also describes this 'dark power' as 'infinite', 'blank dark', 'dumb', appearing in some 'strange and impossible form', 'as if someone hold[ing] a candle led me by the hand and showed me some huge and repulsive tarantula and started assuring me that this was that dark blank, and all-powerful being, and laugh[ed] at my indignation' (409). This description sounds familiar because Ippolit uses the same phrases to describe the *Dead Christ*: 'The painting seems precisely to express this notion of a dark, insolent, and senseless eternal power, to which everything is subjected, and it is conveyed to you involuntarily' (408).

As I suggested in the beginning, the dead Christ represents that 'something without an image', the dead body which resembles nothing but itself. It is nowhere but everywhere. Everyone is subject to it as everyone has to confront their own death. The notion of the senseless eternal power appears to be that of death. If that is the case, death takes the position of the subject and casts its power over the living. Ippolit is passively led to gaze at the repulsive dark blank being which appears in an impossible form. He says he commits suicide because he cannot remain in a life that is subject to this power, that is, the power of death. In other words, he commits suicide only because he is seized by that mystical power. He wants to prevent himself from dying under the power of death and therefore he wants to kill himself first in order to have absolute control over his own death. The 'materialist' who discusses Holbein's *Dead Christ* empirically turns out not to be very different from an idealist, who sees himself subordinated to some unknowable power. Ippolit is too serious about mastering his death and overlooks the enigmatic side of it. Such seriousness has a comical side, which will be explored through Kirilov in *Demons*, who plans to commit suicide for his whole life.

Ippolit attempts to resolve the question he has raised: in view of the very power of the laws of nature, how can we believe in the Resurrection? How can death be overcome? He responds to these questions by committing suicide to express his will power. But, paradoxically, the eighteen-year-old decides to ends his life only because he is nauseated by the power of death. To put it figuratively, he is passively subject to the power of death when he thinks he is going actively to meet death. Similarly, the Prince is always already subject to the power of the guillotine and epilepsy, which crushes and seizes. Ippolit's attempted suicide opens up other questions, which will be addressed in the next chapter: how is it possible for Dostoevsky's heroes to overcome death by committing suicide? To what extent can one's will power overcome the laws of nature? To answer these questions I shall move on to *Demons*.

Notes to Chapter 3

1. 'This fourth part and its conclusion is the most important thing in my novel, i.e., the novel was almost written and conceived for the novel's denouement'. Written in November 1868 to Sofia Ivanova, cited in Richard Pevear's introduction to the novel, see *The Idiot* (New York: Vintage, 2003), xii. On the novel, see Victor Terras, *The Idiot: An Interpretation* (Boston, MA: Twayne Publishers, 1990); Eric J. Ziolkowski, *The Sanctification of Don Quixote: From Hidalgo to Priest* (University Park: Pennsylvania State University Press, 1991), pp. 127–65. Also see Walter Benjamin, 'Dostoevsky's *The Idiot*', in *Selected Writings 1913–1926*, ed. by Marcus P. Bullock and Michael W. Jennings, trans. by Rodney Livingstone, I (Cambridge, MA and London: Harvard University Press, 2004), pp. 78–81.
2. See Jostein Børtnes, 'Dostoevskij's *Idiot* or the Poetics of Emptiness', *Scando-Slavica*, 40 (1994), 5–14 (p. 14).
3. Rogozhin lives in a three-storied mansion, which houses a money-exchange shop owned by the Castrates. The sect of the Castrates splintered off from the older non-Orthodox Russian religious sect of the Flagellants, who believed in the repeatable incarnation of Christ in human beings. To obtain spiritual purity, the Castrates preached physical mutilation of the sexual organs for both male and female. The members of the sect were mainly rich merchants, moneylenders, and goldsmiths. As a widespread cultural myth of the mid-nineteenth century has it, the Castrates redirected their sexual drive into a passion for amassing wealth. That Rogozhin at the end murders Nastasya and uses ointment to preserve the corpse suggests that he desires to possess the woman as material property. See William J. Comer, 'Rogozhin and the "Castrates": Russian Religious Traditions in Dostoevsky's *The Idiot*', *The Slavic and East European Journal*, 40 (1996), 85–99.
4. Quoted from Pevear, 'Introduction', *The Idiot*, p. viii. For the entire entry of the letter, see Nikolai Karamzin, 'Nikolai Karamzin: Letters of a Russian Traveller', trans. by Andrew Kahn, *Studies on Voltaire and the Eighteenth Century*, 4 (2003), 127–28.
5. Quoted from Leonid Grossman, *Dostoevsky: A Biography*, trans. by Mary Mackler (London: Allen Lane, Penguin, 1974), p. 425.
6. The corpse is the primary example of abjection for Kristeva. See her *Powers of Horror: An Essay on Abjection* (New York: Columbia University Press, 1982), pp. 3–4. The experience of the abject can also be seen as the return of the repressed, as Kristeva writes at the end of her book:

   > For abjection, when all is said and done, is the other facet of religious, moral, and ideological codes on which rest the sleep of individuals and the breathing spells of societies. Such codes are abjection's purification and repression. But the return of their repressed makes up our 'apocalypse', and that is why we cannot escape the dramatic convulsions of religious crises. (209)

That Dostoevsky is captured by the body of the dead Christ suggests a religious crisis, in which the corpse is so vividly depicted that the writer is about to lose his faith in the Resurrection and ponders the border between life and death. To use Kristeva's term, the apocalyptic moments in Dostoevsky's works would refer to those moments where the life/death border is doubted and interrogated. Apart from the *Dead Christ*, the guillotine and the epileptic seizure point to these moments.

7. Grossman, *Dostoevsky*, p. 426. For the entire entry, see Anna Dostoevsky, *Dostoevsky: Reminiscences*, trans. and ed. by Beatrice Stillman (London: Wildwood House, 1976), p. 134.
8. Jeanne Elizabeth Nuechterlein, *Translating Nature into Art: Holbein, the Reformation, and Renaissance Rhetoric* (University Park, PA: Pennsylvania State University Press, 2011), p. 85.
9. On Dostoevsky and Holbein's *Dead Christ*, see Jefferson J. A. Gatrall, 'Between Iconoclasm and Silence: Representing the Divine in Holbein and Dostoevskii', *Comparative Literature*, 53 (2001), 214–32; Julia Kristeva, 'Holbein's *Dead Christ*', in *Black Sun: Depression and Melancholia*, trans. by Leon S. Roudiez (New York: Columbia University Press, 1989), pp. 105–38.
10. Pevear, p. xi. For the entire entry, see *Selected Letters of Fyodor Dostoyevsky*, ed. by Joseph Frank and David I. Goldstein, trans. by Andrew R. MacAndrew (New Brunswick and London: Rutgers University Press, 1989), pp. 260–72.
11. The phrase 'Prince Christ' appears several times in the notebooks. See *The Notebooks for 'The Idiot'*, ed. by Edward Wasiolek, trans. by Katharine Strelsky (Chicago and London: University of Chicago Press, 1967), pp. 198, 201, 205.
12. Milan Kundera, *Unbearable Lightness of Being* (New York: Harper & Row, 1984), p. 248.
13. See Mark 9:17–27 and Luke 9:42.
14. On apocalyptic imagery, see William J. Leatherbarrow, 'Apocalyptic Imagery in *The Idiot* and *The Devils*', *Dostoevsky Studies*, 3 (1982), 43–52; David Bethea, *The Shape of Apocalypse in Modern Russian Fiction* (Princeton and Oxford: Princeton University Press, 1989), pp. 62–104; Andrew Wachtel, 'Dostoevsky's *The Idiot*: The Novel as Photograph', *History of Photography*, 26 (2002), 205–15.
15. On the subject of imagery in general, see Jefferson J. A. Gatrall, 'The Icon in the Picture: Reframing the Question of Dostoevsky's Modernist Iconography', *The Slavic and East European Journal*, 48 (2004), 1–25.
16. Robert L. Jackson, *Dostoevsky's Quest for Form: A Study of His Philosophy of Art* (New Haven: Yale University Press, 1966), p. 68.
17. For instance, at the end of the chapter, Jackson quotes:

> 'And thus man strives on earth for an ideal which is contrary to his nature', Dostoevsky wrote in his notebook in 1864. 'When man does not fulfill the law of striving for the ideal ... he experiences suffering and has called his condition sin. And thus man continually must experience suffering, which is balanced by the divine pleasure in fulfillment of the law, i.e. sacrifice. Precisely here, then, is earthly equilibrium. Otherwise the earth would be senseless'. (70)

18. Maurice Blanchot, 'Two Versions of the Imaginary', in *The Station Hill Blanchot Reader: Fiction and Literary Essays*, trans. by Lydia Davis (New York: Station Hill Press, 1999), pp. 417–27 (p. 419).
19. See Pevear's note in *The Idiot*, p. 620.
20. Critics have commented on the significance of the face. See Leslie A. Johnson, 'The Face of the Other in *Idiot*', *Slavic Review*, 50 (1991), 867–78; Val Vinokurov, 'The End of Consciousness and the Ends of Consciousness: A Reading of Dostoevsky's *The Idiot* and *Demons* after Levinas', *Russian Review*, 59 (2000), 21–37. For discussion of the execution, see Gary Cox, *Between Earth and Heaven: Shakespeare, Dostoevsky and the Meaning of Christian Tragedy* (New York: Holt, Rinehart and Winston, 1969), pp. 161–91; Robert Hollander, 'The Apocalyptic Framework of Dostoevsky's *The Idiot*', *Mosaic*, 6 (1974), 123–39; Liza Knapp, *The Annihilation of Inertia: Dostoevsky and Metaphysics* (Evanston, IL: Northwestern University Press, 1996), pp. 66–101.
21. Mikhail Bulgakov, *The Master and Margarita* (1938), trans. by Richard Pevear and Larissa Volokhonsky (London: Penguin, 2007), p. 46.
22. Mikhail Bakhtin, *Problems of Dostoevsky's Poetics*, ed. and trans. by Caryl Emerson (Minneapolis and London: University of Minnesota Press, 1984), p. 37.

23. The phrase is used again in *Demons* to describe the murder of Shatov and Kirilov's suicide, both carried out with a revolver: 'Death occurred almost instantly' (3.6.603); 'Death must have occurred instantly' (3.6.625).
24. Daniel Arasse, *The Guillotine and the Terror*, trans. by Christopher Miller (London: Allen Lane, Penguin, 1989), p. 11. Quoted from David Wykes, 'Gillray's Guillotines', *Word & Image*, 21 (2005), 213–22. The guillotine was originally built by the piano-maker Tobias Schmidt. The first execution by guillotine took place on 25 April 1792 to behead the footpad Nicolas Jacques Pelletier.
25. G. W. F. Hegel, *The Phenomenology of Spirit*, trans. by A. V. Miller (Oxford: Clarendon Press, 1977), p. 360.
26. A letter written on 11 June 1870 to the critic Nikolai Strakhov, quoted in Robert Jackson, 'The Ethics of Vision I', in *Dialogues with Dostoevsky: the Overwhelming Questions* (Stanford: Stanford University Press, 1993), pp. 29–54 (p. 39). Dickens commented on an execution he saw during his stay in Italy in 1844–45: 'Every tinge and hue of life had left it in that instant. It was dull, cold, livid, wax. The body also'. See Charles Dickens, 'An Execution near S. Giovanni Decollato', in *Pictures from Italy* (Harmondsworth: Penguin, 2006), pp. 140–44 (p. 144). Also see William Thackeray, 'Going to See a Man Hanged', in *The Works of William Makepeace Thackeray*, xv (London: Smith, Elder & Co., 1869), pp. 384–92.
27. See H. D. Jocelyn, '*Homo sum: humani nil a me alienum puto* (Terence, *Heauton Timorumenos* 77)', *Antichthon*, 7 (1973), 14–46.
28. Victor Hugo writes, 'Qui assiste au crime, assiste le crime'. Quoted in Jackson, *Dialogues with Dostoevsky*, p. 36.
29. Ibid.
30. For an interpretation of the use of this phrase, see Steven Cassedy, *Dostoevsky's Religion* (Stanford, CA: Stanford University Press, 2005), pp. 124–28.
31. For comparative studies on Hegel and Dostoevsky, see Malcolm V. Jones, 'Echoes of Hegel in Dostoyevsky', *The Slavonic and East European Review*, 49 (1971), 500–20; Steven Cassedy, 'The Shape of Russian Idealism', in *Cold Fusion: Aspects of the German Cultural Presence in Russia*, ed. by Gennady Barabtarlo (New York: Berghahn Books, 2000), pp. 137–52.
32. Quoted in Jones, 'Echoes of Hegel in Dostoyevsky', p. 511.
33. Hegel discusses the death penalty in *Elements of the Philosophy of Right* (1820), par. 100. On this, see Allen W. Wood, *Hegel's Ethical Thoughts* (Cambridge: Cambridge University Press, 1990), pp. 121–22.
34. The Prince's ambivalent attitude towards his epileptic condition — perceiving it as a banal illness and the opening up of a blissful state at the same time — is picked up by Kristeva, who suggests that Bakhtin's dialogism is another way to articulate this ambivalence:

> One might wonder, on the other hand, whether or not the well-known *ambivalence* of Dostoyevsky's heroes, which led Bakhtin to postulate a 'dialogism' at the foundation of his poetics, was an attempt to *represent*, through the ordering of discourses and the conflicts between characters, the opposition, without a synthetic solution, of the two forces (positive and negative) specific to drive and desire. (Kristeva, 'Dostoyevsky, the Writing of Suffering, and Forgiveness', in *Black Sun*, pp. 185–87.)

CHAPTER 4

❖

The Will to Epilepsy: Suicide, Writing, and Modernity

'A great will and a great thought'

> Just as the man who is hanging himself, after kicking away the stool on which he stood, the final shore, rather than feeling the leap which he is making into the void feels only the rope which holds him, held to the end, held more than ever, bound as he had never been before to the existence he would like to leave. (*Thomas the Obscure*)[1]

Thus Maurice Blanchot describes a man who commits suicide by hanging. The man who kills himself would like to 'leave existence' and 'make a leap into the void', which turns out to be impossible. Instead of the 'void', the man experiences only the physical tightening around his neck. The rope 'holds him, held to the end, held more than ever' until the man loses consciousness and therefore can no longer experience anything. The man wills to enter a metaphysical void, but all he can experience is the physical pain. The lofty will to leave one's own existence is obstructed by the mundane tightening of the rope. The rope represents an unbridgeable gap which experience cannot surpass.

This chapter further formulates the epileptic mode of being by examining *Demons* (*Бесы*), particularly the building engineer Alexei Nilych Kirilov's project of suicide.[2] Kirilov wishes to attain an infinite existence by ending his life. His case reflects what I will call the will to death, namely, a desire for finishing the existing life in exchange for a meaningful and utopian afterlife. Similarly, regarding the will to death, I will suggest that Kirilov also has a will to epilepsy. That is, a desire for the ecstatic moments just before the attack of an epileptic seizure. Yet, these ecstatic moments, as I have shown in the previous chapter, last for a minimal time and will be annihilated by the seizure itself. The will to death and the will to epilepsy share a similar pattern: the subject wishes to experience metaphysical existence, but that wish cannot be materialized in the face of death and seizure. To illuminate this point, apart from Kirilov's suicide, I will look at the novel's political context, particularly the idea of Shigalyovism. I will also discuss Nietzsche's *On the Genealogy of Morals* (1887), his notebook commentary on *Demons*, and Maurice Blanchot's discussion of Kirilov in *The Space of Literature* (1955).

The second half of the chapter explores how the will is related to the notion of time by focusing on Nicholai Stavrogin's confession and his suicide. He is extremely sensitive to the course of time and anxious to master the present. With respect to the transient quality of time, this anxiety of freezing the present anticipates Michel Foucault's redefinition of modernity through Baudelaire, that is, the will to 'heroize' the present.[3] The chapter will suggest that the will to epilepsy works in the same way as the will to 'heroize' the present, thereby showing that the epileptic mode of being illuminates the understanding of modernity.[4]

The chronicler Anton Lavrentievich Govorov narrates a series of events in three parts that happened recently in an anonymous Russian province over the course of about twelve days in 1871.[5] Govorov appears to come from an educated and reactionary Russian class. The first part tells the story of the life of his close friend Stepan Trofimovich, who used to be a university teacher and an active intellectual. He is the father of Pyotr Stepanovich, a character based on Sergei Nechaev, a revolutionary leader who murdered his group member I. I. Ivanov for disagreeing with the idea of distributing revolutionary propaganda.[6] Divorced twice and virtually penniless, Stepan depends financially on Varvara Petrovna, who is the widow of a rich and powerful man. Stepan is also the private tutor of Varvara's son Stavrogin. Varvara tries hard to bring Stepan back to the current intellectual circle. She also tries to marry him off to her maid Darya.

The chronicle really begins when Pyotr Stepanovich returns from Switzerland with Stavrogin and other revolutionaries. Pyotr claims to be the representative of a secret, worldwide, revolutionary organization situated vaguely in Europe. The organization is structured in groups of five, and each member is separately affiliated to another group of five. Pyotr returns to Russia in order to incite chaos in the town and eventually destroy the tsarist order. Part 1 mainly deals with the portrayal of the older generation, namely Stepan and Stavrogin's mother.

Part 2 spends most of its time depicting the sons. Pyotr talks to important people in the town to prepare for inciting chaos. Part of it is to organize a fête. On the other hand, Stavrogin, whom Pyotr sees as the spiritual leader of the group, is uninterested in all kinds of collective activities. Stavrogin is challenged to a duel during which he deliberately misses his shot. Four years before the duel, he pulls a socially high-ranking man's nose at a local bar, kisses another man's wife at a party, and bites the ear of the governor. He has a brain fever after that and is sent by his mother to Europe to recover his health. Among the many offences he commits, he has raped a ten-year-old girl who consequently hangs herself. He also marries the epileptic cripple Marya Timofeevna, the sister of Lebyadkin. A banned chapter ('At Tikhon's') narrates his confession of his crimes to Bishop Tikhon. Stavrogin ends up hanging himself in the attic in his mother's house, before which he writes in a letter: 'One can argue endlessly about everything, but the only thing to emanate from me is negation without magnanimity, without power' (754).

The fête, which is organized by the wife of the governor, takes place in part 3. It turns out to be a farce, during which a group of factory workers commit arson at the other side of the town. Liza Tushina, who is a relative of the governor's wife and has a relationship with Stavrogin, rushes to the burnt village to see the wife of Stavrogin (Marya) and is murdered in the crowd. In the same party the literary writer Karmazinov — a caricature of Turgenev — delivers a lengthy speech, which is severely criticized by a group of unexpected guests from the town's lower class.

Shatov, based on I. I. Ivanov, is a former student of Stepan and a trained printer. Four years earlier, he went to America with Kirilov to work in an exploited condition. Having returned to Russia, he wants to quit the revolutionary group but is later murdered by the group leader Pyotr. Kirilov, taking responsibility for the murder and the arson, shoots himself in order to actualize his suicide plan. The murder of Shatov and other crimes are discovered. Pyotr flees to Moscow and the rest of the group members are arrested. The revolutionary group disintegrates before it manages to cause enough chaos to affect the tsarist order.

In chapter 7 of part 3, the chronicle finishes by going back to Stepan Trofimovich, who decides to walk to the countryside in order to get to know the Russian people (538). He falls ill during his 'pilgrimage' and dies within a week (630). On his deathbed, Stepan interprets an episode from the Bible which is quoted by the chronicler in the epigraph. A man from Gerasenes is possessed by demons. Christ casts them away into a flock of swine, which rush into a lake where they drown (Luke 8:32–35). For Stepan, Russia is analogous to the possessed man in the Bible, and the educated class, such as Stavrogin and Shatov, are analogous to the demons. Stepan prophesies that

> a great will and a great thought [великая мысль и великая воля] will descend to [Russia] from on high, as upon that insane demoniac, and out will come all these demons, all the uncleanness, all the abomination that is festering on the surface ... (3.7.655, 10:499)

Just as the possessed man in the Bible is healed by Christ, Russia will be healed by the great will and the great thought.

I would like to expand the discussion of the 'great will' in order to move towards Kirilov's task in proving his self-will. Alluding to the biblical scene, Stepan's formulation of the 'great will' apparently refers to God's will, which will save Russia from being 'contaminated' by European ideologies. Similarly, on another occasion, the Slavophile Shatov, paraphrasing Stavrogin, says that a navigational force is needed to sustain the operation of a country:

> Not one nation has ever set itself up on the principles of science and reason [...] Nations are formed and moved by another ruling and dominating force, whose origin is unknown and inexplicable. This force is the force of the unquenchable desire to get to the end, while at the same time denying the end. It is the force of a ceaseless and tireless confirmation of its own being and a denial of death. (2.1.250)

Instead of reason and science which represent a fixed set of logic and values, the formation of a nation is driven by an inexplicable force, which is similar to Stepan's 'a great will and a great thought'. The will refers to an incessant drive which rules and dominates. The will is distinguished from reason and science as the will can move both ways: it is the drive of denying an end but also that which can strive towards an end; it is the drive to shed blood in strengthening a nation and at the same time a paranoid force to secure the boundaries of the nation. This will is both an infinite affirmation of 'its own being' and the 'denial of death'. The way in which the will operates to sustain a nation can be seen as a successive weaving of generative forces. The life of the nation is affirmed by appropriating the dead, as commemorated in national festivals and monuments. On the other hand, corpses showing the mundane existence of death are cast away under the nation's life-affirming force.

As long as the nation is not motivated by reason or science, the will holds the authority to make subjective judgement. 'There's never been a nation', says Shatov, 'without religion, that is, without a conception of good and evil. Every nation has its own conception, and its own particular good and evil' (251). Whether a deed is good or evil is determined by the will, which transforms the exceptionally good and evil into eternal values.

For Shatov, an example of this kind of decisionism is pseudoscience, which possesses the power to confuse good and evil by utilizing reason:

> Half-science is a despot such as has never been seen before. A despot with its own priests and slaves, a despot before whom everything has bowed down with a love and superstition unthinkable till now, before whom even science itself trembles and whom it shamefully caters to. (251)

The advocate of pseudoscience is similar to the Jesuit figure Smerdyakov in *The Brothers Karamazov* who challenges the existence of God through a casuist reading of Genesis.[7] Pseudoscience also justifies Raskolnikov's classification of humankind into ordinary and extraordinary persons, of whom the extraordinary ones such as Napoleon have the right to commit bloodshed, break the old law, and found a new one. Shigalyov, a member of the group which is influenced by Fourier's utopian socialism, formulates a similar world-view, which is refracted through the voice of Pyotr. Shigalyovism (шигалевщина), a term which later entered the Russian language, divides humanity into two unequal parts:

> One tenth is granted freedom of person and unlimited rights over the remaining nine tenths. These must lose their person and turn into something like a herd, and in unlimited obedience, through a series of regenerations, attain to primeval innocence, something like the primeval paradise — though, by the way, they will have to work. The measures proposed by the author for removing the will from nine tenths of mankind and remaking them into a herd, by means of a re-educating of entire generations — are quite remarkable, based on natural facts, and extremely logical. (2.7.403–04)

The freedom of the one tenth is dependent on the enslavement of the nine tenths. Shigalyov himself confesses: 'Starting from unlimited freedom, I conclude with unlimited despotism' (402). He anticipates the Grand Inquisitor in *The Brothers Karamazov*, who thinks that the majority of men would prefer enslavement to absolute freedom.[8] When creating the idea of Shigalyovism, Dostoevsky may have had in mind a speech that was delivered by the anarchist Mikhail Bakunin at the 'Congress of Peace' in Geneva in 1867, during which he preached atheism, and the abolition of large government and private property.[9] The fact that Bakunin thought that violence was necessary to achieve these goals appalled Marx and Engels, who evicted Bakunin and his followers from the First International. 'These all-destroying anarchists', they write, 'who wish to reduce everything to amorphousness in order to replace morality by anarchy, carry bourgeois immorality to its final extreme'.[10]

Shigalyovism is a kind of pseudoscience which classifies humanity into a small group of elites and a big group of 'herd' which have no individuality. Shigalyov's idea goes further than Raskolnikov's formulation of humankind by saying that the nine tenths have to abandon their will and work ceaselessly for the good of the one tenth.[11]

After a series of deprivations the nine tenths will reach 'primeval innocence', an eternal state of stability in which there will be absolute obedience and they will be deprived of self-will under the rule of the 'greater will'. Removing the majority's will, the despot wishes to create a future that is controllable and measureable. The anxiety to will an apocalyptic end is marked on the face of Shigalyov (here we recall Lebedev, who spends his whole life studying the Apocalypse, and Prince Myshkin, who continually reflects on the last moments of the condemned man):

> He looked as if he were expecting the end of the world, not at some indefinite time in the distant future according to the prophecies (which might never come true), but at some very definite time, let's say the day after tomorrow, precisely at twenty-five past ten in the morning. (1.4.136)

Kirilov's 'fearsome freedom'

Both Shatov's comments on the nation and Pyotr's refraction of Shigalyovism have introduced the structure of the ruler's will, especially the way in which it affirms regeneration by negating death and desire for an eternal state of stability. If rulers impose their will on the nations, *Demons* also illuminates how a person carries out his will power to discipline the self. Alexei Nilych Kirilov, one of the 'demons' that 'contaminates' Russia with European ideologies, is a despot of himself. He is a 27-year-old structural engineer who wishes to obtain a job constructing the railway bridge.[12] He is 'somewhat pensive and absentminded'; he speaks ungrammatical Russian, 'somehow strangely shuffling his words, and became confused when he had to put together a long phrase' (1.3.91). He is studying the increasing suicide rate in Russia and wants to know why people are afraid to kill themselves. Stepan Trofimovich is confused by Kirilov's occupation and his interest in nihilism: 'One thing puzzles me: you want to build our bridge, and at the same time you declare yourself for the principle of universal destruction. They'll never let you build our bridge!' (95). Stepan's comical comment exposes a deep-rooted problem of the nihilist movement in 1860s Russia. On the one hand, Kirilov and other revolutionaries promote universal destruction (the middle name 'Nilych' implies 'nothing'). But on the other hand, he endorses bridge engineering, seeing science as a pathway for Russia to move towards a better future.

The idea of universal destruction, characteristic of the nihilist movement in the 1860s, recalls Turgenev's *Fathers and Children*, which is the first Russian novel to coin the phrase 'nihilist' (from the Latin *nihil*, 'nothing'). Turgenev's hero Bazarov is a medical student who promotes the value of science and the destruction of the tsarist order. He defines a nihilist as someone 'who doesn't bow down before authorities, doesn't accept even one principle or faith, no matter how much respect surrounds that principle'.[13] Whether a new and better system will replace the existing one is not his concern; all idealistic creation or affirmation must be negated and abandoned. Bazarov refracts a phrase which originally comes from Herzen and other progressives: 'The ground must be cleared' (5.38).

But there is a flaw in Bazarov's nihilism. If every principle has to be abandoned, science as a principle of study should also be negated. Bazarov does not negate everything: he believes in at least one value, that is the truth of empirical science. Placing science on a higher level, the nihilist's apparent negation is actually an affirmative discourse. Even more, Bazarov's affirmation of the truth in science is ironic: he contracts a virus when he performs an autopsy to a man with typhus and at the end dies. Bazarov is a preacher of science rather than a professional practitioner. As Isaiah Berlin comments, 'his dissection of frogs is not genuine pursuit of the truth, it is only an occasion for rejecting civilized and traditional values'.[14] In *Demons*, Stepan also comments on Bazarov, saying that the character is 'fake', 'doesn't exist at all', 'cavort[s] and squeal[s] with joy like puppies in the sun', and desires 'to cause a sensation around his name' (215). Or, as Stavrogin puts it, the nihilist is 'the lackey in thought and lackey in soul'.[15]

Kirilov's nihilism is equally problematic. The engineer lives an ascetic life. He eats little, drinks tea throughout the night and goes to bed at dawn (113). He has the ability to wake up whenever he wants (2.1.239). Kirilov is anxious to prove his will power by leading a disciplined life. But that is not enough: to prove that man has absolute control over the self he has to commit suicide, an action which Albert Camus would describe as the absurd.[16] Dostoevsky keeps coming back to the subject of self-killing through his characters such as Svidrigailov in *Crime and Punishment*, Ippolit in *The Idiot*, and the wife in 'The Meek Girl'.[17] It is through Kirilov that we can find the most extensive reflection on the subject. He discusses his project with three figures in the novel: the chronicler Govorov, Stavrogin, and Pyotr. I shall look at each dialogue in order to unfold Kirilov's suicide plan.

Kirilov explains his research on the subject of suicide to Govorov. He admits that he knows little about why people dare not kill themselves (114). But he suggests two possible reasons: first, men are afraid of the pain of death. He imagines a stone the size of a house falling upon an individual. He or she will not feel the pain but will be afraid of such an idea. The second reason is 'the other world', which Kirilov does not explain any further (114). This recalls Myshkin saying that the ignorance of what will happen after death is a form of mystical terror. Kirilov's plan aims to overcome the fear of death. He says:

> God is the pain of the fear of death. He who overcomes pain and fear will himself become God. Then there will be a new life, a new man, everything new ... The history will be divided into two parts: from the gorilla to the destruction of God, and from the destruction of God to ... the physical changing of the earth and man. Man will be God and will *change physically* [*переменитъся физически*]. And the world will change, and deeds will change, and thoughts, and all feelings. (1.3.115, 10:94, emphasis mine)

Kirilov envisages the 'other world' in which everything will change as men will have proven their autonomy. Notice his use of the language of regeneration, specifically the phrase 'to change physically': Kirilov borrows the idea of the Resurrection and applies it to the individuals. The same phrase appears in Kirilov's reflection on epilepsy, which I will discuss later. Meanwhile it is sufficient to say that the suicide project adopts a metaphysical language to describe an afterlife which cannot be known.

In a dialogue with Pyotr, Kirilov clearly states the goal of his suicide: 'If there is a God, then the will is all his, and I cannot get out of his will. If not, the will is all mine, and it is my duty to proclaim self-will' (3.6.617). Kirilov is not against the idea of God. Rather, he sees himself as God: 'For three years I have been searching for the attribute of my divinity — self-will!' (619). If Kirilov is able to kill himself freely out of pure reason but not fear or anger, he will be the master of his existence. Life does not finish according to God's will anymore. After his suicide, he will have proved the death of God and men will not need to kill themselves (619).

In view of his determination to kill himself and the monastic life he lives, Kirilov has little enthusiasm in living the existing life. But, in his third account of the project to Stavrogin, he says that he loves life and he does not see any contradiction between self-killing and loving his life: 'What of it? Why together? Life's separate, and that's separate. Life is, and death is not at all'. Kirilov's ungrammatical reply suggests that there is no such concept as death because death is also life in so far as death will bring Kirilov a new afterlife. He reconfigures the life/death dichotomy into life/afterlife. Stavrogin continues to ask Kirilov:

> 'You've started believing in the future eternal life?'
> 'No, not future eternal, but here eternal. There are moments, you reach moments, and time suddenly stops, and will be eternal.'
> 'You hope to reach such a moment?'
> 'Yes'. (2.1.236)

Kirilov seeks eternity in the present instead of the future, just as Myshkin envisages eternal harmonies in the ecstatic moments of epilepsy. The above dialogue suggests that eternity can even be attained within life. Here we begin to move from the will to death to the will to epilepsy. Not only envisaging a perfectly beautiful afterlife, the bridge engineer also sees eternity within the present moment. In this way, the notion of time has no significance for Kirilov, as he says earlier: 'There will be entire freedom when it makes no difference whether one lives or does not live. That is the goal to everything' (115). When Stavrogin evokes the passage from the Book of Revelation in which the seventh angel swears that time will cease to exist, Kirilov replies: 'When all mankind attains happiness, time will be no more, because there's no need. A very correct thought. [...] Time isn't an object, it's an idea. It will die out in the mind' (237). Kirilov experiences something akin to a revelation at this point, seeing everything as good and happy (237). He says: 'If someone's head gets smashed in for the child's sake, that's good, too; and if it doesn't get smashed in, that's good, too. Everything is good' (237). The blissful engineer even breaks his clock in order to commemorate the moment when he finds happiness:

> 'And when did you find out that you were so happy?'
> 'Last week, on Tuesday, no, Wednesday, because it was Wednesday by then, in the night. [...] I was pacing the room ... it makes no difference. I stopped my clock, it was two thirty-seven'. (238)

In chapter 5 of part 3 ('A Traveller'), Marya Ignatievna, a follower of the nihilist movement and the wife of Shatov, is pregnant with Stavrogin's son and returns to Shatov's flat after three years of separation. While Shatov is running around trying to find a midwife and the items needed for Marya's labour, Kirilov, pacing through the night in the room next door, contemplates some moments of eternal harmony. He says to Shatov:

> There are seconds, they come only five or six at a time, and you suddenly feel the presence of eternal harmony, fully achieved. It is nothing earthly; not that it's heavenly, but man cannot endure it in his earthly state. One must *change physically* or die. The feeling is clear and indisputable. As if you suddenly sense the whole of nature and suddenly say: yes, this is true. God, when he was creating the world, said at the end of each day of creation: 'Yes, this is true, this is good'. [...] What's most frightening is that it's so terribly clear, and there's such joy. If it were longer than five seconds — the soul couldn't endure it and would vanish. In those five seconds I live my life through, and for them I would give my whole life, because it's worth it. To endure ten seconds one would have to *change physically*. (3.5.590, emphasis mine)

During the moment, Kirilov would say 'yes, this is true', which he compares to God, who he imagines would also speak the same phrase. In this way, Kirilov implies that he shares God's vision; he can also be God. It is not accidental that he uses the phrase 'change physically' twice. He also used it previously in the passage where he explains his suicide plan. The phrase suggests that he wants to transform himself into a man-god. Kirilov says he has these ecstatic moments about once every three days. He says he does not have epilepsy, but Shatov says he will get it:

> 'An epileptic described to me in detail this preliminary sensation before a fit, exactly like yours; he, too, gave it five seconds and said it couldn't be endured longer. Remember Muhammad's jug that had no time to spill while he flew all over paradise on his horse? The jug is those five seconds; it's all too much like your harmony, and Muhammad was an epileptic. Watch out, Kirilov, it's the falling sickness!'
>
> 'It won't have time', Kirilov chuckled softly. (591)

Kirilov's reflection echoes his view on the 'now eternal'. Eternity not only comes after life but can also be obtained in the few seconds before a seizure takes place. Like Myshkin's reflection, Kirilov says he would give his whole life for the few seconds. But what is new in this passage is his attempt to endure those moments for a longer time. To achieve this, Kirilov has to change physically, suggesting a transformation from a man to a man-god who has supernatural power. Previously, he used 'to change physically' (115) to explain the requirement to overcome the fear of death and attain a new world where everything will be changed. Now he uses the same phrase twice in the above paragraph to describe the requirement to endure the few seconds of harmonious moments that take place just before an epileptic seizure. In both cases Kirilov tries to attain a state of eternity through a physical transformation. Kirilov sees himself as the exceptional man, recalling Shigalyovism, in which the one tenth of the population must make decisions for the remaining nine tenths.

What fascinates Kirilov is the ecstatic pre-seizure moment. He essentializes this moment, dismisses the convulsion and the collapse of consciousness that take place during the seizure. The will to epilepsy refers to this incessant desire for the state of eternal harmony where 'time will be no more'. As the engineer elaborates on his ecstasy:

> You don't forgive anything, because there's no longer anything to forgive. You don't really love — oh, what is here is higher than love! [...] I think man should stop giving birth. Why children, why development, if the goal has been achieved? (591)[18]

In these moments, the relation between Kirilov and the world is cut off. There is no responsibility involved, and there is no need to produce offspring because the individual can live eternally. This denial of reproducing new lives goes hand in hand with the affirmation of regenerating one's existing life.

That Kirilov does not have epilepsy but only experiences moments of eternal harmony leads Nietzsche to call Kirilov a self-alienated 'conceptual epileptic', a phrase the philosopher also uses to describe the Dominican priest Savonarola, Luther, Robespierre, and Saint-Simon.[19] Among Dostoevsky's novels — *Humiliated and Insulted*, *Notes from Underground*, *The Idiot*, and *Demons* — Nietzsche read *Demons* in its entirety and even excerpted a series of passages and fragments in his notebook. C. A. Miller's in-depth study of the notebook gives an invaluable comparison between Kirilov and Nietzsche's Zarathustra. The article demonstrates how Nietzsche understands Kirilov as the figure of decadence who annihilates 'God' only to assert a 'freedom' that negates life. Kirilov is in contrast to the Dionysian principle refracted through the voice of Zarathustra, who represents the affirmation of 'body and earth' (*Leib und Erde*).[20] Zarathustra suggests that a 'new pride' can be attained by repudiating God as a phantom. But this is crucially different from the way Kirilov dismisses God as fiction. Kirilov's goal is self-deification, to see himself as the substitute of God. By doing so he will achieve absolute freedom; death, as he says, will have no meaning anymore. The existing life, the body, has to be transcended, changed physically, in order to attain a new life.[21]

Kirilov perceives his epilepsy only conceptually by ignoring the seizure that torments the body and annihilates consciousness, and by wanting to endure the unendurable few seconds of ecstasy through a physical transformation. The emphasis on the physical change suggests the transcendence of life and the repression of the body and its instincts. Kirilov would rather sacrifice his bodily needs in order to obtain truth, or what he calls the new life or eternal harmony. He does not believe in the truth given to him by Christianity. In a dialogue with Pyotr, he says that Christ tells lies to his fellow convicts on the cross and therefore the perfectly beautiful God does not exist. For Kirilov, Christ 'was the highest on all the earth, he constituted what it was to live. Without this man the whole planet with everything on it is — madness only' (3.6.618). Christ is supposed to represent truth. In his interpretation of the crucifixion, Kirilov annihilates the truth given by Christ and creates truth by turning himself into a man-god. His anxiety to understand truth is confirmed in Dostoevsky's notebook for *Demons*, which says that Kirilov would 'sacrifice everything for truth', which is a national trait of the generation: 'For the whole problem amounts to no more than the question as to what ought to be considered "truth". That is what this novel is all about'.[22] Kirilov does not accept the truth explained by an objective and transcendental power: he seeks truth by constructing it on his own.

Nietzsche's *On the Genealogy of Morals* is helpful to understand Kirilov's desperate will to truth, which is refracted through his will to death and epilepsy. In the very last section of the book, continuing his critique of Christianity, Nietzsche writes that men are desperate to seek for meanings, specifically in the case of suffering:

> Man was surrounded by a gaping *void* — he did not know how to justify, explain, affirm himself, he suffered from the problem of his meaning. [...] Man, the boldest animal and the one most accustomed to pain, does *not* repudiate suffering as such; he desires it, he even seeks it out, provided that he has been shown a meaning for it, a *reason* for suffering.[23]

Kirilov finds a 'meaning' for his life through self-deification. He even comes to desire the fear of death by suicide in order to obtain his 'fearsome freedom'. Kirilov is indifferent to the reaction of his body to this grandiose plan. He has a minimal diet and stays awake all night to reflect on the epileptic moment (the chronicler says he is so good at formulating his thoughts on this moment that it seems he has written them down (590)). The problem of Kirilov's anxiety to understand what truth ought to be is integral to the engineer's despising of his body and its instinct. As Nietzsche goes on to write:

> This hatred of the human, and even more of the animal, of the material, this revulsion from the senses, from reason itself, this fear of happiness and beauty, this yearning to pass beyond all appearance, change, becoming, death, desire, beyond yearning itself. All this represents [...] a will to *nothingness*, an aversion to life, a rebellion against the most fundamental pre-conditions of life, but which is and remains none the less a will! ... And, to say once again in conclusion what I said at the beginning: man would rather will *nothingness* than *not* will at all ... (136)

This passage summarizes the problem of nihilism that has been discussed thus far. The negation of the body is an affirmation of self-will. Kirilov says he 'loves life'. But the life he loves is a metaphysical one, which does not involve the body. The will to death and the will to epilepsy feed on the anxiety to provide a meaning to death and epilepsy, which are by definition always ungraspable.

'Death as Possibility'

In a chapter entitled 'Death as Possibility' in *The Space of Literature*, Maurice Blanchot comments on Kirilov's suicide project, showing that death does not belong to the realm of experience and questioning whether one can die one's own death. As in *Thomas the Obscure* in the epigraph, the man who hangs himself does not experience the entering of the void but the tightening of the rope.

In part 3, Pyotr visits Kirilov and forces him to take responsibility for the arson and Shatov's murder, and then commit suicide. Kirilov signs his name in a testimony, excitedly changing his title twice, giving himself an aristocratic title ('de Kirilloff') and then a cosmopolitan one ('gentilhomme-séminariste russe et citoyen du monde civilisé') (3.6.621). He snatches his revolver and shuts himself in a dark room. After ten minutes, Pyotr enters the room but cannot see Kirilov, who is hiding next to the window. The chronicler writes that Kirilov is

> motionless, drawn up, his arms flat at his sides, his head raised, the back of his head pressed hard to the wall, in the very corner, as if he wished to conceal and efface all of himself. By all tokens, he was hiding, yet it was somehow not possible to believe it. (623)

The engineer, who wants to overcome the fear of death and prove his insubordination and fearsome freedom, is paralysed by fear and is hiding in his room to postpone the suicide. Govorov continues to describe Kirilov:

> he did not even move, did not even stir one of his members — as if it were made of stone or wax. The pallor of his face was unnatural, the black eyes were completely immobile, staring at some point in space. (624)

Pyotr moves closer to touch the petrified engineer, who in return bites Pyotr's left fingers. The group leader strikes the engineer's head three times and leaves the room. Terrible shouts come from the room. Kirilov says 'now' ten times or so, and then shoots himself (624).

In this last moment before Kirilov kills himself, we witness the petrified Kirilov losing his self-will; his attack on Pyotr suggests that he virtually enters into a state of madness. That Kirilov turns wax-like recalls the consumptive Ippolit who freezes in his bed when he sees Rogozhin visiting his room in his dream. Ippolit explains that what causes him to decide to commit suicide is the revulsion of some dark, peculiar, impossible tarantula-like power (3.6.409). The above scene also recalls Ippolit's Nature, which crushes Christ into a motionless corpse. The petrified Kirilov seems to be subordinated to the same power here. All the ideals that Kirilov anticipates from death collapse at the moment when actual death is imminent. Death is no longer an idea which the mind can fathom from a distance. It arrives as an instant of singularity, which the subject can no longer idealize. Kirilov's 'defeat' would be a case in point for Søren Kierkegaard when reflecting on what it means to die:

> I would have to ask whether it is at all possible to have an idea of death, whether death can be anticipated and *anticipando* [by being anticipated] be experienced in an idea, or whether it is only when it actually is. And since its actual being is a non-being, [I would have to ask] whether it therefore is only when it is not, in other words, whether the ideality can ideally vanquish death by thinking it, or whether materiality conquers in death, so that a human being dies like a dog, whereas death can be annulled only by the dying person's idea of death at the moment of death.[24]

That a human being dies like a dog recalls the image of cutting off the head of a cabbage (Hegel) — both point to death's banality. Yet, death is not merely barren materiality. A movement involves Kirilov trying to 'vanquish death by thinking it' and him being petrified as all the tangible knowledge of death goes astray in view of the actuality of death. Blanchot, this time focusing on the singularity of death, questions to what extent Kirilov can control his own death, or whether it is death which sentences him to death:

> Even when, with an ideal and heroic resolve, I decide to meet death, isn't it still death that comes to meet me, and when I think I grasp it, does it not grasp me? Does it not loosen all hold upon me, deliver me to the ungraspable? Do I die, humanly, a death which will be that of a man and which I will imbue with all of human intention and freedom? Do I myself die, or do I not rather die always other from myself, so that I would have to say that properly speaking *I* do not die? Can I die? Have I the power to die?[25]

Would Kirilov still be able to prove himself a man-god if his death was not willed?

The petrified moment in the dark room suggests that Kirilov does not die his own death. For him, suicide is the resolute step that will bring him to a new life. But the will to overcome death is refuted by the impossibility of death, as it is not and cannot be experienced. In other words, we can say that the 'direction' of Kirilov's will to death is 'reversed':

> It is the fact of dying that includes a radical reversal, through which the death that was the extreme form of my power not only becomes what loosens my hold upon myself by casting me out of my power to begin and even to finish, but also becomes that which is without any relation to me, without power over me — that which is stripped of all possibility — the unreality of the indefinite. (106)

The suicidal will is not vanquished by another will as in a combat. The former loses potency as it fails to form any relation to death. The possibility of dying is met with the impossibility of death. The wish to seek eternal harmony by committing suicide is invalid as death is ungraspable and does not belong to the realm of experience. The will to death is 'reversed': suicide as a re-solution is disempowered at the confrontation with the unknown.

For Blanchot, death is always doubled. On the one hand, death is understood in the realm of symbolization. For instance, suicide can put an end to an intolerable life; it represents courage, liberty, etc. But on the other hand, there is this death which one cannot comprehend, which is closer to Lacan's idea of the real:

> There is one death which circulates in the language of possibility, of liberty, which has for its furthest horizon the freedom to die and the capacity to take mortal risks; and there is its double, which is ungraspable. It is what I cannot grasp, what is not linked to *me* by any relation of any sort. It is that which never comes and toward which I do not direct myself. (104)

Kirilov sees the first meaning of death but perhaps not its second meaning. He wills for the 'second' death but always ends up falling into the 'first', namely, the death that is idealistically thought of as conquerable and knowable. The second meaning of death is outside the limit of human experience; it is beyond mastery, but Kirilov wants to conquer it. Blanchot compares his incessant but futile pursuit of death to the suicide of a phantom:

> Kirilov's feverishness, his instability, his steps which lead nowhere, do not signify life's agitation or a still vital force; they indicate, rather, that he belongs to a space where no one can rest [...] he who, through clumsiness, has missed his own death, is like a ghost returning only to continue to fire upon his own

> disappearance. He can only kill himself over and over. This repetition is as frivolous as the eternal and as grave as the imaginary. (102)

Kirilov justifies his suicide project at least three times in the novel. He spends all his time at night reflecting on the same problems of death and eternal harmony in epilepsy. On the one hand, this repetitive activity of consciousness is of little importance, as we know that Kirilov's suicide will lead to the transformation of neither the self nor the world. But on the other hand, this repetitive reflection of death is important because it expresses Kirilov's remarkable wish to contemplate and even to seize hold of the ungraspable, which would haunt any individual person who is conscious of his own death.

Notice how Blanchot describes Kirilov as a ghost. He tries to comprehend his death, but since death is always ungraspable, he always 'misses' death. He keeps 'missing' it as he keeps reflecting on it. Because he is always already vulnerable with respect to death, he is as if already 'dead' before he shoots himself. Each 'shooting' of death will be 'missed' as death has already taken place, turning the 'heroic' engineer from being resolutely active into radically passive.

Stavrogin's Crimes of Writing

Now I move on to Stavrogin in order to illuminate further the problem of the will. In the case of Kirilov, his negation of life is shown to be an affirmation of metaphysical life. By envisaging a physical transformation he will become a man-god. Put another way, Kirilov is apparently sceptical of the truth of Christianity but he actually believes in divinity more than anyone else, recalling Pyotr who says that the engineer believes in 'God worse than any priest' (3.6.623). The engineer believes in certain principles but he is not aware of them, just as he comments on men who are not happy because they don't know they are happy (2.1.237). Or, as Stavrogin comments on him: 'If you found out that you believe in God, you would believe; but since you don't know yet that you believe in God, you don't believe' (239). The problem with Kirilov is that he does not know he believes, just like Bazarov who is ignorant of his rooted belief in scientific principles.

The case of Stavrogin, who is also concerned with the question of faith, is more complicated. We know fragments of the life of Nikolai Vsevolodovich Stavrogin. He is a 25-year-old, well-educated, sociable person, and was tutored by Stepan Trofimovich. He is put on trial because he kills and wounds his opponents in duels. He is exiled to serve in infantry regiments. He is promoted for participating in the suppression of the Polish uprising. After his promotion, Stavrogin suddenly resigns and enjoys living with the 'outcasts' in Petersburg. He recalls Lermontov's Pechorin in *A Hero of Our Time*, who also returns to his country from war and turns into a man of indifference.

Stavrogin has been to various cities and he is registered as a citizen of the canton of Uri in Switzerland (1.2.54, 'At Tikhon's', 701). Later he writes that he did not choose to live in a gloomy place such as Uri. Everywhere for him is equally alienated: 'Nothing binds me to Russia — everything in it is as foreign to me as everywhere else. True, I dislike living in it more than elsewhere, but even in it I was unable to come to hate anything!' (675).

Stavrogin fights a duel and deliberately fires his shot into the air, which his opponent takes as a worse insult. Kirilov, who acts as the second for Stavrogin's duel, says that he has a tendency to seek a burden (289). He further comments: 'If Stavrogin believes, he does not believe that he believes. And if he does not believe, he does not believe that he does not believe' (3.6.616). If Kirilov is possessed by European ideologies, Stavrogin is 'eaten' up by the idea that he resists to believe in any of them.

I would like to examine Stavrogin's confession. It was supposed to form chapter 9 of part 2, but it was banned as the publisher thought it was too shocking. The chapter was discovered in 1921 and published a year later. The confession is written after Stavrogin has raped the ten-year-old girl Matryosha (who is sometimes described as fourteen).

Stavrogin tells Bishop Tikhon that he has been unwell. At night he has hallucinations and sees before him 'some malicious being, scoffing and "reasonable", and "various" faces and characters' (686). This ghostly image turns out to be Matryosha. He says that his chief goal in visiting Tikhon is to forgive himself and seek boundless suffering. Only by doing so will the apparition vanish (710). Tikhon reads out Stavrogin's confession, which is full of expressions that emphasize Stavrogin's self-will. The confessant compares his piece with Jean-Jacques Rousseau's *Confessions*, in which the French writer mentions his 'vice' (masturbation). Stavrogin's confession reads: 'I stopped it the moment I decided I wanted to, in my seventeenth year. I am always master of myself when I want to be' (692).[26] This recalls Govorov saying that Stavrogin, after being slapped in the face by Shatov, demonstrates his mastery over the self by not hitting Shatov back, as though he is seizing a red-hot bar of iron in his hand in order to measure his strength of mind (204). Stavrogin's mentioning of his 'vice' is not so much a confession out of a sense of guilt as a show of vanity. The reference to Rousseau recalls what the Underground Man says about the impossibility of writing a faithful autobiography:

> Rousseau, for example, most certainly told a pack of lies about himself in his confessions, and even did so intentionally, out of vanity ... I understand very well how one can sometimes slap whole crimes on oneself solely out of vanity ... (1.37)

Writing in this case becomes a process of self-fashioning, where meaning is unfinalized and develops according to reader's response.

Matryosha is the daughter of a family which rents a flat from Stavrogin. One day his penknife is lost. When Stavrogin finds the penknife, he decides to stay silent so that Matryosha will be blamed and birched by her mother (692). On another day, Stavrogin and the girl are left alone in the flat. Stavrogin approaches the daughter, kissing her hands, face, knees, and feet. Matryosha kisses him back, after which she becomes terribly ill, murmuring words like 'I have killed God'. Three days later, he returns to the flat, deciding to 'finish it all' (698). He sees Matryosha leave the flat and enter into a tiny shed in order to hang herself. Stavrogin makes note of the time and waits in the flat for the suicide to finish. He describes a fly buzzing and a red spider crawling on the wall in order to demonstrate the degree of clarity he possesses in his mind (700). After more than half an hour, he leaves the flat and peeps inside the shed to make sure the girl has killed herself, as he writes in the confession: 'I look through that crack for a long time, it was dark inside, but not totally. At last I made out what I needed ... I want to be totally sure' (700).

Stavrogin is not so much remorseful of the rape as he is anxious to demonstrate his ability to manipulate his memory:

> I am setting this down precisely in order to prove the extent of my power over my memories, and how unfeeling for them I had become. I would reject them all in a mass, and the whole mass would obediently disappear each time the moment I wanted it to. (702)

The confession is more like a manifesto written to show the man's complete control over his criminal act. Instead of reminiscence, he constructs, arranges, and even creates his memories through writing, recalling Kirilov saying that time is merely an idea that can be abolished by the will.

The young man writes that he can annihilate any section of his memory if he wants to. But on the other hand, this attempt to master memory is not always workable. Stavrogin records a haunting dream:

> I saw before me (oh, not in reality! And if only, if only it had been a real vision!), I saw Matryosha, wasted and with feverish eyes, exactly the same as when she had stood on my threshold and shaking her head, had raised her tiny little fist at me. And nothing had ever seemed so tormenting to me! The pitiful despair of a helpless ten-year-old being with a still unformed mind, who was threatening me (with what? What could she do to me?), but, of course, blaming only herself! Nothing like it had ever happened to me. I sat until nightfall, not moving and *forgetting about time* [...] No — what is unbearable to me is only this image alone, and precisely on the threshold, with its raised and threatening little fist, only that look alone, *only that minute alone*, only that shaking head. This is what I cannot bear, because since then it appears to me almost every day. It does not appear on its own, but I myself evoke it, and cannot help evoking it, even though I cannot live with it. Oh, if only I could ever see her really, at least in a hallucination! (703–04, emphasis mine)

The apparition of Matryosha represents a different operation of time in Stavrogin's confession. The apparition suspends Stavrogin's will to master time as measurable and retrievable. Throughout the confession, time is often mentioned by Stavrogin to emphasize his precise memory of what happens during the rape. But in view of the haunting of the apparition, the will to manipulate time is paralysed by the operation of another framework of time, which is marked by the recurring of a particular moment in the past. The Matryosha ghost eludes Stavrogin's attempt to demonstrate his self-mastery through writing the confession.

Tikhon describes Stavrogin's confession as an attempt to 'portray' himself as rougher than he wishes to. He says it is in parts 'stylistically accentuated', 'as if you admire your own psychology and seize upon every little detail just to astonish the reader with an unfeelingness that is not in you' (706). For Tikhon, Stavrogin has an egoistical wish for martyrdom and self-sacrifice. He wants to circulate his confession, hoping to be condemned by the public, constructing himself as a great sinner. But what he will not be able to endure are unexpected responses including people's laughter (709). Tikhon warns Stavrogin that he will commit another crime in order to postpone the plan to publish the confession (714). Indeed, he later makes himself marry the epileptic girl Marya Timofeevna — not technically a crime but a revolting act. If Tikhon is right in thinking that the intention to publish the confession is to refashion the self as the great criminal, committing another crime will be equally effective in achieving that. 'Cursed psychologist!' replies Stavrogin, who then leaves the monastery in trembling (714).

The confession remains unpublished and its author apparently does not commit any more crimes. At the end of the novel, Stavrogin returns to his mother's house and hangs himself in the attic. The location and method are the same as Matryosha's suicide, suggesting that her haunting image is part of the reason he kills himself. Earlier he writes:

> I know I can remove the girl even now, whenever I wish. As before, I am in perfect control of my will. But the whole point is that I have never wanted to do it, I myself do not want to and will not want to; that I do know. And so it will go on, right up to my madness. (704)

Stavrogin does not want to be free from the Matryosha ghost because, as Tikhon points out, he desires to be a martyr who continually bears a guilty conscience and seeks suffering. In the attic he writes on a scrap of paper: 'Blame no one; it was I' (678). Recalling Tikhon saying that Stavrogin is 'portraying' and 'posturing' in the confession, the suicide itself is part of the postures of producing the self. This is hinted at in his last letter written to his nursemaid Darya:

> I know I ought to kill myself, to sweep myself off the earth like a vile insect; but I'm afraid of suicide, because I'm afraid of showing magnanimity. I know it will be one more deceit — the last deceit in an endless series of deceits. (676)

Stavrogin did kill himself, which he has already foreseen as merely another deception amongst many.

Perpetual Transformations

I would like to conclude by evoking a definition of modernity in relation to the will. In his essay 'What is Enlightenment?', Michel Foucault discusses modernity from the perspective of how men respond to the course of time. On the one hand, there is an awareness of the transient nature of our modern life, or what Baudelaire would call the 'ephemeral, the fleeting, the contingent'.[27] On the other hand, modern man reacts to the transience by attempting to recapture something eternal within the very present moment. 'Modernity', Foucault writes, 'is the attitude that makes it possible to grasp the "heroic" aspect of the present moment. Modernity is not a phenomenon of sensitivity to the fleeting present; it is the will to "heroize" the present'.[28] What is described here is the modern consciousness's reaction to the transient nature of everyday life. Having severed the link with traditions, the self is placed randomly in the passage of time. The will to 'heroize' the present marks the anxiety to master that randomness. Instead of passively acknowledging the fragments, repetitions, and forgetfulness experienced in the city, consciousness resists by perpetually freezing the present. Stavrogin's confession and suicide echo the above definition of modernity. His anxiety to manipulate time by confessing his crime in writing, his emphasis on the ability to be unaffected by the ghostly past (Matryosha), his insistence on proving his will power to stop masturbation and other bodily desires — all these suggest the will to 'heroize' the present, to recapture a sense of eternity within the present moment.

The will to 'heroize' the present can also be understood as the desire to refashion the self. Foucault elaborates:

> Modern man, for Baudelaire, is not the man who goes off to discover himself, his secrets and his hidden truth; he is the man who tries to invent himself. This modernity does not 'liberate man in his own being'; it compels him to face the task of producing himself. (312)

Stavrogin's 'accentuated stylization', 'portrayal', and 'posturing' in his confession are evidence of a modern man's writing. In it he desires martyrdom and self-sacrifice by publicizing the piece. When the chronicler Govorov mentions that Stavrogin's face resembles a mask — hair too black, eyes too calm and clear, complexion too delicate and white, colour too bright and clean, his teeth like pearls and lips like coral (1.2.43) — there is no face behind the mask, the face literally is the mask. On the other hand, that the modern man does not 'liberate [himself] in his own being' suggests that Kirilov's project of liberating men and becoming a man-god is a quixotic idea in modernity. The language of liberty and freedom is outmoded because it still sees the possibility of achieving these ideals. After returning from the war, Stavrogin has no hope of changing or defending his country. He resigns and becomes a capricious dandy, continually switching masks, perpetually transforming himself, turning the politics of the country onto his own body.[29]

Having discussed how Kirilov and Stavrogin seize upon the fleeting moment of the present in order to deal with the unknown future, the next chapter, on *The Brothers Karamazov*, I will examine how the youngest brother Alyosha Karamazov idealizes a particular moment of the past in order to cope with the trauma of his family history. Could Alyosha overcome his trauma? Does Alyosha's relationship with trauma resemble Kirilov's relationship with death, which cannot be mastered? In order to answer these questions I move on to the final novel.

Notes to Chapter 4

1. Quoted in Simon Critchley, *Very Little ... Almost Nothing: Death, Philosophy, Literature* (London: Routledge, 2004), p. 35.
2. The novel's title has been translated variously into English: *The Possessed* (Constance Garnett, 1967); *The Devils* (David Magarshack, 1971); *Demons* (Richard Pevear and Larissa Volokhonsky, 1994); and *Devils* (Michael R. Katz, 1999).
3. Michel Foucault, 'What is Enlightenment?', in *Essential Works of Foucault*, 1 (London: Penguin, 2000), pp. 303–19 (p. 310).
4. On *Demons*, see William J. Leatherbarrow, *A Devil's Vaudeville: The Demonic in Dostoevsky's Major Fiction* (Evanston, IL: Northwestern University Press, 2005); Nancy K. Anderson, *The Perverted Ideal in Dostoevsky's 'The Devils'* (New York: Peter Lang, 1997). Also see Hannah Arendt's illuminative commentary on the novel, 'Notes on Dostoevsky's *Possessed*', in *Reflections on Literature and Culture* (Stanford: Stanford University Press, 2007), pp. 275–81. For discussions of Stavrogin, see Richard Pope and Judy Turner, 'Toward Understanding Stavrogin', *Slavic Review*,

49 (1990), 543–52; Joseph Frank, 'The Masks of Stavrogin', *The Sewanee Review*, 77 (1969), 660–69; R. M. Davison, '*The Devils*: The Role of Stavrogin', in *New Essays on Dostoyevsky*, ed. by Malcolm V. Jones and G. M. Terry (Cambridge and London: Cambridge University Press, 1983), pp. 95–114. For the source of Stavrogin, see G. Katkov, 'Steerforth and Stavrogin: On the Sources of *The Possessed*', *The Slavonic and East European Review*, 69 (1949), 469–88; Craig Cravens, 'The Strange Relationship of Stavrogin and Stepan Trofimovich as Told by Anton Lavrent'evich G-v', *Slavic Review*, 59 (2000), 782–801; Jostein Børtnes, 'The Last Delusion in an Infinite Series of Delusions: Stavrogin and the Symbolic Structure of *The Devils*', *Dostoevsky Studies*, 4 (1983), 53–67. Also see Georg Lukács, 'Stavrogin's Confession' (1922), in *Reviews and Articles from 'Die rote Fahne'*, trans. by P. Palmer (London: Merlin Press, 1983), pp. 44–45.

5. On the significance of the anonymity of the province in relation to the revolutionary plot, see Anne Lounsbery, 'Dostoevskii's Geography: Centers, Peripheries, and Networks in *Demons*', *Slavic Review*, 66 (2007), 212–29.
6. On the Nechaev Affair, see Joseph Frank, '*The Devils* and the Nechaev Affair', in *Through the Russian Prism: Essays on Literature and Culture* (Princeton: Princeton University Press, 1990), pp. 137–52.
7. 'The Lord God created light on the first day, and the sun, moon, and stars on the fourth day. Where did the light shine from on the first day?' (3.6.124). I will discuss this quote in Chapter 5.
8. The Grand Inquisitor speaks to Christ who is silent throughout his speech: 'You overestimated mankind, for, of course, they are slaves, though they were created rebels' ('The Grand Inquisitor', 5.5.256).
9. Konstantin Mochulsky, *Dostoevsky: His Life and Work*, trans. by M. J. Minihan (Princeton: Princeton University Press, 1967), pp. 329–30.
10. Quoted in Joseph Frank, *Dostoevsky: The Miraculous Years, 1865–1871* (Princeton: Princeton University Press, 1995), p. 448.
11. Dostoevsky's response to Bakunin's anarchism can be compared to his scepticism towards French Revolution: see Dmitry Shlapentokh, *The French Revolution in Russian Intellectual Life: 1865–1905* (Westport, CT and London: Praeger, 1996), pp. 52–59. For Dostoevsky's relationship to the Russian revolution, see Stuart Finkel, *On the Ideological Front: The Russian Intelligentsia and the Making of the Soviet Public Sphere* (New Haven: Yale University Press, 2007); Semen Frank, 'The Ethics of Nihilism', in *Vekhi: A Collection of Articles About the Russian Intelligentsia*, ed. by Marshall Shatz and Judith E. Zimmerman (Armonk, NY and London: M. E. Sharpe, 1994), pp. 131–56. For the writer's view on democracy, see Nancy Ruttenburg, *Dostoevsky's Democracy* (Princeton and Oxford: Princeton University Press, 2008).
12. Railway construction in Russia had been developing rapidly when *Demons* was written. Cf. Lebedev's comment on railways discussed in Chapter 4.
13. Ivan Turgenev, *Fathers and Sons*, trans. by Michael Katz (New York and London: W. W. Norton, 1994), 5.18.
14. Sir Isaiah Berlin, '*Fathers and Children*: Turgenev and the Liberal Predicament', in *Fathers and Sons* (New York and London: W. W. Norton, 1994), pp. 228–37 (p. 234).
15. Quoted in Mochulsky, *Dostoevsky: His Life and Work*, p. 623. On the subject of Russian nihilism, see Charles Moser, *Antinihilism in the Russian Novel of the 1860s* (The Hague and London: Mouton, 1964); Ronald Hingley, *Nihilists: Russian Radicals and Revolutionaries in the Reign of Alexander II, 1855–81* (London: Weidenfeld & Nicolson, 1967); Franco Venturi, *Roots of Revolution: A History of the Populist and Socialist Movements in Nineteenth Century Russia*, trans. by Francis Haskell (London: Weidenfeld & Nicolson, 1960). On a broader view of the history of nihilism, see Michael A. Gillespie, 'The Demons Unbound: Russian Nihilism and the Pursuit of the Promethean', in *Nihilism before Nietzsche* (Chicago and London: University of Chicago Press, 1996), pp. 135–73.
16. Camus discusses Kirilov in '*Le Mythe de Sisyphe*' to illuminate the concept of the absurd. See Ervin C. Brody, 'Dostoevsky's Kirilov in Camus's *Le Mythe de Sisyphe*', *The Modern Language Review*, 70 (1975), 291–305.
17. On the subject of suicide in Dostoevsky, see Irina Paperno, *Suicide as a Cultural Institution in Dostoevsky's Russia* (Ithaca and London: Cornell University Press, 1997); N. N. Shneidman, *Dostoevsky and Suicide* (Oakville and New York: Mosaic Press, 1984). Also see Susan K.

Morrissey, *Suicide and the Body Politic in Imperial Russia* (New York: Cambridge University Press, 2006), pp. 1–18, 238–72.

18. The comment on marriage is an inaccurate reference to Matthew 22:30 and Mark 12:25, where it is said: 'They neither marry nor are given in marriage, but are like angels in heaven'. See Pevear's note, p. 731.
19. C. A. Miller, 'The Nihilist as Tempter-Redeemer: Dostoevsky's "Man-God" in Nietzsche's Notebooks', *Nietzsche-Studien* (1980), 165–226 (p. 206).
20. Quoted ibid., p. 187, originally from Nietzsche's notebook.
21. For comparison between Dostoevsky and Nietzsche, see C. A. Miller, 'Nietzsche's "Discovery" of Dostoevsky', *Nietzsche-Studien* (1973), 202–57; Janko Lavrin, 'A Note on Nietzsche and Dostoevsky', *Russian Review*, 28 (1969), 160–70; Eric V. D. Luft and Douglas G. Stenberg, 'Dostoevskii's Specific Influence on Nietzsche's Preface to *Daybreak*', *Journal of the History of Ideas*, 52 (1991), 441–61; Robert Jackson, 'Counterpoint: Nietzsche and Dostoevsky', in *Dialogues with Dostoevsky* (Stanford: Stanford University Press, 1993), pp. 237–50; Edith W. Clowes, 'Self-Laceration and Resentment: The Terms of Moral Psychology in Dostoevsky and Nietzsche', in *Freedom and Responsibility in Russian Literature: Essays in Honour of Robert Louis Jackson*, ed. by Elizabeth C. Allen and Gary S. Morson (Evanston, IL: Northwestern University Press, 1995), pp. 119–33.
22. Dostoevsky, *The Notebooks for 'The Possessed'*, ed. by Edward Wasiolek, trans. by Victor Terras (Chicago and London: University of Chicago Press, 1968), p. 408.
23. Friedrich Nietzsche, *On the Genealogy of Morals: A Polemic*, trans. by Douglas Smith (New York: Oxford University Press, 1996), 3.28.136.
24. Søren Kierkegaard, *Concluding Unscientific Postscript to Philosophical Fragments*, ed. and trans. by Howard V. Hong and Edna H. Hong (Princeton: Princeton University Press, 1992), p. 168.
25. Maurice Blanchot, *The Space of Literature* (Lincoln, NB and London: University of Nebraska Press, 1989), p. 98.
26. For the significance of Rousseau in *Demons*, see Robin Feuer Miller, *Dostoevsky's Unfinished Journey* (New Haven and London: Yale University Press, 2007), pp. 86–104. The Underground Man in *Notes from Underground* says that Rousseau 'told a pack of lies about himself in his confessions, and even did so intentionally, out of vanity' (1.37). The Underground Man also points out the impossibility of writing a faithful autobiography (37), which can be seen as a comment on Stavrogin's confession, in which the confessant is more concerned with his writing style than whether the content is true or not. For discussion of the subject of confession in Dostoevsky, see Jeremy Tambling, *Confession: Sexuality, Sin, the Subject* (Manchester: Manchester University Press, 1990), pp. 164–79; Barbara F. Howard, 'The Rhetoric of Confession: Dostoevskij's *Notes from Underground* and Rousseau's *Confessions*', *The Slavic and East European Journal*, 25 (1981), 16–32.
27. Quoted in Foucault, 'What is Enlightenment?', in *Essential Works of Foucault*, 1, 310. For Dostoevsky's relationship to modernity, see Marshall Berman, *All that is Solid Melts into Air: The Experience of Modernity* (London: Verso, 1983), pp. 176–248.
28. Ibid.
29. Christopher Norris suggests that modernity can be characterized by the spirit of perpetual transformation. See his '"What is Enlightenment?": Kant according to Foucault', in *The Cambridge Companion to Foucault*, ed. by G. Gutting (Cambridge: Cambridge University Press, 1994), pp. 156–96 (p. 174).

CHAPTER 5

❖

The Karamazovs' Other History: Childhood, Violence, and the Shriekers[1]

Contexts for the Novel

The Brothers Karamazov (*Братья Карамазовы*) is Dostoevsky's last novel (1878–80). It is divided into four parts and an epilogue, with three Books in each part. In the December 1877 issue of *A Writer's Diary*, Dostoevsky said that he was occupied by a certain 'artistic work', which turned out to be the last novel he would write. At that time, he had written *The Adolescent* (*A Raw Youth*, 1875), a novel about a young man who wants to become a Rothschild, and his relationship with his biological father and stepfather. The notebooks for *The Adolescent* indicate that Dostoevsky wanted to write a novel called *Disorder*, an idea which finds its fullest expression in the dysfunctional family in *The Brothers Karamazov*. He also wanted to write a piece called *Fathers and Children*, which he said he had tried as an idea by writing *The Adolescent*. Other relevant plans included the massive project *The Life of a Great Sinner*, which emerged from *Atheism*, another unwritten novel which narrates how a great criminal becomes a hermit and wanders all over Russia to redeem his crime.[2]

In May 1878, Dostoevsky's three-year-old son Alyosha died after a series of attacks of epilepsy, which he had presumably inherited from his father. In the same year, the writer visited the monastery of Optina Pustyn with the philosopher Vladimir Solovyev and spoke to the elder Ambrose about his son's death. In the middle of his voyage to the monastery, Dostoevsky stopped in Moscow and sold the periodical rights of *The Brothers Karamazov* to the journal *Russian Messenger* published by Mikhail Katkov. On his return to Petersburg the writer worked most of the night and slept all morning. He dictated the draft of the novel to his wife Anna Grigoryevna, who would make a typed copy for Dostoevsky to make further corrections, before sending the finalized copy to Katkov.

The first two Books ('A Nice Little Family', 'An Inappropriate Gathering') appeared in January 1879. Book 3 — including a hysterical fit of Alyosha Karamazov — was published in February. Books 4 and 5 ('Strains', 'Pro and Contra') were out between April to June; the latter included the chapter 'The Grand Inquisitor'. In July, Dostoevsky travelled to Bad Ems, a place he disliked, to seek treatment for emphysema. Books 6 and 7 ('The Russian Monk', 'Alyosha') appeared in August and September. Books 8 -10 were published before Dostoevsky went to Moscow for the inaugural ceremony of the monument to Pushkin in May 1880, during which he gave the legendary speech on the prophetic quality of Pushkin. Books 11 and 12 — including Ivan's dialogue with the devil-figure — came out monthly from July. In November 1880, after he had sent out the epilogue, including Alyosha's revolutionary speech at Ilyusha's funeral, Dostoevsky wrote: 'Well here, the novel is finished! I've worked it for three years, I have been printing it for two — a significant moment for me'.[3] Two months later, on 28 January 1881, the writer died of a lung haemorrhage. The funeral, which was held three days later in Petersburg, was attended by over 30,000 people.

The Brothers Karamazov is supposed to be a biography of Alyosha Karamazov in two parts, as the narrator writes in the preface:

> Starting out on the biography of my hero, Alexei Fyodorovich Karamazov, I find myself in some perplexity [...] while I have just one biography, I have two novels. The main novel is the second one — about the activities of my hero in our time, that is, in our present, current moment. As for the first novel, it already took place thirteen years ago and is even almost not a novel at all but just one moment from my hero's early youth. (4)

What is that 'one moment' Dostoevsky aims to record? The novel was published in 1879; thirteen years ago was 1866, during which a Petersburg student Karakozov attempted to assassinate Alexander II in his carriage. The student was arrested and put on trial. He was deprived of his civil rights and sentenced to death by hanging. The coincidence of the names (Karamazov and Karakozov) and the time when the story takes place suggest that Alyosha Karamazov is based on the revolutionary figure from real life. The revolutionary motif is hinted at when Alyosha is described as transforming into a fighter in Book 7 ('Cana of Galilee') and when he boosts the solidarity of his disciples with a commemorative speech in Book 12 ('At Ilyusha's Stone'). Although Dostoevsky did not live to complete the second part of the biography, according to his wife and his friend A. S. Suvorin, the grown-up Alyosha would become a revolutionary in the sequel, and would be arrested and executed for a political crime.[4] Rumours in Petersburg said that Alyosha would even arrive at the idea of assassinating the Tsar.[5] It should also be noted that up to seven assassination attempts were organized by the People's Will during the time the novel was being written (1879–81). Alexander II was assassinated by the same group of revolutionaries in March 1881, just after Dostoevsky had died. The revolutionary motif is not unrelated to the parricidal motif in *The Brothers Karamazov*. I suggest we can consider the father's violence to women and his sons in the novel along with tsarist violence to his people. The killing of the father will be read as an allegory of the killing of the Tsar; the novel's sequel, as it were, is already written in an allegorized form.[6]

The Mothers Karamazov

I will analyse the plot with emphasis on the Karamazov family history. The novel is based on what happens to a broken family in a town called Skotoprigonyevsk ('Cattle Run'), located about 150 miles south-east of Petersburg. Fyodor Karamazov is a landowner with four sons, from two marriages and a rape. Mitya (Dmitri), twenty-eight, is the first-born son by the first wife Adelaida. Ivan and Alyosha, who are twenty-four and twenty, are from the second wife Sofia Ivanovna. The three sons are abandoned by the father at birth.

Before the main action of the novel takes place, the father, who is attracted to all kinds of females, has raped Lizaveta Smerdyashchaya, a holy fool who gives birth to the fourth son, Smerdyakov. The son is discovered and raised by the family servant Grigory and his wife. The neighbours call the son Fyodorovich (assuming he is Fyodor's son), but the old Karamazov prefers to call him Smerdyakov (Смердяков), meaning 'the son of the stinking woman'.

The surrogate father Grigory had a six-fingered son who only lived for two weeks. He called the son a dragon and thought he ought not to be baptized. The son's death has left 'a stamp' on the father's soul. Since then he has been concerned with 'the divine', reading portions of religious writings such as the Book of Job and the sermons of 'Our God-bearing Father, Isaac the Syrian' (96). He is also interested in the non-Orthodox sectarians, the Flagellants (96), who promote castrations as a means of obtaining spiritual purity.[7] On the same night Grigory's son is buried, Stinking Lizaveta, who is pregnant, climbs over the fence and falls onto Fyodor's backcourt. The mother is strangely silent throughout the night, 'for the simply reason that she had never been able to speak', suggesting that she is not only a holy fool but also deaf and dumb (96). Painfully, she gives birth to Smerdyakov and dies on the spot.

Smerdyakov is twenty-four when the narrative begins. His physiognomy is 'disproportionate to his age' and is like that of a eunuch (125). The young Smerdyakov feeds dogs food mixed with nails. He also has the habit of hanging and burying cats with ceremonies, which he may have learnt from Grigory, who is associated with the Flagellants.[8] The surrogate father discovers the son's habit and punishes him with a 'painful birching': 'You are not a human being, you were begotten of bathhouse slime, that's who you are' (124). It turns out that Smerdyakov never forgives Grigory for what he has said. In a Scripture lesson, the son asks his surrogate father a question concerning cosmic origins: 'The Lord God created light on the first day, and the sun, moon, and stars on the fourth day. Where did the light shine from on the first day?' (124).[9] The question of the cosmic origin is also the question of Smerdyakov's origin of birth: where do I come from? Or more precisely, who is my father? Grigory, shocked by the question, replies 'I will show you where!' and gives the son a violent blow on his cheek. The question of origin — both religious and biological — is returned with a blow, a violent event which recalls Smerdyakov's traumatic birth. A week later, the son has his first epileptic fit. Smerdyakov's epileptic condition marks his traumatic birth, i.e. he was begotten because of a rape. It is not accidental that Smerdyakov passes violence to animals. Retrospectively, the son says:

> I came from Stinking Lizaveta without a father [...] Grigory Vasilievich reproaches me for rebelling against my nativity: 'you opened her matrix,' he says. I don't know about her matrix, but I'd have let them kill me in the womb, so as not to come out into the world at all. (224)

This chapter explores how Smerdyakov's epileptic seizure and hysterical fits in the case of other brothers become an indexical moment to a violent family history which was silenced. To read epilepsy in *The Brothers Karamazov* means to rearticulate a history of violence and at the same time the violence of history. Smerdyakov's traumatic birth will illuminate the other three brothers' traumatic past, which also has to do with the father's violence.

In the third night of the story, Smerdyakov shams an epileptic fit and pretends to have fallen into unconsciousness. When the servants are asleep, he wakes up and murders Fyodor by smashing his skull with a paperweight. He also steals 3,000 roubles which he never uses. He has a real and severe epileptic fit shortly after the murder. A week later he hangs himself. There is a strange repetition of the two fits of Smerdyakov: the first one takes place after being punished by the surrogate father Grigory; the second one happens after killing the biological father. The two seizures are reminders of Smerdyakov's traumatic birth and the violence of the two fathers in the past.[10]

As for Mitya, he is completely forgotten by the old Karamazov (1.2.10). The first-born son changes hands five times in the course of his upbringing. He never finishes high school; he studies in a military school and later serves in the Caucasus. He leads a wild life and spends a great deal of money, often thinking that his father is hiding his deceased mother's inheritance. Book 1 opens with the family history; Book 2 moves on to the father meeting his sons (except Smerdyakov) in the monastery to settle the money issue. Mitya several times hints that he will murder the father. This is also hinted at when Zosima kneels down before Mitya: 'Forgive me! Forgive me, all of you!' (1.6.75). The elder senses that parricide is going to happen. He orders Alyosha to leave the monastery and stay with the other brothers.

On the night of the murder, Mitya visits the father's house to see if Grushenka — a woman for whom he and the father are competing — is with him. Mitya mistakenly wounds Grigory while he is leaving the house, causing the family servant to think that Mitya is the murderer. Owing to all sorts of disadvantageous evidence — such as his manifest aggression, Smerdyakov being physically too weak to kill, etc. — Mitya is arrested for parricide.

During the police interrogation in Book 9, Mitya insists on his innocence. But something happens at the end which changes his mind: 'He had a strange sort of dream, somehow entirely out of place and out of time' (507). The brother dreams of himself in a carriage, flying past a burnt-down village. A line of peasant women — thin, wasted, with brownish faces — is standing in front of it. The scene suggests that the women have just committed arson. As Cathy Frierson points out, arson was a popular form of protest of 'a beleaguered daughter-in-law or wife against patriarchal powers in her household'.[11] Burning houses would also attract hysterical women and some of them would throw themselves into the fire.[12] The women standing in a line in Mitya's dream could be a group of oppressed women who have committed arson or they could be hysterics who are attracted to it — in both cases the women in Mitya's dream appear to suffer from patriarchal powers in their household.

One of the women in the line, with her breast dried-up and possibly hysterical, is holding a baby who is 'crying, reaching out its bare little arms, its little fists somehow all blue from the cold' (507). Mitya 'wants to weep, he wants to do something for them all, so that the wee one will no longer cry [...] And it must be done at once, without delay and despite everything, with all his Karamazov unrestraint' (508). What is to be done exactly is not said. The Karamazovian force can be benevolent or destructive, recalling the contemplative Smerdyakov, who in the next second can either redeem his sin or burn down his village (3.6.127). Mitya wakes up at this ambivalent point and declares that he will accept any charges against him. 'I had a good dream', he says. Just before the trial he says to Alyosha: 'I've sensed a new man in me, a new man has arisen in me! [...] Why did I have a dream about a "wee one" at such a moment? [...] It's for the "wee one" that I will go. Because everyone is guilty for everyone else' (591). The 'wee one' dream causes Mitya to accept punishment even though he is innocent. Perhaps he is trying to bear the responsibility for the violence committed by his father in the past, of which the result allegorically appears in this dream. In fact, Mitya has written a note and hid it in his pocket: 'For my whole life I punish myself, I punish my whole life!' (8.5.403). The note recalls the theme of *The Life of a Great Sinner* and suggests a kind of confessional writing. Mitya is eventually sentenced to hard labour in Siberia. The ending shows Ivan, who also feels guilty of parricide, trying to arrange an escape for Mitya to America.

In Book 11, Ivan has three consecutive meetings with Smerdyakov, during which the latter explains the details of the murder. He accuses Ivan: 'I want to prove it to your face tonight that in all this the chief murderer is you alone, sir, and I'm just not the real chief one, though I did kill him. It's you who are the most lawful murderer!' (11.8.627). According to Smerdyakov's casuistry, Ivan knows the parricide is going to happen but he still decides to leave Skotoprigonyevsk for Moscow, unconsciously allowing Smerdyakov to take his father's life. Ivan is confused and seems to agree with what the casuist has said to him. After the meeting, he has a hallucination, in which he sees a devil-figure telling him about the life in hell. Ivan is split between his thoughts, not knowing whether the devil-figure is his own hallucination or a living individual, suggesting a kind of schizophrenia. Ivan becomes seriously ill and has an attack of brain fever. In the trial, Ivan claims that Smerdyakov killed the father, but no one believes him: 'He killed him, and killed him on my instructions ...Who doesn't wish for his father's death ...?' (686).

Ivan is academically gifted and has studied at the university. He sustains himself by writing sketches of street lives in newspapers, for which he signs 'Eyewitness'. In Book 5 ('Rebellion'), he talks to Alyosha about cases of child abuse which he has collected from newspapers. Calling the cases 'lovely pictures' ('картинки прелестные', 14:220), Ivan introduces each story as if creating a cinematic montage (241). The first of the collection is about the Turks' torture of Slav children in Bulgaria; the second is about a young man, who has grown up like a 'little wild beast', being guillotined for killing an old man in Geneva; the last three have to do with Russian parents torturing their children and images of mutilation. Not accidentally, Ivan is also abandoned at birth by his father, suggesting that the son is actually complaining against his father in his fascination with child abuse.[13]

Ivan's last picture is about an eight-year-old boy having mistakenly thrown a stone at the paw of a general's favourite dog. The general captures the child and locks him up for the night. On the next day he strips the child naked and orders his flock of hounds to devour him. The general also has the child's mother witness the killing. Ivan questions Alyosha: 'Well ...what to do with [the general]? Shoot him? Shoot him for our moral satisfaction? Speak! Alyoshka!' (243). 'Shoot him!', Alyosha replies softly with a remarkably twisted smile (243), suggesting a kind of hidden aggression against the father figures in Ivan's 'lovely pictures'.

Alyosha's mother Sofia Ivanovna dies when he is four-year-old. He is snatched away by her benefactress and comes to live with various guardians of the female sex. From adolescence, he has a 'wild, frantic modesty and chastity' (20). His unconditional generosity is compared to that of a holy fool. He cannot bear certain words and conversations about women among his schoolmates' discussions. Just before he finishes high school, he returns home and visits his mother's grave, after which he enters the monastery and becomes the disciple of Zosima. Alyosha has a vivid memory of her mother's face and caresses: 'As if she were standing alive before me' (18). Alyosha's memory of the mother is described as that which 'emerge[s] throughout one's life as specks of light, as it were, against the darkness, as a corner torn from a huge picture, which has all faded and disappeared except for that little corner' (18).[14]

But on the other hand, something quite contrary to what Alyosha remembers happened. The sixteen-year-old orphan Sofia Ivanovna married the old Karamazov in order to run away from her tormenting benefactress, an aristocratic old lady. Sofia 'was once taken out of a noose that she had hung from a nail in the closet' (13). The relationship between Sofia and her benefactress recalls *Humiliated and Insulted*, where Nelly is also constantly abused by her landlady (2.4.118). It should be noted that they both suffer from hysteria and epilepsy. Fyodor is particularly attracted to Sofia, whose 'innocent eyes cut [his] soul like a razor' (13). Seeing himself as her benefactor who has saved her life, Fyodor pays no respect to Sofia. He invites various women to launch orgies in his house. The terrorized experiences she has with Fyodor and her benefactress cause her to suffer from hysterical seizures:

> this unhappy young woman, who had been terrorized since childhood, came down with something like a kind of feminine nervous disorder, most often found among simple village women, who are known as shriekers because of it. From this disorder, accompanied by terrible hysterical fits, the sick woman would sometimes even lose her reason. (13)

Sofia's shrieking, which is symptomatic of this 'terrible woman's disease', is prominent in peasant women who are oppressed by exhausting work, improper birth giving, desperate grief, and beating (47). Medical research suggested that the shrieks of the peasant women were often caused by the 'exceptionally harsh conditions of rural life', implying that the shrieking is a symptom produced under patriarchal oppression.[15] References to the shrieker permeate the novel: apart from Sofia, a peasant woman who visits Zosima suddenly starts 'screeching, hiccupping and shaking all over as if in convulsions' (1.3.47). Shrieking is also associated with Katerina Ivanovna and Grushenka. It also happens to Alyosha's fiancée Lise, who imagines crucifying a four-year-old boy by cutting off his fingers (11.3.584). Ilyusha's mother also has a seizure in front of her deceased son at the end of the novel (770). Liza Knapp points out that the shriekers like Sofia are equivalent to hysterical women in Western Europe.[16] In fact, in the same period when *The Brothers Karamazov* was published, the neurologist Jean Martin Charcot was conducting a notorious study on hysterical women in the Salpêtrière Hospital in Paris. One of his approaches to the hysterics was to photograph and publicize their seizures. Charcot's studies in hysteria became a spectacle, causing the surrealist writers Breton and Aragon to republish some of Charcot's photographs of the hysterics, saying that hysteria was the greatest poetic discovery of the nineteenth century.[17] Just as the shriekers were oppressed under patriarchy in Russia, the hysterics in Western Europe, as Charles Bernheimer suggests, also suffered from the split between their own personal impulses and the demands of patriarchy.[18] That hysteria refers to sufferings produced by patriarchy has initiated a long history of feminist critique.[19]

Besides, in the dictionary of Russian folklore culture by Vladimir Dal (1863–66), shrieking (кликлуша) was defined as 'one possessed by a form of falling sickness, to which peasant women are especially susceptible'.[20] The medical phrase *hystérie-épilepsie* was still often used to describe hysterical symptoms in later nineteenth-century Europe; the two diseases were virtually indistinguishable, and I am going to accept this identification.[21]

'A moment of danger'

Alyosha on the one hand has a tendency towards creating a 'good memory' of his mother. But on the other hand, there are other memories — such as Sofia being terrorized by Fyodor — which have to do with the traumatic side of the family history. There are moments in which the novel points back to the strained relationship between the son and parents. Smerdyakov's epileptic seizures, Mitya's dream of the dried-up hysterical women, Ivan's 'lovely pictures' in which the mother witnesses her son being tortured, Alyosha's mother's hysterical shrieks — these images flit by in the course of the narrative, exposing the other side of the 'good memory', the 'other' history of the brothers Karamazov. This 'other' history finds its expression during the attack of hysteria and epilepsy, the two major illnesses which haunt all the Karamazovs. This chapter explores these moments, examining how they point to an alternative, silenced side of history. My approach is informed by Walter Benjamin in *Theses on the Philosophy of History* (1950), where he writes: 'The true picture of the past flits by. The past can be seized only as an image which flashes up at the instant when it can be recognized and is never seen again'.[22] In the next section he adds: 'To articulate the past historically does not mean to recognize it "the way it really was". It means to seize hold of a memory as it flashes up at a moment of danger' (VI, 247).

Diane Thompson suggests that the function of memory in *The Brothers Karamazov* is to propel the narrative and exemplify the discourse of Christian Orthodoxy.[23] Her argument neglects a less predictable memory, which always disrupts the voluntary ones. In contrast to Thompson's approach, I am interested in the point that what Alyosha seems to remember coherently about his mother is actually fragmentary. These fragmentary memories of the past have to do with a series of violent acts afflicted by the father, which often involved sexual activities. I will consider three moments in the novel. First, Alyosha's memory of his mother in Book 1, which involves a mixture of disconnected images. One of them is derived from Claude Lorrain's *Acis and Galatea*, a painting which Dostoevsky saw in Dresden, suggesting that Alyosha is idealizing his memory of the past. Second, Alyosha's first hysterical seizure in Book 2, which is virtually identical to his mother's. The repetition suggests that the mother's trauma of being abused by the father is passed on to the son. Third, Alyosha's second hysterical fit in Book 7 ('Cana of Galilee'), in which he dreams of Zosima and Christ. I suggest that Fyodor also appears in the dream, causing an overlapping of three fathers. This carnivalization of fatherly images — the elder, the divine, and the rapist — destabilizes Alyosha's relationships with his fathers, resisting the attempt to write a single and undisturbed family history. I will conclude with Book 12 ('At Ilyusha's Stone') where Alyosha delivers a speech for Ilyusha, showing how the brother is anxious to preserve a 'good' memory of the past, to create a history which is fixed with beautiful images.

A Corner of the Picture

In Book 1, where Alyosha is introduced, his memory of his mother is presented vividly:

> This is exactly how it was with [Alyosha]: he remembered a quiet summer evening, an open window, the slanting rays of the setting sun (these slanting rays he remembered most of all), an icon in the corner of the room, a lighted oil-lamp in front of it, and before the icon, on her knees, his mother, sobbing as if in hysterics, with shrieks and cries, seizing him in her arms, hugging him so tightly that it hurt, and pleading for him to the Mother of God, holding him out from her embrace with both arms towards the icon, as if under the protection of the Mother of God ... and suddenly a nurse rushes in and snatches him from her in fear. What a picture! [Вот картина!] Alyosha remembered his mother's face, too, at that moment: he used to say that it was frenzied, but beautiful, as far as he could remember. (19, 14:18)

This picture can be divided into at least five separate images. These images are pre-cinematic in so far as they, like a camera, penetrate different levels of the field of vision. First, the picture depicts the quiet summer evening with the slanting rays of the setting sun, resembling a 'long shot'. Second, the picture zooms into the house of the father, showing the icon, oil-lamp, the mother and the son. Third, there is an extreme close-up of the mother's prayer. The picture shows the mother hysterically pressing against her son, hoping to protect him by borrowing the power from the Mother of God. Fourth, just after an ellipsis, the nurse comes and takes away the son. Fifth, there is another close-up picture of the mother. These images seem to form a story about the mother and son. Indeed this story is what has been forged in Alyosha's memory. However, a rereading of these images will suggest that they did not necessarily take place in a linear sequence. It appears that Alyosha has recreated his own memory of his mother.

In *A Writer's Diary* (1873), Dostoevsky comments on historical painting after visiting an exhibition. He writes:

> Ask any psychologist you like and he will tell you that if you imagine some event of the past, especially of the distant past — one that is completed and historical (and to live without imagining the past is impossible) — then the event will *necessarily* be imagined in its completed aspect, i.e., with the addition of all its subsequent developments that had not yet occurred at the historical moment in which the artist is trying to depict a person or event. And thus the essence of a historical event cannot even be imagined by an artist exactly as it probably happened in reality. ('Apropos of the Exhibition', 1.215)

The difficulty of representing a historical event is a commentary on Alyosha trying to 'paint' his mother's history. Rereading Alyosha's memory means to examine how he imagines the past in relation to his mother, and how he supplements that imagination with additional images drawn from the present. For instance, it is not accidental that Alyosha remembers the 'slanting rays of the setting sun', which appears again in Zosima's biography in Book 6. The elder says:

> I bless the sun's rising each day and my heart sings to it as before, but now I love its setting even more, its long slanting rays, and with them quiet, mild, tender memories, dear images from the whole of a long and blessed life — and over all is God's truth, moving, reconciling, all forgiving! (292)

As Zosima's disciple, perhaps Alyosha has supplemented his memory of his mother with a phrase used by his mentor. It should be noted that the biography is written down from memory by Alyosha sometime after Zosima's death. So it is equally possible that he has 'borrowed' the memory of his mother and used it when writing the biography. In other words, the image of the setting sun is not attached to any original voice presented in the novel.

Moreover, the 'slanting rays of the setting sun' is a phrase used frequently in other novels. In Stavrogin's confession in *Demons*, he writes that he dreams of seeing Claude Lorrain's painting *Acis and Galatea* in the gallery of Dresden, a painting he likes to call 'The Golden Age'. For Stavrogin, the painting represents the best period of Europe before it was contaminated by civilization:

> A corner of the Greek archipelago; blue, caressing waves, islands and rocks, a luxuriant coastline, a magic panorama in the distance, an inviting sunset — words cannot express it. Here European mankind remembered its cradle, here were the first scenes from mythology, its earthly paradise ... Here beautiful people lived! ('At Tikhon', 703)

Stavrogin's dream reflects the desire for a utopia. He continues: 'The rocks and sea, the slanting rays of the setting sun — it was as if I still saw it all when I woke up and opened my eyes, for the first time in my life literally wet with tears' (703).

And yet, Stavrogin's fantasy is disrupted by the image of a girl: Matryosha — the girl he has raped and who is now dead — reappears in his dream, shaking her head and raising her fist at him (703). The golden-age fantasy is dissolved by the traumatic image of the dead child. Similarly, in *The Adolescent*, the surrogate father comments on the same painting before his son, pointing to the disappearance of the golden age:

> I had woken up and opened my eyes which were literally wet with tears [...] By that time it was already evening [...] And then you see, dear boy, the setting

FIG. 7. Claude Lorrain, *Coastal Landscape with Acis and Galatea* (1657)

> sun of the first day of European humanity which I had seen in my dream was instantly transformed for me when I woke up into the setting sun of the last day of European humanity! (3.2.492)

Claude's *Acis and Galatea* on the one hand represents the image of happiness, origin, and love. But on the other hand, the painting is always already a marker of the decline of humanity. In fact, the painting has frozen a seemingly joyful moment of a Greek myth. In Sicily, a Grecian colony, Acis and Galatea are in love with each other and are oblivious of the world around them. This prelapsarian moment is associated with 'the golden age', a Slavophile's notion of retrospective utopianism.[24] And yet, what is not shown in the painting is that the Cyclops Polyphemus, the guardian of the shore, is also in love with Galatea. Distracted by her, Polyphemus leaves the incoming boats unchallenged. As Ovid writes: 'His unstaunched thirst for blood is quenched: ships may pass and repass safely'.[25] According to the myth, the Cyclops will hurl a rock at Acis and kill him. As Richard Peace comments: 'Claude has caught the scene at an idyllic moment of repose, but it is an idyll soon cruelly and violently to be shattered' (21). Alyosha's 'slanting rays of the setting sun' is integral to an image of destruction, which is unspoken in his memory of the mother. Just as Claude excludes violence in his painting, Alyosha chooses to 'paint' the nicer part of his childhood for his picture-memory.

The image of the setting sun is followed by a close-up of the mother, who is pleading hysterically before the icon, 'as if under the protection of the Mother of God' (19). The image of pleading is followed by an ellipsis and then a nurse comes and takes away the child ('under the protection of the Mother of God ... and suddenly a nurse rushes in'). The ellipsis suggests a narrative break between the mother pleading and the nurse's appearance. Alyosha remembers his mother in a 'quiet summer evening'. Strangely, it is also an evening when the little Alyosha and Ivan are snatched away by their mother's benefactress:

> Exactly three months after Sofia Ivanovna's death, the general's widow [the benefactress] suddenly appeared in person in our town [...] It was evening. [... She] made straight for the cottage and the two boys. Seeing at a glance that they were unwashed and in dirty shirts, she gave one more slap to Grigory himself and announced to him that she was taking both children home with her, then carried them outside just as they were, wrapped them in a plaid, put them in the carriage, and took them to her own town. (14)

At the age of four, Alyosha may have mistaken the benefactress for a nurse. Besides, Sofia is already dead when the benefactress takes the children away, meaning that the last image of Alyosha's memory ('a nurse rushes in') cannot possibly happen in the mother's presence. Every image in his memory represents a separate event in a different time and space. Only through Alyosha's recollections are different images pieced together and turned into a seemingly uninterrupted narrative.

Alyosha's Hysteria

There are other questions we can ask about the beautiful picture of the mother. For instance, why is Alyosha's mother weeping in the seemingly beautiful memory? Another part of the novel repeats this image of the mother's sobbing. In Book 3 ('Over the Cognac'), the drunken old Karamazov meets Ivan and Alyosha in his house. Speaking of the charm of the female sex, he gives an account of how he sexually abused Sofia:

> Listen, Alyoshka, I always used to take your late mother by surprise, only it worked out differently. I never used to caress her, but suddenly, when the moment came — suddenly I'd lay myself down before her, crawling on my knees, kissing her feet, and I always, always sent her — I remember it as if it were today — into that little laugh, a showery, tinkling, soft, nervous, peculiar little laugh. It was the only kind she had. I knew that that was how her sickness usually began, that the next day she'd start her shrieking again, and that this present little laugh was no sign of delight — well, it may have been false, but still it was delight. (3.8.136–37)

The passage hints at a primal scene, in which the son 'witnesses' the father sexually abusing the mother. That Sofia is only a sixteen-year-old in the above passage suggests that the scene is also a form of child abuse. The primal scene is not unconsciously evoked in Alyosha's mind but directly told by the father. The passage also suggests that the father seduces the mother just in order to provoke her hysterical fit, implying a kind of sadism in him.

The father moves on to recount another abuse of his 'little shrieker' (137) ('кликушечка', 14:126). In the first year of the marriage, he thinks the mother is praying too much. He picks up her icon and threatens her: 'Look ... look, here's your icon, here it is, I'm taking it down. Now watch. You think it's a wonder-working icon, and right now, before your eyes, I'm going to spit on it, and nothing will happen to me ...!' (137). Spitting de-consecrates the icon, severing the relationship between the Mother of God and Alyosha's mother. The spitting of saliva not only profanes the mother's prayer, but also evokes the image of the abject. That is, the saliva, which exists in liminal space, both inside and outside the membrane, engenders a threat to body boundaries.[26] It is at this point of boundary intrusion that the mother breaks into a hysterical fit. The father says: 'Lord, I thought, now she's going to kill me! But she just jumped up, clasped her hands, then suddenly covered her face with them, shook all over, and fell to the floor ... just sank down...' (137).

Alyosha, listening to his father telling how he abused his mother, suddenly breaks into a hysterical fit, which is identical to his mother's:

> The old man jumped up in fright. From the time he began talking about his mother, a change had gradually come over Alyosha's face. He flushed, his eyes burned, his lips trembled ... The drunken old man went on spluttering and noticed nothing until the moment when something very strange suddenly happened to Alyosha — namely, the very same thing he had just told about the 'shrieker' repeated itself with him. He suddenly jumped up from the table just as his mother was said to have done, clasped his hands, then covered his face with them, fell back in his chair as if he'd been cut down, and suddenly began shaking all over in a hysterical attack of sudden trembling and silent tears. The remarkable resemblance to his mother especially struck the old man. (137)

Now we have a clearer picture to explain why the mother is sobbing and pleading before the icon in Alyosha's memory. She might have been abused by the father and wanted to protect his son from being abused. Alyosha chooses to remember a scene just after the primal scene — that he was seized tightly in the mother's arms — suggesting that his memory has a tendency to disavow the traumatic past. The mother's hysterical sobbing and seizing of the son are symptoms hinting that violence had taken place. Likewise, Alyosha's seizure is the moment where the 'good' memory of the mother is burst open with images of sexual abuse. It is also the moment at which a history of violence resurfaces in consciousness. Furthermore, the history of violence has no origin, as we know the benefactress also maltreated Sofia. Alyosha's seizure therefore is indexical not to a single but multiple images of violence which involve different tormentors of both sexes.

A psychoanalytic reading of Alyosha's memory will help us further understand the seizure. In 1886, Freud returned from Paris after studying hysteria with Charcot in the Salpêtrière Hospital. Freud began to write extensively on the subject of hysteria. He suggested that there were three distinctive phases in a complete hysterical fit:

> The first, 'epileptoid', phase which resembles an epileptic fit. [...] The second phase, that of the '*grands mouvements*', manifests movements of wide compass, such as what are known as 'salaam' movements, arched attitude (*arc de cercle*), contortion and so on. [...] The third, hallucinatory, phase of a hysterical attack, the '*attitudes passionnelles*', is distinguished by attitudes and gestures which belong to scenes of passionate movement, which the patient hallucinates and often accompanies with the corresponding words.[27]

One of the discoveries Freud made in the Salpêtrière is that the above symptoms have no organic cause. This leads him to explore the meanings 'beneath' these symptoms. He is particularly interested in the hallucinatory phase of hysteria. The patients' hallucination is often connected to the memory of the past, particularly traumatic memory. He, in collaboration with his colleague Josef Breuer, writes in *Studies in Hysteria*:

> Our attempted explanation takes its start from the third of these phases, that of the '*attitudes passionnelles*'. Where this is present in a well-marked form, it exhibits the hallucinatory reproduction of a memory which was important in bringing about the onset of the hysteria — the memory either of a single major trauma (which we find *par excellence* in what is called traumatic hysteria) or of a series of interconnected part-traumas (such as underlie common hysteria). Or, lastly, the attack may revive the events which have become emphasized owning to their coinciding with a moment of special disposition to trauma.[28]

The passage can be summarized by an observation by Freud and Breuer: '*Hysterics suffer mainly from reminiscences*' (2:7). That is, hysteria has to do with the physical suffering conditioned by a selective blockage of memory.[29] Freud furthers these observations in the essay 'Screen Memories' (1899), in which he says that the formation of hysterical symptoms has to do with the 'building up of our store of memories'.[30] In a dialogue with an educated man aged thirty-eight, Freud asks his patient to recollect his childhood memories. In the process of his recounting, the analyst notices that the man has amalgamated two sets of phantasies of his childhood: '[he] projected the two phantasies on to one another and made a childhood memory of them' (3:315). The kind of memory which is constructed from various phantasies and genuine events is what Freud calls a 'screen memory'. He shows that when the man recollects his childhood scenes, the subject does not experience the scene from the perspective of the child who was in the scene, but rather as an observer from outside the scene: 'A picture cannot be an exact repetition of the impression that was originally received. For the subject was then in the middle of the situation and was attending not to himself but to the external world' (3:321). Not memory from the past, but memory of the past — hence Freud concludes his essay by raising the question of whether we have any memories at all from our childhood:

> Memories *relating to* our childhood may be all that we possess. Our childhood memories show us our earliest years not as they were but as they appeared at the later periods when the memories were aroused. In these periods of arousal, the childhood memories did not, as people are accustomed to say, *emerge*; they were *formed* at that time. (3:322)

Through looking into the slips, gaps and silences in the patient's stories, the psychoanalyst examines how a symptom in the present is linked to the past. The memory of a certain event told by the patient can be that which happened before or after the event which the subject has unconsciously disavowed. In other words, a seemingly trivial event can be the trace of the silenced area in memories. This part of memories of childhood has often to do with sexual elements which were not developed into consciousness (317).

Freud's studies in hysteria offer a way of reading which sees trivial words as symptoms. The epileptic/hysterical seizure is read as the symptom of a traumatic past. Smerdyakov's epilepsy is indexical to the fact that his mother was raped by Fyodor and he himself was abused by Grigory. Alyosha's seizure points to the primal scene where his mother was sexually abused. Ivan's obsession with his 'lovely pictures', including the child who is torn to pieces in front of his mother, rearticulates a history of abused children (including himself). The dried-up women with the baby crying in Mitya's dream imply they suffer under patriarchal oppression in their household.

Cana of Galilee

In Book 7 ('Cana of Galilee'), Zosima has passed away and his body deteriorates. Alyosha is disillusioned; he leaves the monastery and meets Rakitin, who wants to destroy his purity by making Grunshenka seduce him. After meeting her, Alyosha returns to the monastery and prays 'almost mechanically' next to Zosima's corpse (359). Meanwhile, he hears an elder reading a passage from the Gospel of St John, in which Christ turns water into wine in a wedding banquet (John 2:1–11). As the reading goes on, Alyosha falls into a dream, in which he sees Zosima serving wine in the banquet: 'I, too, my dear', says Zosima,

> I, too, have been called, called and chosen [...] Why are you hiding here, out of sight...? Come and join us. We are rejoicing [...] We are drinking new wine, the wine of a new and great joy. (361)

Alyosha's dream amalgamates the wedding banquet with the death of Zosima. The dream continues to create new images, as Zosima addresses Alyosha:

> And you, quiet one, you, my meek boy, today you, too, were able to give a little onion to a woman who hungered. Begin, my dear, begin, my meek one, to do your work! And do you see our Sun, do you see him? (361)

Alyosha replies: 'I am afraid ... I don't dare to look' (361). The Sun in the wedding banquet represents Christ. Alyosha, who is tempted to fall for sensuality, is ashamed to look at the Sun. Zosima replies strangely:

> Do not be afraid of him. Awful is his greatness before us, terrible is his loftiness, yet he is boundlessly merciful [...] He is waiting for new guests, he is ceaselessly calling new guests, now and unto ages of ages. See, they are bringing the new wine, the vessels are being brought in ... (362)

In the Gospel of St John, Christ did not call new guests endlessly and there was no new wine being brought into the banquet.[31] This carnivalesque detail of the dream, however, has a parallel to what would happen in an orgy organized by Alyosha's other father, that is, the old Karamazov. It is no coincidence that Fyodor is completely drunk when he recounts the sexual abuse in Book 3 ('Over the Cognac'). We do not see Alyosha helping Zosima to serve in the banquet; the dream finishes after the image of the drunken father is hinted: 'Something burned in Alyosha's heart, something suddenly filled him almost painfully, tears of rapture nearly burst from his soul ... He stretched out his hands, gave a short cry, and woke up' (362). Three fathers have visited in Alyosha's dream: Zosima, Christ, and the old Karamazov. These three images are interchangeable in the dream. The father figure is both the divine and the debauched, recalling the Karamazovian beauty, which is always marked by the ideal of Madonna and Sodom at the same time (3.3.108). The father figure represents both the elder who teaches the doctrine of immortality as well as the rapist who abused Alyosha and his mother. The condensed image of the father suggests an ambivalent meaning of patriarchy. That the son is asked to join the orgy also suggests a homosexual attraction between the fathers and son.

It is said that Alyosha will become a revolutionary and decide to assassinate the Tsar in the sequel. If we take the Tsar as another father figure for Alyosha, his attitude towards his fathers will become more ambivalent. He would be killing the father figure of Russia, echoing Smerdyakov killing the father of the Karamazov brothers. Although the sequel is unwritten, we can read it symptomatically and say that Alyosha's assassination of the Tsar is indexical to the country's trauma, i.e. the long history of sufferings produced under autocracy, just as the parricide opens up the silenced and painful side of the Karamazovs' history.

After the dream, Alyosha steps out of the monastery and has his second hysterical fit:

> He stood gazing and suddenly, as if he had been cut down, threw himself to the earth. He did not know why he was embracing it, he did not try to understand why he longed so irresistibly to kiss it, but he was kissing it, weeping, sobbing, and watering it with his tears, and he vowed ecstatically to love it, to live it unto ages of ages. (362)[32]

Susanne Fusso suggests that the earth evokes the image of the maternal. She sees Alyosha's frenzied kissing as some sort of masturbatory moment, after which the son ceases to be a virgin.[33] But if we take into account the idea that Alyosha is having a hysterical fit, the kissing will be more likely to indicate his traumatic past. As we recall, in his vivid memory, the mother embraces Alyosha so tightly that it creates pain. She is pleading for the protection of the Mother of God. Here, outside the monastery, Alyosha re-enacts the picture he used to paint: he embraces his mother (the earth), weeps over it and loves it without reserve. He embraces not only the biological mother:

> The silence of the earth seemed to merge with the silence of the heavens, the mystery of the earth touched the mystery of the stars ... [...] With each moment he felt clearly and almost tangibly something as firm and immovable as this heavenly vault descend into his soul. (363)

Figuratively, the son merges himself with the earth, which is then merged with the heavens. From the reference to the drunken father to the ecstatic kissing of the motherly earth, Cana of Galilee ends with a fantasy of reuniting with the mother, which empowers the son:

> He fell to the earth a weak youth and rose up a fighter, steadfast for the rest of his life, and he knew it and felt it suddenly, in that very moment of his ecstasy. Never, never in all his life would Alyosha forget that moment. (363)

Just as he would never forget the memory of his mother, his transformation into a fighter is founded upon some 'good' memory, and at the same time on the disavowal, the screening out of his traumatic past.

It is significant that the traumatic history of the Karamazovs is set in the countryside: while the Petersburgers, as Svidrigailov in *Crime and Punishment* puts it, are half-mad and like to talk to themselves on the street (6.3.467), the Russian rural inhabitants are traumatized by their parents at birth. 'Our Russian destiny', Dostoevsky writes in *A Writer's Diary*, 'will not be finally resolved by Petersburg. Therefore every *new* feature, even the smallest, that serves to characterize these "new people" may be worthy of our attention' ('Vlas', 1.160). Dostoevsky's reading of Russia does not end with the Petersburg novels (*Humiliated and Insulted*, *Notes from Underground*, *Crime and Punishment*, and *The Idiot*). He extends it to the countryside by producing *Demons* and *The Brothers Karamazov*. If Petersburg is 'epilepsy-inducing', creating the epileptic mode of being, Alyosha's countryside is equally 'epileptic' considering the fact that the family repressed its traumatic history, which only appears in flashes in the moment of seizures.

At Ilyusha's Stone

Three days after Zosima's death, Alyosha leaves the monastery. In Book 12, he delivers a speech to commemorate Ilyusha, who dies of consumption after fighting against the Karamazovs for humiliating his father Snegiryov. What happened was that before the main action of the novel takes place, Mitya 'seized [Snegiryov] by the beard in front of everyone, led him outside in that humiliating position, and led him a long way down the street' (4.5.193). Ilyusha witnessed the entire process. He 'saw it and went running along beside them, crying loudly and begging for his father, and rushing up to everyone asking them to defend him, but everyone laughed' (193).

Standing by Ilyusha's stone, the place where the son wants to be buried, Alyosha gives an uplifting speech to Ilyusha's friends. Alyosha is anxious to build a 'good' memory of Ilyusha: 'Let us remember his face, and his clothes, and his poor boots, and his little coffin, and his unfortunate, sinful father, and how he bravely rose up against the whole class for him!' (775). Alyosha pushes further to suggest that a 'good' memory is the key to salvation:

> Some such beautiful, sacred memory, preserved from childhood, is perhaps the best education. If a man stores up many such memories to take into life, then he is saved for his whole life. And even if only one good memory remains with us in our hearts, that alone may serve some day for our salvation. (774)

A powerful brotherhood, as Alyosha's speech suggests, has to be built upon some beautiful memory *from* childhood. Such memory will ensure that the grown-up children can remember their capacity to love and keep themselves away from 'great evil' (775). But if we recall Freud's analysis, there is no such thing called memory from the past, but only present-day memory of the past. The way in which the children remember Ilyusha depends largely on how Alyosha interprets the dead child's past. The 'beautiful and sacred' memories from childhood are always already mediated by Alyosha's speech on forming the brotherhood.

Before the speech, Alyosha is haunted by another picture of Ilyusha, which is very different from what he proposes to his young disciples:

> They all silently stopped at the big stone. Alyosha looked and the whole picture of what Snegiryov had once told him about Ilyushechka, crying and embracing

> his father, exclaiming: 'Papa, papa, how he humiliated you!' rose at once in his memory. Something shook, as it were, in his soul. (774)

There is another part of Alyosha's memory which is not addressed in his speech, that is, the very fact that Ilyusha's father was humiliated by Mitya. This segment of memory — which again returns in the form of a picture — tells the traumatic moment when Ilyusha witnessed his father being humiliated in public. This image remembered recalls a desperate complaint. Yet the humiliation done to the father has not been expiated. This little picture of Ilyusha is screened out from the massive, beautiful, and even sacred picture which Alyosha wants to paint before his disciples.

When the children are carrying Ilyusha's coffin to the churchyard, his mad mother has a hysterical fit. But like the previous picture of Ilyusha pleading with his father, the image of hysteria flits by and the mother is absent in Alyosha's speech:

> They picked up the coffin, but as they carried it past his mother, they stopped in front of her for a moment and set it down, so that she could say her farewells to Ilyusha. But suddenly looking so closely at that dear little face, which for the past three days she had only seen from a distance, she began suddenly shaking all over, wagging her gray head back and forth hysterically above the coffin. 'Mama, cross him, bless him, kiss him,' Ninochka [her daughter] cries to her. But she kept wagging her head like an automaton, and then silently, her face twisted with burning grief, she suddenly began beating her breast with her fist. They moved on with the coffin. (770)

Just as Alyosha's hysterical fit points back to the violence done to his mother, here we have Ilyusha's mother falling into a fit before the corpse of her son, who tried to fight for his humiliated father. The hysterical mothers permeate the novel: the line of dried-up peasant women in Mitya's dream; Ivan's woman who is forced to witness her son's torture; Alyosha's mother who has been terrorized since childhood; and Smerdyakov's holy fool mother who was raped. The album of abused women is made complete by the picture of Ilyusha's mad mother. The above passage shows another scene where the traumatic side of Ilyusha's family history is implied. This side of the history only finds its expression in the form of severe seizure.

The tension between the return of traumatic memory and the urgency in crystallizing a good memory can be summarized by one last picture. In section nine of *Theses on the Philosophy of History*, Walter Benjamin discusses Paul Klee's *Angelus Novus*, calling the figure in the painting the angel of history:

> His eyes are staring, his mouth is open, his wings are spread. This is how one pictures the angel of history. His face is turned toward the past. Where we perceive a chain of events, he sees one single catastrophe which keeps piling wreckage upon wreckage and hurls it in front of his feet. The angel would like to stay, awaken the dead, and make whole what has been smashed. But a storm is blowing from Paradise; it has got caught in his wings with such violence that the angel can no longer close them. This storm irresistibly propels him into the future to which his back is turn, while the pile of debris before him grows skyward. This storm is what we call progress.[34]

The good memory Alyosha wants to create, the sacred family history he would like

FIG. 8. Paul Klee, *Angelus Novus* (1920)
photograph: Elie Posner (© The Israel Museum, Jerusalem)

to imagine — these are what we are inclined to envisage and what Benjamin calls 'a chain of events'. But the angel in shock sees something different: he wants to awaken the dead, to rearticulate the traumatic past. This is forbidden by 'progress', which idealizes history, taking it as a chain of events. Likewise, the children disciples 'moved on with [Ilyusha's] coffin', overlooking his mother's seizure (770). The storm is blowing from Paradise, suggesting that the movement driven by the storm is not purely negative. To affirm the traumatic past is not always positive either. The passage offers a double vision for reading the family history of the Karamazovs: it urges a reading of what is screened out, silenced, and traumatized in the past. At the same time, such reading has to be placed in a dialectical relationship with a progressive reading of the future, such as Alyosha's memorial speech. Only in this way can the subject be hopeful that he will not remain in the state of shock and will strive to reach Paradise.

Notes to Chapter 5

1. The title is inspired by Beatrice Hanssen's book, *Walter Benjamin's Other History: Of Stones, Animals, Human Beings, and Angels* (Berkeley: University of California Press, 1998).
2. For details of Dostoevsky's unwritten projects, see Robert L. Belknap, *The Genesis of 'The Brothers Karamazov'* (Evanston, IL: Northwestern University Press, 1990), pp. 45–53; Joseph Frank, *Dostoevsky: The Mantle of the Prophet, 1871–1881* (Princeton: Princeton University Press, 2002), pp. 390–548; Leonid Grossman, *Dostoevsky: A Biography*, trans. by Mary Mackler (London: Allen Lane, Penguin, 1974), pp. 455–60, 569–83; Konstantin Mochulsky, *Dostoevsky: His Life and Work*, trans. by M. A. Minihan (Princeton: Princeton University Press, 1967), pp. 565–96.
3. Quoted in Mochulsky, *Dostoevsky*, p. 565.
4. James L. Rice, 'Dostoevsky's Endgame: The Projected Sequel to *The Brothers Karamazov*', *Russian History/Histoire Russe*, 33 (2006), 50–62.
5. A reviewer, after attending the public reading of Book 10, wrote in the Odessa daily *Novorossiiskii Telegraf* in 1880:

   > from a few rumours about the further contents of the novel, rumours current in Petersburg literary circles, I can say only that Aleksei [Karamazov] in time becomes the village schoolmaster, and influenced by some sort of special psychological processes at work in his soul, he actually arrives at the idea of assassinating the Tsar.

   Quoted in Rice, 'Dostoevsky's Endgame', p. 45.
6. On the novel, see Gary L. Browning, 'Zosima's "Secret of Renewal" in *The Brothers Karamazov*', *The Slavic and East European Journal*, 33 (1989), 516–29; Carol A. Flath, 'The Passion of Dmitrii Karamazov', *Slavic Review*, 58 (1999), 584–99; Kate Holland, 'Novelizing Religious Experience: The Generic Landscape of *The Brothers Karamazov*', *Slavic Review*, 66 (2007), 63–81; Robin Feuer Miller, *The Brothers Karamazov: Worlds of the Novel* (New Haven: Yale University Press, 2008); Nina Perlina, *Varieties of Poetic Utterance: Quotation in 'The Brothers Karamazov'* (Lanham, MD: University Press of America, 1985); Victor Terras's detailed annotation of the novel is particularly helpful: *A Karamazov Companion: Commentary on the Genesis, Language, and Style of Dostoevsky's Novel* (Madison: University of Wisconsin Press, 1981).
7. See Chapter 3 for discussion of the Flagellants.
8. Smerdyakov is the eunuch figure and his surrogate father is associated with the Flagellants. Similarly, Rogozhin in *The Idiot* lives in the house of the Castrates and his father sympathizes with the sectarians. Both Smerdyakov and Rogozhin are associated with the image of a Castrate and have committed a murder. For further comparison, see Irene Masing-Delic, 'The "Castrator" Rogozhin and the "Castrate" Smerdiakov: Incarnations of the Dostoevskii's "Devil-Bearing" People?', *Dostoevsky Studies*, n.s., 10 (2006), 88–114.
9. Smerdyakov claims that he is the casuist disciple of Ivan Karamazov, who says that if there is no immortality, then everything is permitted. Ivan's casuistry is most articulated in 'Rebellion' and 'The Grand Inquisitor' in Book 5 ('Pro and Contra'). For the relationship of Smerdyakov and Ivan, see Marina Kanevskaya, 'Smerdiakov and Ivan: Dostoevsky's *The Brothers Karamazov*', *Russian Review*, 61 (2002), 358–76.
10. For further discussion of Smerdyakov's epilepsy, see Nathan Rosen, 'Freud on Dostoevsky's Epilepsy: A Revaluation', *Dostoevsky Studies*, 9 (1988), 108–27. Other psychoanalytic studies of the novel include: J. R. Maze, 'Dostoevsky: Epilepsy, Mysticism and Homosexuality', *American Imago*, 38 (1981), 155–83; Geoffrey Carter, 'Freud and *The Brothers Karamazov*', *Literature and Psychology*, 31 (1981), 15–31.
11. Cathy A. Frierson, *All Russia is Burning! A Cultural History of Fire and Arson in Late Imperial Russia* (Seattle: University of Washington Press, 2002), p. 145.
12. Ibid., p. 57.
13. Geoffrey C. Kabat writes: 'What [Ivan] formulates as a general, global indictment of creation has its origin in his personal history' (Geoffrey C. Kabat, *Ideology and Imagination: The Image of Society in Dostoevsky* (New York: Columbia University Press, 1978), p. 149). For the conflict of the father and the four sons, see ibid., pp. 111–62; Michael Holquist, *Dostoevsky and the Novel*

(Princeton and Guildford: Princeton University Press, 1977), pp. 165–91; Neal Bruss, 'The Sons Karamazov: Dostoevsky's Characters as Freudian Transformations', *The Massachusetts Review*, 27 (1986), 40–67; Harriet Murav, 'From Skandalon to Scandal: Ivan's Rebellion Reconsidered', *Slavic Review*, 63 (2004), 756–70.

14. On the importance of maternity, see Carol Apollonio, 'The Mothers Karamazov', in *Dostoevsky's Secrets: Reading Against the Grain* (Evanston, IL: Northwestern University Press, 2009), pp. 145–62.
15. James Rice, 'The Covert Design of *The Brothers Karamazov*: Alesha's Pathology and Dialectic', *Slavic Review*, 68 (2009), 355–75 (p. 362).
16. Liza Knapp, 'Mothers and Sons in *The Brothers Karamazov*: Our Ladies of Skotoprigonevsk', in *A New Word on The Brothers Karamazov* (Evanston; IL: Northwestern University Press, 2004), pp. 31–52 (p. 37).
17. Elisabeth Bronfen, 'The Performance of Hysteria', in *Identities: Time, Difference, and Boundaries*, ed. by Heidrun Friese (New York: Berghahn Books, 2002), pp. 153–69 (p. 159). The two surrealists write in 1928: 'Hysteria is a mental state [...] characterized by the subversion of the relationship established between the subject and the moral world [...] It can, from every point of view, be considered as a supreme means of expression'. Quoted in Rae Beth Gordon, 'From Charcot to Charlot: Unconscious Imitation and Spectatorship in French Cabaret and Early Cinema', *Critical Inquiry*, 27 (2001), 515–49 (p. 549).
18. 'In an increasingly industrialized society, the Victorian woman was looked up to as representative of the purity, order, and serenity of earlier, less anxious times. Gentle, submissive, naïve, and good, she was also expected to be strong in her righteousness, perfectly controlled in her decorous conduct, and skilled in her domestic managerial capacities. Faced with this conflict, numerous Victorian women developed unconscious defensive strategies whereby they disavowed the intense anger and aggressive impulses for which the culture gave them no outlet. [...] Women transformed their repressed hostility and desire into physical symptoms that simultaneously acknowledged and disowned those feelings.' Quoted in *In Dora's Case: Freud — Hysteria — Feminism*, ed. by Charles Bernheimer and Claire Kahane (New York: Columbia University Press, 1990), pp. 5–6.
19. For feminist studies in hysteria, see Bernheimer and Kahane's *In Dora's Case*, which is a collection of essays critiquing Freud's analysis of his hysterical patient Ida Bauer; Elaine Showalter, *The Female Malady: Women, Madness, and English Culture, 1830–1980* (New York: Pantheon, 1985); Hélène Cixous and Catherine Clément, *The Newly Born Woman* (London: I. B. Tauris, 1996). Georges Didi-Huberman examines the photographic images of hysterics developed by Charcot, *Invention of Hysteria: Charcot and the Photographic Iconography of the Salpêtrière* (Cambridge, MA and London: MIT Press, 2003).
20. Quoted in Rice, 'The Covert Design of *The Brothers Karamazov*', p. 362.
21. On the distinction between epilepsy and hysteria, see Mark S. Micale, *Approaching Hysteria: Disease and its Interpretations* (Princeton: Princeton University Press, 1995), pp. 171–72; Rice, 'The Covert Design of *The Brothers Karamazov*', pp. 355–375; Owsei Temkin, *The Falling Sickness: A History of Epilepsy from the Greeks to the Beginnings of Modern Neurology*, 2nd edn (Baltimore and London: Johns Hopkins University Press, 1971), pp. 351–59; Vicky Lebeau, *Psychoanalysis and Cinema: The Play of Shadows* (London: Wallflower, 2001), p. 16; Jean-Paul C. J. Selten, 'Freud and Dostoevsky', *The Psychoanalytic Review*, 80 (1993), 441–55.
22. Walter Benjamin, *Illuminations*, trans. by Harry Zorn (London: Pimlico, 1999), p. 247.
23. Diane O. Thompson, *The Brothers Karamazov and the Poetics of Memory*, 2nd edn (Cambridge: Cambridge University Press, 2009). On the subject of memory, see Robert Belknap, 'Memory in *The Brothers Karamazov*', in *Dostoevsky: New Perspectives*, ed. by Robert L. Jackson (Englewood Cliffs, NJ: Prentice-Hall Publishers, 1984), pp. 227–42; Michael Katz, 'The Theme of Maternity in Aleša Karamazov's Four-Year-Old Memory', *The Slavic and East European Journal*, 34 (1990), 506–10. Also see Michael Katz, *Dreams and the Unconscious in Nineteenth-Century Russian Literature* (Hanover, NH: University Press of New England, 1984).
24. *A History of Russian Philosophy 1830–1930: Faith, Reason, and the Defense of Human Dignity*, ed. by G. M. Hamburg and Randall A. Poole (Cambridge: Cambridge University Press, 2010), p. 36.
25. Quoted in Richard Peace, 'Dostoevsky and "The Golden Age"', *Dostoevsky Studies*, 3 (1982), 62–78 (p. 74). Also see Gary Shapiro's discussion of Dostoevsky on the painting: *Archaeologies of*

Vision: Foucault and Nietzsche on Seeing and Saying (Chicago and London: University of Chicago Press, 2003), pp. 39–60.

26. Saliva is disgusting but because it is part of the body secretion, it cannot be fully rejected. See Julia Kristeva, *Powers of Horror: An Essay on Abjection* (New York: Columbia University Press, 1982), pp. 1–31. Cf. Georges Bataille, who sees spit as the image of formlessness, which is comparable to the power of destabilizing boundaries in abjection. See *Visions of Excess: Selected Writings 1927–1939* (Manchester: Manchester University Press, 1985), p. 31.
27. 'Hysteria' (1888), in *The Standard Edition of the Complete Psychological Works of Sigmund Freud*, trans. and ed. by James Strachey and others, I (London: Vintage, 2001), pp. 42–43.
28. 'Studies in Hysteria' (1893–95), in *The Standard Edition*, II (London: Vintage, 2001), p. 14, partly cited in Ilza Veith, *Hysteria: The History of a Disease* (Chicago and London: University of Chicago Press, 1965), p. 272.
29. See Bernheimer and Kahane, *In Dora's Case*, p. 11.
30. Freud, 'Screen Memories' (1899), in *The Standard Edition*, III (London: Vintage, 2001), pp. 301–22 (p. 321).
31. Zosima's words regarding Christ inviting new guests could refer to another passage in the Gospel: 'In my Father's house are many mansions: if it were not so, I would have told you. I go to prepare a place for you' (John 14:2). I am interested in how Zosima's speech has carnivalized the biblical scenes.
32. The image of Alyosha being cut down echoes the same image used to describe his first hysterical fit: '[He] fell back in his chair as if he'd been cut down, and suddenly began shaking all over in a hysterical attack of sudden trembling and silent tears' (3.8.137).
33. Susanne Fusso, *Discovering Sexuality in Dostoevsky* (Evanston, IL: Northwestern University Press, 2006), pp. 69–79.
34. Benjamin, *Illuminations*, p. 249.

CONCLUSION

❖

Death Sentences: Infinite Postponement

This book has traced and examined the appearances of epilepsy in five of Dostoevsky's novels, suggesting that the writer's works are characterized by the epileptic mode of being. For this particular existence, I have referred to the infinite alternation between the desire to seize upon the present moment and the impossibility of seizing it. The moment which is impossible to seize upon has been understood as the caesura, the moment of incomprehensibility which ruptures the sense of continuity of the novels' narratives. This is the moment where Dostoevsky's heroes are thrown into a state of traumatic shock, even the collapse of consciousness.

On the other hand, I have also demonstrated that the heroes are compelled to return to the traumatic side of their life, hoping to make sense of and even master it. The dualistic pattern of existence echoes Dostoevsky's comparison of epilepsy to the experience of death, which advances and retreats. The alternation can also be compared to Freud's Fort/Da game, in which the child obtains postponed pleasures by repeatedly throwing out a cotton wheel and pulling it back.[1] In this conclusion, I want to suggest that the epileptic existence demands that Dostoevsky's heroes live in infinite postponement. That is to say, there is a sense of delay in the epileptic existence, which necessitates a subjectivity which is always deferred and unfinalized.

I would like to illuminate the point about postponement by looking at Maurice Blanchot's *The Instant of My Death* (*L'Instant de ma mort*, 1994). This short story about a young man surviving a firing squad is said to be Blanchot's own reminiscence of surviving a German military shooting during his involvement with the French Resistance in 1944.[2] The writer discusses the subject of death in his fictions and literary essays, such as 'Two Versions of the Imaginary', *Thomas the Obscure*, *The Space of Literature* (I have discussed these in Chapters 3 and 4), 'Literature and the Right to Death', and *Death Sentence* (*L'Arrêt de mort*). In the last example, a short story published in 1948, the narrator tells a story of his female friend who suffers from a fatal disease but goes on to survive for an unexpectedly long period of time.[3] It would be fifty years before Blanchot articulated the trauma of survival in *The Instant of My Death*. Similarly, in 1849, Dostoevsky was also reprieved at the last moment from his death sentence, which was then commuted to hard labour and conscription to the army. The first time he extensively articulated his experience of execution was eighteen years later, when Prince Myshkin in *The Idiot* relates a story told by 'a certain man', who is given a death sentence for a political crime and is pardoned at the last minute (1.4.60–61). Another instance of delay, among many others, is found in *Notes from Underground* (1864), where the Underground Man tells an anecdote in part 2 ('Apropos of the Wet Snow') which took place sixteen years ago in the year of Revolution, and which 'refuses to be gotten rid of' (1.11.38).

The Instant of My Death tells the story of a young man who lives with his family in a country house in France. One day, he opens the door to a group of Nazi soldiers who order the family to go outside the house: 'The Nazi placed his men in a row in order to hit, according to the rules, the human target'.[4] On the young man's request, the children and elderly are allowed to stay until the rest of them are killed. At this point, the narrator writes:

> I know — do I know it — that the one at whom the Germans were already aiming, awaiting but the final order, experienced then a feeling of extraordinary lightness, a sort of beatitude (nothing happy, however) — sovereign elation? The encounter of death with death? (5)

The narrator, knowing that he may have misread the moment, suggests that the young man experiences a kind of 'extraordinary lightness' in his encounter with death. The encounter with death has a sort of beatitude, but it has little to do with the beauty of resurrection or an afterlife. Rather, the young man engages in a peculiar relationship with death: 'he was bound to death by a surreptitious friendship' (5).

Just before the guns are fired, the lieutenant is distracted by the noise of an explosion in a nearby battle. As he moves away to investigate the noise, the soldiers suspend the shooting. One of them, approaching the young man with a laugh, makes a sign for him to disappear. He runs away and hides himself in a distant forest. Except for the country house, the entire area is searched and burnt. Three farmers' sons are slaughtered but the young man — whom the lieutenant perceives to be of noble class — survives.

The young man, who should have already died, continues to live by injustice. Here I follow Jean-François Lyotard's definition of the survivor: 'One who has come into contact with death in some bodily or psychic fashion and has himself remained alive'.[5] Concerning Auschwitz and the question of bearing testimony of what happened there, Lyotard says that 'survivor implies that an entity that is dead or ought to be is still alive'.[6] Thereafter, the ecstasy which elates the young man at the firing squad is gone: 'No doubt what then began for the young man was the torment of injustice. No more ecstasy' (7). The instant of the young man's death does not pass away with the narrative; it stays inside him as he continues to live:

> There remained, however, at the moment when the shooting was no longer but to come, the feeling of lightness that I would not know how to translate: freed from life? The infinite opening up? Neither happiness, nor unhappiness. Nor the absence of fear and perhaps already the step beyond. I know, I imagine that this unanalyzable feeling changed what there remained for him of existence. As if the death outside of him could only henceforth collide with the death in him. 'I am alive. No, you are dead'. (9)

The young man is alive in so far as he has survived the firing squad; hence the death which is outside of him. Yet, he is already dead in the sense that the shooting, which was missed, is 'no longer but to come', suggesting a state of suspension, endless waiting. This suspended mode — in which death is always about to come

— marks the young man's 'posthumous' existence. He has survived and yet he is always already dead. At the end the narrator summarizes: 'All that remains is the feeling of lightness that is death itself or, to put it more precisely, the instant of my death henceforth always in abeyance (*en instance*)' (11).[7] The phrase 'in abeyance' (*en instance*) has a legal implication: 'instance' can mean the process in a court of justice, e.g. court of first instance (OED). In this way, 'in abeyance' (*en instance*) involves the story's title (*L'instant de ma mort*), suggesting that the instant of my death is always pending, just as the process in the court. The opening line reads: 'I remember a young man — a man still young — prevented from dying by death itself — and perhaps the error of injustice' (3). It is death which 'disallows' the young man to die. Death is like the judge in the court who sentences the young man to a death penalty which is always to be executed. Rather than I who die my own death, it is death which stops me from dying. Death as the object turns into the subject which puts me into incessant trials, recalling Kafka's *The Trial*, in which Joseph K is told that his trial is always pending and yet he will be arrested at any time.[8]

Death shows its power in the life of the survivor, announcing to him a death sentence which is infinitely postponed. Hent de Vries writes: 'Death does not stop to arrive, yet a death that at every instant goes on to arrive never arrives as such. Put otherwise, its arrival as such retains an element or structure of ineffaceable delay or postponement'.[9] Death is ungraspable but, at the same time, consciousness keeps running after death. Consciousness attempts to come closer to but never arrive at death, and yet death is always pending in life. Dostoevsky and Blanchot had experienced death sentences. But death can also be the 'subject' which 'sentences', putting the survivors into a state in which they are always already dead.

The point about postponement in *The Instant of My Death* can be seen as a commentary on Dostoevsky's post-execution, post-Siberian, and posthumous novels. In *Humiliated and Insulted*, the Schillerian hero Vanya is mocked by the Sadean libertine Prince Valkovsky. The mockery terrorizes Vanya, challenging the moral ideals he wants to achieve. This moment of shock has been compared to the mystic terror which strikes him in the middle of writing. The Schillerian hero is subject to mockery of his romantic pursuit of moral ideals. His project of building lofty ideals is continually delayed, thus marking an existence which is characterized by postponement.

In my discussion of *Crime and Punishment*, I have demonstrated that the murder of the pawnbroker happens completely by chance in the carnivalesque Haymarket. The chance-effect fits into what the Underground Man calls the unintentional side of the city (I.2.8). Raskolnikov meticulously plans the murder and he wishes to become a Napoleon, to be able to speak the 'new word' by killing the pawnbroker. Yet, the randomness of the murder has proved that it is actually a postponement of what he intended to achieve. The Napoleonic ideal, like any other justifications Raskolnikov creates for his crime, is unachieved, missed, and delayed.

In *The Idiot*, Prince Myshkin attempts to analyse what the convict has in mind at the very last moment before the guillotine blade is released. The Prince indulges in thinking about that particular moment, even hoping to experience it himself. Likewise, the consumptive boy Ippolit is fascinated by Holbein's *The Body of the Dead*

Christ in the Tomb, which causes him to doubt the Resurrection. Both the Prince and Ippolit are fascinated by the instant of death; they are anxious to reflect on it and hope to understand it. This is what happens to the Prince's epileptic condition. He compares the moment of attack to the biblical phrase 'time shall be no more'. The Prince wishes to see the moment in epilepsy as a beautiful and timeless instant which can be retrieved when it is wanted. He desires for no postponement. But on the other hand, the Prince also admits that the seizure is nothing more than a banal illness which continually torments him. The logic of the writing of epilepsy never moves towards a single conclusion and therefore never confirms a single identity. What is reached at the end of the Prince's conclusion is another delay in his thoughts. He knows very well that the 'highest moments' are idealistic but all the same, he will go on to reflect on them. Consciousness is torn between the fascination of epilepsy and the awareness that such fascination is idealistic, creating a delay, a 'dis-appointment' in existence.

Demons has further demonstrated that the desire to seize the present is infinitely postponed. This is proved in Kirilov's attitude towards his own death and his imaginary epilepsy. By committing suicide, he wants to master death, to prove his fearsome freedom and his insubordination to God. Yet, the death which Kirilov has mastered is only the death which circulates in the language of liberty. The second death, which has no relation to the living Kirilov, is beyond the realm of experience and is therefore ungraspable. Kirilov can kill himself but he cannot master his own death. Death is infinitely postponed.

Kirilov says he will transform physically and become a man-god after the suicide. Similarly, he desires a physical transformation through which he will be able to overcome the pain of the epileptic attack and to enjoy the ecstasy of it. The desire to master death in Kirilov is meant to be identical with the desire to overcome epilepsy: both are the attempts to create meanings, to appropriate the ungraspable to the realm of experience. However, death and epilepsy — appearing in the form of 'sudden death' — always elude these desires, causing them to be infinitely missed and postponed.

In *The Brothers Karamazov*, Alyosha is anxious to keep a good memory of his mother, holding on to an image of the past. But a symptomatic reading of his remembrance and dream has shown that the seemingly beautiful and sacred images of the mother hardly exist. What the brother recalls instead are fragmented memories of the past. These pieces of memory are indexical to the traumatic past of his mother and himself. Alyosha's reading of his family history is idealistic, and I have contrasted him with other heroes who want to seize the moment. While Kirilov in *Demons* wants to control the indefinite future by killing himself, Alyosha desires to sculpt an untainted and eternal past. It is this beautifully preserved history he wants to pass on to his children disciples. Yet, there is always the other side, the traumatic side of memory which is silenced and which flashes through the moment of seizure. In this way, Alyosha's good pictures of memory are always marked by a caesura which remains unbridgeable and therefore causes delays and postponements in his remembrance. His attempt to draw a faithful picture of the past is futile because it always misses the traumatic parts of history.

The infinite postponement necessitates the Dostoevskian subject being repeatedly thrown into the condition of unfinishedness and deferment. This is what I have called the epileptic mode of being, a heterogeneous state of existence which distinguishes the posthumous writings of the epileptic survivor.

Notes to the Conclusion

1. Sigmund Freud, *Beyond the Pleasure Principle*, in *On Metapsychology, Penguin Freud 11*, trans. and ed. by James Strachey and others (Harmondsworth: Penguin, 1984), pp. 283–87.
2. Leslie Hill, *Blanchot: Extreme Contemporary* (London and New York: Routledge, 1997), p. 12.
3. Maurice Blanchot, *Death Sentence*, in *The Station Hill Blanchot Reader: Fiction and Literary Essays*, trans. by Lydia Davis (New York: Station Hill Press, 1999), pp. 129–87.
4. Maurice Blanchot, *The Instant of My Death*, with Jacques Derrida, in *Demeure: Fiction and Testimony*, trans. by Elizabeth Rottenberg (Stanford: Stanford University Press, 2000), pp. 1–11 (p. 5).
5. Quoted in Andrew Slade, *Lyotard, Beckett, Duras, and the Postmodern Sublime* (New York: Peter Lang, 2007), p. 4.
6. Jean-François Lyotard, *Toward the Postmodern*, ed. by Robert Harvey and Mark S. Roberts (Atlantic Highlands, NJ: Humanities Press, 1993), p. 144.
7. The original text reads: 'Seul demeure le sentiment de légèreté qui est la mort même ou, pour le dire plus précisément, l'instant de ma mort désormais toujours en instance' (10). Hent de Vries's translation renders: 'What remains is solely the sentiment of lightness which is death itself or, to put it more precisely, the instant of my death which is from now on always pending'. See Hent de Vries, '"Lapsus Absolu": Notes on Maurice Blanchot's *The Instant of My Death*', *Yale French Studies*, 93 (1998), 30–59 (p. 41).
8. See the chapter 'Lawyer, Manufacturer, Painter', in Franz Kafka, *The Trial*, trans. by Breon Mitchell (New York: Schocken Books, 1998), pp. 111–66.
9. De Vries, '"Lapsus Absolu"', p. 39.

BIBLIOGRAPHY

❖

ABRAHAM, KARL, *Selected Papers of Karl Abraham*, trans. by Douglas Bryan and Alix Strachey (London: Maresfield Library, 1988)

ADORNO, THEODOR W. and MAX HORKHEIMER, *Dialectic of Enlightenment*, trans. by John Cumming (London: Verso, 1979)

ALLEN, ELIZABETH C. and GARY S. MORSON, eds, *Freedom and Responsibility in Russian Literature: Essays in Honour of Robert Louis Jackson* (Evanston, IL: Northwestern University Press, 1995)

ALLEN, STANLEY, 'Piranesi's "Campo Marzio": An Experimental Design', *Assemblage*, 10 (1989), 70–109

ANDERSON, NANCY K., *The Perverted Ideal in Dostoevsky's 'The Devils'* (New York: Peter Lang, 1997)

ANTSIFEROV, NIKOLAI, *Dostoevsky's Petersburg* (Leningrad: Lenizdat, 1991)

APOLLONIO, CAROL, *Dostoevsky's Secrets: Reading Against the Grain* (Evanston, IL: Northwestern University Press, 2009)

ARASSE, DANIEL, *The Guillotine and the Terror*, trans. by Christopher Miller (London: Allen Lane, Penguin, 1989)

ARENDT, HANNAH, *Reflections on Literature and Culture* (Stanford: Stanford University Press, 2007)

AVSEY, IGNAT IGOR, 'Unizhennye I oskorblennye', *The Literary Encyclopedia.* First published 14 July 2007 <http://www.litencyc.com/php/sworks.php?rec=true&UID=11266>

BAKHTIN, MIKHAIL, *Problems of Dostoevsky's Poetics*, ed. and trans. by Caryl Emerson (Minneapolis and London: University of Minnesota Press, 1984)

—— *Art and Answerability: Early Philosophical Essays*, ed. by Michael Holquist and Vadim Liapunov, trans. by Vadim Liapunov (Austin: University of Texas Press, 1990)

BANERJEE, MARIA NEMCOVA, *Dostoevsky: The Scandal of Reason* (New York: Lindisfarne Books, 2006)

BARABTARLO, GENNADY, ed., *Cold Fusion: Aspects of the German Cultural Presence in Russia* (New York: Berghahn Books, 2000)

BATAILLE, GEORGES, *Visions of Excess: Selected Writings 1927–1939* (Manchester: Manchester University Press, 1985)

BELKNAP, ROBERT L., *The Genesis of 'The Brothers Karamazov'* (Evanston, IL: Northwestern University Press, 1990)

BENJAMIN, WALTER, *Illuminations*, trans. by Harry Zorn (London: Pimlico, 1999)

—— *Selected Writings 1913–1926*, ed. by Marcus P. Bullock and Michael W. Jennings, I (Cambridge, MA and London: Harvard University Press, 2004)

BERMAN, MARSHALL, *All that is Solid Melts into Air: the Experience of Modernity* (London: Verso, 1983)

BERNHEIMER, CHARLES and CLAIRE KAHANE, eds, *In Dora's Case: Freud — Hysteria — Feminism* (New York: Columbia University Press, 1990)

BETHEA, DAVID, *The Shape of Apocalypse in Modern Russian Fiction* (Princeton and Oxford: Princeton University Press, 1989)

BLANCHOT, MAURICE, *The Space of Literature* (Lincoln, NB and London: University of Nebraska Press, 1989)

—— *The Station Hill Blanchot Reader: Fiction and Literary Essays*, trans. by Lydia Davis (New York: Station Hill Press, 1999)

—— *The Instant of My Death*, with Jacques Derrida, in *Demeure: Fiction and Testimony*, trans. by Elizabeth Rottenberg (Stanford: Stanford University Press, 2000)

BØRTNES, JOSTEIN, 'The Last Delusion in an Infinite Series of Delusions: Stavrogin and the Symbolic Structure of *The Devils*', *Dostoevsky Studies*, 4 (1983), 53–67

——'Dostoevskij's *Idiot* or the Poetics of Emptiness', *Scando-Slavica*, 40 (1994), 5–14

BREGER, LOUIS, 'Dostoevskii and Medicine', *Slavic Review*, 45 (1986), 735–37

——*Dostoevsky: The Author as Psychoanalyst* (New York: New York University Press, 1989)

BRODY, ERVIN C., 'Dostoevsky's Kirilov in Camus's *Le Mythe de Sisyphe*', *The Modern Language Review*, 70 (1975), 291–305

BROWNING, GARY L., 'Zosima's "Secret of Renewal" in *The Brothers Karamazov*', *The Slavic and East European Journal*, 33 (1989), 516–29

BRUMFIELD, WILLIAM C., '*Thérèse philosophe* and Dostoevsky's Great Sinner', *Comparative Literature*, 32 (1980), 238–52

BRUSS, NEAL, 'The Sons Karamazov: Dostoevsky's Characters as Freudian Transformations', *The Massachusetts Review*, 27 (1986), 40–67

BUCHANAN, HENRY, *Dostoevsky's Crime and Punishment: An Aesthetic Interpretation* (Nottingham: Astra Press, 1996)

BUCKLER, JULIE A., *Mapping St. Petersburg: Imperial Text and Cityshape* (Princeton and Oxford: Princeton University Press, 2007)

BURNHAM, WILLIAM, 'The Legal Context and Contributions of Dostoevsky's *Crime and Punishment*', *Michigan Law Review*, 100 (2002), 1227–48

BUTIKOV, GEORGHY, *St. Isaac's Cathedral Museum* (Leningrad: SMART, 1990)

CARTER, GEOFFREY, 'Freud and *The Brothers Karamazov*', *Literature and Psychology*, 31 (1981), 15–31

CASSEDY, STEVEN, *Dostoevsky's Religion* (Stanford, CA: Stanford University Press, 2005)

CATTEAU, JACQUES, *Dostoyevsky and the Process of Literary Creation*, trans. by Audrey Littlewood (Cambridge: Cambridge University Press, 1989)

CAWTHORNE, TERENCE, 'Julius Caesar and the Falling Sickness', *Proceedings of the Royal Society of Medicine*, 51 (1957), 1–4

CHAITIN, GILBERT D., *Rhetoric and Culture in Lacan* (Cambridge: Cambridge University Press, 1996)

CHERKASOVA, EVGENIA, *Dostoevsky and Kant: Dialogues on Ethics* (Amsterdam: Rodopi, 2009)

CIXOUS, HÉLÈNE and CATHERINE CLÉMENT, *The Newly Born Woman* (London: I. B. Tauris, 1996)

CLARK, KATERINA and MICHAEL HOLQUIST, *Mikhail Bakhtin* (Cambridge, MA and London: Harvard University Press, 1984)

COMER, WILLIAM J., 'Rogozhin and the "Castrates": Russian Religious Traditions in Dostoevsky's *The Idiot*', *The Slavic and East European Journal*, 40 (1996), 85–99

COX, GARY, *Between Earth and Heaven: Shakespeare, Dostoevsky and the Meaning of Christian Tragedy* (New York: Holt, Rinehart and Winston, 1969)

—— *'Crime and Punishment': A Mind to Murder* (Boston: Twayne Publishers, 1990)

CRACRAFT, JAMES, ed., *Peter the Great Transforms Russia* (Lexington, MA: D. C. Heath, 1991)

CRAVENS, CRAIG, 'The Strange Relationship of Stavrogin and Stepan Trofimovich as Told by Anton Lavrent'evich G-v', *Slavic Review*, 59 (2000), 782–801

CRITCHLEY, SIMON, *Very Little . . . Almost Nothing: Death, Philosophy, Literature* (London and New York: Routledge, 2004)

DALTON, ELIZABETH, *Unconscious Structure in 'The Idiot': A Study in Literature and Psychoanalysis* (Princeton, NJ: Princeton University Press, 1979)

Dickens, Charles, *Pictures from Italy* (Harmondsworth: Penguin, 2006)

Didi-Huberman, Georges, *Invention of Hysteria: Charcot and the Photographic Iconography of the Salpêtrière* (Cambridge, MA and London: MIT Press, 2003)

Dodds, E. R., *The Greeks and the Irrational* (Berkeley, Los Angeles, and London: University of California Press, 1951)

Dostoevsky, Anna, *Dostoevsky: Reminiscences*, trans. and ed. by Beatrice Stillman (London: Wildwood House, 1976)

Dostoevsky, Fyodor, *The Insulted and Injured*, trans. by Constance Garnett (London: Heinemann, 1915)

—— *The Idiot*, trans. by David Magarshack (Harmondsworth: Penguin, 1955)

—— *The Brothers Karamazov*, trans. by David Magarshack (Harmondsworth: Penguin, 1958)

—— *The Notebooks for 'The Idiot'*, ed. by Edward Wasiolek, trans. by Katharine Strelsky (Chicago and London: University of Chicago Press, 1967)

—— *The Notebooks for 'Crime and Punishment'*, ed. and trans. by Edward Wasiolek (Chicago and London: University of Chicago Press, 1967)

—— *The Notebooks for 'The Possessed'*, ed. by Edward Wasiolek, trans. by Victor Terras (Chicago and London: University of Chicago Press, 1968)

—— *The Brothers Karamazov*, trans. by Constance Garnett (New York: Norton, 1976)

—— *Crime and Punishment*, ed. by George Gibian, trans. by Jessie Coulson (New York and London: Norton, 1989)

—— *Selected Letters of Fyodor Dostoyevsky*, ed. by Joseph Frank and David I. Goldstein, trans. by Andrew R. MacAndrew (New Brunswick and London: Rutgers University Press, 1989)

—— *An Accidental Family*, trans. by Richard Freeborn (Oxford, New York: Oxford University Press, 1994)

—— *A Writer's Diary*, trans. by Kenneth Lantz, 2 vols (Evanston, IL: Northwestern University Press, 1994)

—— *Dostoevsky's Occasional Writings*, trans. by David Magarshack (Evanston, IL: Northwestern University Press, 1997)

—— *Winter Notes on Summer Impressions*, trans. by David Patterson (Evanston, IL: Northwestern University Press, 1997)

—— *Crime and Punishment*, trans. by Jessie Coulson (Oxford and New York: Oxford University Press, 1998)

—— *The Karamazov Brothers*, trans. by Ignat Avsey (Oxford: Oxford University Press, 1998)

—— *The Eternal Husband and Other Stories*, trans. by Richard Pevear and Larissa Volokhonsky (New York: Bantam Books, 2000)

—— *Memoirs from the House of the Dead*, trans. by Jessie Coulson (Oxford: Oxford University Press, 2001)

—— *Notes from Underground*, trans. by Michael R. Katz (New York and London: W. W. Norton, 2001)

—— *Notes from Underground and The Double*, trans. by Jessie Coulson (London: Penguin, 2003)

—— *The Devils*, trans. by David Magarshack (London: Penguin, 2004)

Dostoevsky, Fyodor, and Michael R. Katz, 'Petersburg Visions in Prose and Verse', *New England Review*, 24 (2003), 99-116

Egorov, Alekseevich, *The Architectural Planning of St. Petersburg* (Athens, OH: Ohio University Press, 1969)

Eisenstein, Sergei M. 'Piranesi, or the Fluidity of Forms', trans. by Roberta Reeder, *Oppositions*, 11 (1997), 84–110

Emery, John P., 'Othello's Epilepsy', *Psychoanalytic Review*, 46 (1959), 30–32

Euripides, *Bacchae*, ed. by Philip Vellacott (Harmondsworth: Penguin, 1972)

Fanger, Donald, *Dostoevsky and Romantic Realism: A Study of Dostoevsky in Relation to Balzac, Dickens and Gogol* (Cambridge, MA: Harvard University Press, 1965)
Finkel, Stuart, *On the Ideological Front: The Russian Intelligentsia and the Making of the Soviet Public Sphere* (New Haven: Yale University Press, 2007)
Flath, Carol A., 'The Passion of Dmitrii Karamazov', *Slavic Review*, 58 (1999), 584–99
Foucault, Michel, *Essential Works of Foucault*, ed. by Paul Rabinow, I (London: Penguin, 2000)
Frank, Joseph, 'The Masks of Stavrogin', *The Sewanee Review*, 77 (1969), 660–69
—— *Dostoevsky: The Seeds of Revolt, 1821–1849* (Princeton: Princeton University Press, 1976).
—— *Dostoevsky: The Years of Ordeal, 1850–1859* (Princeton: Princeton University Press, 1983)
—— *Dostoevsky: The Stir of Liberation, 1860–1865* (Princeton: Princeton University Press, 1986)
—— *Dostoevsky: The Miraculous Years, 1865–1871* (Princeton: Princeton University Press, 1995)
—— *Dostoevsky: The Mantle of the Prophet, 1871–1881* (Princeton: Princeton University Press, 2002)
—— *Through the Russian Prism: Essays on Literature and Culture* (Princeton: Princeton University Press, 1990)
Freud, Sigmund, 'Hysteria' (1888), in *The Standard Edition of the Complete Psychological Works of Sigmund Freud*, trans. and ed. by James Strachey and others, I (London: Vintage, 2001), pp. 39–59
—— 'Studies in Hysteria' (1893–95), *The Standard Edition*, II (London: Vintage, 2001), pp. 1–311
—— 'Screen Memories' (1899), in *The Standard Edition*, III (London: Vintage, 2001), pp. 301–22
—— 'Some Character-Types Met with in Psychoanalytic Work' (1916), in *Art and Literature, Penguin Freud 14* (Harmondsworth: Penguin, 1990), pp. 291–333
—— 'The "Uncanny"' (1919), in *The Standard Edition*, XVII (London: Hogarth Press and the Institute of Psycho-Analysis, 1955), p. 226–34
—— *Beyond the Pleasure Principle* (1920), in *On Metapsychology, Penguin Freud 11*, trans. and ed. by James Strachey and others (Harmondsworth: Penguin, 1984), pp. 283–87
—— *The Ego and the Id* (1923), in *On Metapsychology, Penguin Freud 11*, trans. and ed. by James Strachey (Harmondsworth: Penguin, 1984), pp. 350–408
—— 'The Economic Problem of Masochism' (1924), in *On Metapsychology, Penguin Freud 11*, trans. and ed. by James Strachey (Harmondsworth: Penguin, 1984), pp. 409–26
—— *Civilization and its Discontents* (1930), in *Civilization, Society and Religion, Penguin Freud 12*, trans. by James Strachey (Harmondsworth: Penguin, 1964), pp. 243–340
—— *New Introductory Lectures on Psychoanalysis* (1933), in *The Standard Edition*, XXII (London: Vintage, 2001), pp. 1–182
—— *Writings on Art and Literature*, trans. by James Strachey (Stanford: Stanford University Press, 1997)
Friedlander, Walter J., *The History of Modern Epilepsy: The Beginning, 1865–1914* (Westport, CT and London: Greenwood Press, 2001)
Frierson, Cathy A., *All Russia is Burning! A Cultural History of Fire and Arson in Late Imperial Russia* (Seattle: University of Washington Press, 2002)
Friese, Heidrun, ed., *Identities: Time, Difference, and Boundaries* (New York: Berghahn Books, 2002)
Fusso, Susanne, *Discovering Sexuality in Dostoevsky* (Evanston, IL: Northwestern University Press, 2006)
Garland, Henry, *Schiller* (London: Harrap, 1949)
Gatrall, Jefferson J. A., 'Between Iconoclasm and Silence: Representing the Divine in Holbein and Dostoevskii', *Comparative Literature*, 53 (2001), 214–32
—— 'The Icon in the Picture: Reframing the Question of Dostoevsky's Modernist Iconography', *The Slavic and East European Journal*, 48 (2004), 1–25

Gillespie, Michael A., *Nihilism before Nietzsche* (Chicago and London: University of Chicago Press, 1996)

Gilman, Sander, *Disease and Representation: Images of Illness from Madness to AIDS* (Ithaca, NY and London: Cornell University Press, 1988)

Gordon, Rae Beth, 'From Charcot to Charlot: Unconscious Imitation and Spectatorship in French Cabaret and Early Cinema', *Critical Inquiry*, 27 (2001), 515–49

Grossman, Leonid, *Dostoevsky: A Biography*, trans. by Mary Mackler (London: Allen Lane, Penguin, 1974)

Gutting, Gary, ed., *The Cambridge Companion to Foucault* (Cambridge: Cambridge University Press, 1994)

Hamburg, G. M. and Randall A. Poole, eds, *A History of Russian Philosophy 1830–1930: Faith, Reason, and the Defense of Human Dignity* (Cambridge: Cambridge University Press, 2010)

Hanssen, Beatrice, *Walter Benjamin's Other History: Of Stones, Animals, Human Beings, and Angels* (Berkeley: University of California Press, 1998)

Hegel, G. W. F., *The Phenomenology of Spirit*, trans. by A. V. Miller (Oxford: Clarendon Press, 1977)

Hill, Leslie, *Blanchot: Extreme Contemporary* (London and New York: Routledge, 1997)

Hingley, Ronald, *The Undiscovered Dostoyevsky* (Westport, CT: Greenwood Press, 1962)

——*Nihilists: Russian Radicals and Revolutionaries in the Reign of Alexander II, 1855–81* (London: Weidenfeld & Nicolson, 1967)

Hölderlin, Friedrich, 'Notes on the *Oedipus* and Notes on the *Antigone*', trans. by Jeremy Adler, in *Comparative Criticism*, v, ed. by William Shaffer (Cambridge: Cambridge University Press, 1983), pp. 205–44

Holland, Kate, 'Novelizing Religious Experience: The Generic Landscape of *The Brothers Karamazov*', *Slavic Review*, 66 (2007), 63–81

Hollander, Robert, 'The Apocalyptic Framework of Dostoevsky's *The Idiot*', *Mosaic*, 6 (1974), 123–39

Holquist, Michael, *Dostoevsky and the Novel* (Princeton and Guildford: Princeton University Press, 1977)

Howard, Barbara F., 'The Rhetoric of Confession: Dostoevskij's *Notes from Underground* and Rousseau's *Confessions*', *The Slavic and East European Journal*, 25 (1981), 16–32

Ishaq, Ibn, *The Life of Muhammad*, trans. by A. Guillaume (Karachi: Oxford University Press, 1967)

Jackson, Robert L., *Dostoevsky's Quest for Form: A Study of his Philosophy of Art* (New Haven: Yale University Press, 1966)

——*Twentieth Century Interpretations of 'Crime and Punishment': A Collection of Critical Essays* (Englewood Cliffs, NJ: Prentice-Hall, 1974)

——ed., *Dostoevsky: New Perspectives* (Englewood Cliffs, NJ: Prentice-Hall Publishers, 1984)

——*Dialogues with Dostoevsky: The Overwhelming Questions* (Stanford: Stanford University Press, 1993)

——ed., *A New Word on 'The Brothers Karamazov'* (Evanston; IL: Northwestern University Press, 2004)

Jocelyn, H. D., '*Homo sum: humani nil a me alienum puto* (Terence, *Heauton Timorumenos* 77)', *Antichthon*, 7 (1973), 14–46

Johnson, Brian R., *The Art of Dostoevsky's Falling Sickness* (Ann Arbor, MI: ProQuest, 2008)

Johnson, Leslie A., 'The Face of the Other in *Idiot*', *Slavic Review*, 50 (1991), 867–78

Jones, Malcolm V., 'Echoes of Hegel in Dostoyevsky', *The Slavonic and East European Review*, 49 (1971), 500–20

——'Dostoevsky and an Aspect of Schiller's Psychology', *Slavonic and East European Review*, 52 (1974), 337–54

JONES, MALCOM and G. M. TERRY, eds, *New Essays on Dostoyevsky* (Cambridge and London: Cambridge University Press, 1983)

JONGE, ALEX DE, *Dostoevsky and the Age of Intensity* (London: Secker & Warburg, 1975)

KABAT, GEOFFREY C., *Ideology and Imagination: The Image of Society in Dostoevsky* (New York: Columbia University Press, 1978)

KAFKA, FRANZ, *The Trial*, trans. by Breon Mitchell (New York: Schocken Books, 1998)

KAGANOV, GRIGORY, *Images of Space: St. Petersburg in the Visual and Verbal Arts*, trans. by Sidney Monas (Stanford: Stanford University Press, 1997)

——*Peterburg v kontekste barokko* (Saint-Petersburg: Stella, 2001)

KANEVSKAYA, MARINA, *N. K. Mikhailovsky's Criticism of Dostoevsky: The Cruel Critic* (Lewiston, NY and Lampeter: Edwin Mellen Press, 2001)

——'Smerdiakov and Ivan: Dostoevsky's *The Brothers Karamazov*', *Russian Review*, 61 (2002), 358–76

KANT, IMMANUEL, *Critique of Practical Reason*, trans. by Lewis White Beck (Indianapolis: Bobbs-Merrill, 1957)

——*Kant: Political Writings*, ed. by Hans S. Reiss (Cambridge: Cambridge University Press, 1991)

KARAMZIN, NIKOLAI, 'Nikolai Karamzin: Letters of a Russian Traveller', trans. by Andrew Kahn, *Studies on Voltaire and the Eighteenth Century*, 4 (2003), 127–28

KATKOV, G., 'Steerforth and Stavrogin: On the Sources of *The Possessed*', *The Slavonic and East European Review*, 69 (1949), 469–88

KATZ, MICHAEL R., *Dreams and the Unconscious in Nineteenth-Century Russian Literature* (Hanover, NH: University Press of New England, 1984)

——'The Theme of Maternity in Aleša Karamazov's Four-Year-Old Memory', *The Slavic and East European Journal*, 34 (1990), 506–10

KIERKEGAARD, SØREN, *Concluding Unscientific Postscript to Philosophical Fragments*, ed. and trans. by Howard V. Hong and Edna H. Hong (Princeton: Princeton University Press, 1992)

KLOSSOWSKI, PIERRE, 'A Destructive Philosophy', *Yale French Studies*, 35 (1965), 61–80

KNAPP, LIZA, *The Annihilation of Inertia: Dostoevsky and Metaphysics* (Evanston, IL: Northwestern University Press, 1996)

KÖRNER, STEPHAN, *Kant* (Harmondsworth: Penguin, 1990)

KRISTEVA, JULIA, *Powers of Horror: An Essay on Abjection* (New York: Columbia University Press, 1982)

——*Black Sun: Depression and Melancholia*, trans. by Leon S. Roudiez (New York: Columbia University Press, 1989)

KUNDERA, MILAN, *Unbearable Lightness of Being* (New York: Harper & Row, 1984)

LACAN, JACQUES, *The Four Fundamental Concepts of Psychoanalysis: The Seminar of Jacques Lacan, Book XI*, ed. by Jacques Alain-Miller, trans. by Alan Sheridan (New York: W. W. Norton, 1977)

——'Kant with Sade', trans. by James Swenson, *October*, 51 (1989), 55–75

——*The Ethics of Psychoanalysis 1959–1960: The Seminar of Jacques Lacan*, ed. by Jacques-Alain Miller, trans. by Dennis Porter (London: Routledge, 1992)

——*Écrits*, trans. by Bruce Fink (New York: W. W. Norton, 2006)

LARY, N. M., *Dostoevsky and Dickens: A Study of Literary Influence* (London: Routledge and Kegan Paul, 1973)

LAVRIN, JANKO, 'A Note on Nietzsche and Dostoevsky', *Russian Review*, 28 (1969), 160–70

LEATHERBARROW, WILLIAM J., 'Apocalyptic Imagery in *The Idiot* and *The Devils*', *Dostoevsky Studies*, 3 (1982), 43–52

——ed., *Dostoevskii and Britain* (Oxford: Berg, 1995)
——*A Devil's Vaudeville: The Demonic in Dostoevsky's Major Fiction* (Evanston, IL: Northwestern University Press, 2005)
——'The Sorcerer's Apprentice: Authorship and the Devil in Dostoevskii's *Poor Folk* and *The Landlady*', *The Slavonic and East European Review*, 83 (2005), 599–616
LEBEAU, VICKY, *Psychoanalysis and Cinema: The Play of Shadows* (London: Wallflower, 2001)
LINCOLN, W. BRUCE, *Sunlight at Midnight: St. Petersburg and the Rise of Modern Russia* (New York: Basic Books, 2000)
LOMBROSO, CESARE, *The Man of Genius* (New York: Charles Scribner's Sons, 1895)
LORD, ROBERT, *Dostoevsky: Essays and Perspectives* (London: Chatto & Windus, 1970)
LOUNSBERY, ANNE, 'Dostoevskii's Geography: Centers, Peripheries, and Networks in *Demons*', *Slavic Review*, 66 (2007), 212–29
LUFT, ERIC V. D. and DOUGLAS G. STENBERG, 'Dostoevskii's Specific Influence on Nietzsche's Preface to *Daybreak*', *Journal of the History of Ideas*, 52 (1991), 441–61
LUKÁCS, GEORG, *Reviews and Articles from 'Die rote Fahne'*, trans. by P. Palmer (London: Merlin Press, 1983)
LYNGSTAD, ALEXANDRA, *Dostoevskij and Schiller* (The Hague: Mouton, 1975)
LYOTARD, JEAN-FRANÇOIS, *Toward the Postmodern*, ed. by Robert Harvey and Mark S. Roberts (Atlantic Highlands, NJ: Humanities Press, 1993)
MACPIKE, LORALEE, *Dostoevsky's Dickens: A Study of Literary Influence* (London: Barnes & Noble, 1981)
MARTYN, DAVID, *Sublime Failures: The Ethics of Kant and Sade* (Detroit: Wayne State University Press, 2003)
MASING-DELIC, IRENE, 'The "Castrator" Rogozhin and the "Castrate" Smerdiakov: Incarnations of the Dostoevskii's "Devil-Bearing" People?', *Dostoevsky Studies*, n.s. 10 (2006), 88–144
MAZE, J. R., 'Dostoevsky: Epilepsy, Mysticism and Homosexuality', *American Imago*, 38 (1981), 155–83
MENNINGHAUS, WINFRIED, 'Walter Benjamin's Variations of Imagelessness', *Critical Horizons: A Journal of Philosophy & Social Theory*, 14 (2013), 407–28
MICALE, MARK S., *Approaching Hysteria: Disease and its Interpretations* (Princeton: Princeton University Press, 1995)
MILLER, C. A., 'Nietzsche's "Discovery" of Dostoevsky', *Nietzsche-Studien* (1973), 202–57
——'The Nihilist as Tempter-Redeemer: Dostoevsky's "Man-God" in Nietzsche's Notebooks', *Nietzsche-Studien* (1980), 165–226
MILLER, ROBIN FEUER, *Dostoevsky's Unfinished Journey* (New Haven and London: Yale University Press, 2007)
——*The Brothers Karamazov: Worlds of the Novel* (New Haven: Yale University Press, 2008)
MOCHULSKY, KONSTANTIN, *Dostoevsky: His Life and Work*, trans. by Michael A. Minihan (Princeton: Princeton University Press, 1973)
MORRISSEY, SUSAN K., *Suicide and the Body Politic in Imperial Russia* (New York: Cambridge University Press, 2006)
MOSER, CHARLES, *Antinihilism in the Russian Novel of the 1860s* (The Hague and London: Mouton, 1964)
——'From Skandalon to Scandal: Ivan's Rebellion Reconsidered', *Slavic Review*, 63 (2004), 756–70
MURPHY, EDWARD L., 'The Saints of Epilepsy', *Medical History*, 3 (1959), 303–11
NIETZSCHE, FRIEDRICH, *Selected Letters of Friedrich Nietzsche*, ed. and trans. by Christopher Middleton (Chicago: University of Chicago Press, 1969)
——*Daybreak: Thoughts on the Prejudices of Morality*, trans. by R. J. Hollingdale (Cambridge: Cambridge University Press, 1982)

——*On the Genealogy of Morals: A Polemic*, trans. by Douglas Smith (New York: Oxford University Press, 1996)

——*The Birth of Tragedy: From the Spirit of Music*, ed. by Douglas Smith (New York: Oxford University Press, 2008)

——*Twilight of the Idols, or How to Philosophize with a Hammer*, trans. by Duncan Large (New York: Oxford University Press, 2008)

NUECHTERLEIN, JEANNE ELIZABETH, *Translating Nature into Art: Holbein, the Reformation, and Renaissance Rhetoric* (University Park, PA: Pennsylvania State University Press, 2011)

PAGEL, WALTER, *Paracelsus: An Introduction to Philosophical Medicine in the Era of the Renaissance* (Basel and London: Karger, 1982)

PANICHAS, GEORGE A., *Dostoevsky's Spiritual Art: the Burden of Vision* (Brunswick, NJ: Transaction Publishers, 2004)

PAPERNO, IRINA, *Suicide as a Cultural Institution in Dostoevsky's Russia* (Ithaca and London: Cornell University Press, 1997)

PEACE, RICHARD, 'Dostoevsky and "The Golden Age"', *Dostoevsky Studies*, 3 (1982), 62–78

——*Dostoyevsky: An Examination of the Major Novels* (London: Bristol Classical Press, 1992)

——ed., *Fyodor Dostoevsky's 'Crime and Punishment': A Casebook* (Oxford: Oxford University Press, 2006)

PERLINA, NINA, *Varieties of Poetic Utterance: Quotation in 'The Brothers Karamazov'* (Lanham, MD: University Press of America, 1985)

PLATO, *Timaeus*, trans. by R. G. Bury (Cambridge, MA and London: Harvard University Press, 1929)

POPE, RICHARD and JUDY TURNER, 'Toward Understanding Stavrogin', *Slavic Review*, 49 (1990), 543–52

PUSHKIN, ALEXANDER, *Selected Works in Two Volumes*, trans. by Irina Zheleznova (Moscow: Progress Publisher, 1974)

RANCOUR-LAFERRIERE, DANIEL, *The Slave Soul of Russia: Moral Masochism and the Cult of Suffering* (New York and London: New York University Press, 1995)

REINHARD, KENNETH, 'Kant with Sade, Lacan with Levinas', *Modern Language Notes*, 110 (1995), 785–808

RICE, JAMES L., 'Dostoevsky's Medical History: Diagnosis and Dialectic', *Russian Review*, 42 (1983), 131–61

——*Dostoevsky and the Healing Art: An Essay in Literary and Medical History* (Ann Arbor, MI: Ardis, 1985)

——'Dostoevsky's Endgame: The Projected Sequel to *The Brothers Karamazov*', *Russian History/Histoire Russe*, 33 (2006), 50–62

——'The Covert Design of *The Brothers Karamazov*: Alesha's Pathology and Dialectic', *Slavic Review*, 68 (2009), 355–75

ROSEN, NATHAN, 'Freud on Dostoevsky's Epilepsy: A Revaluation', *Dostoevsky Studies*, 9 (1988), 108–27

ROSENSHIELD, GARY, *Crime and Punishment: The Techniques of the Omniscient Author* (Lisse: Peter de Ridder Press, 1978)

——*Western Law, Russian Justice: Dostoevsky, the Jury Trial, and the Law* (Madison: University of Wisconsin Press, 2005)

ROSENTHAL, BERNICE G., ed., *Nietzsche in Russia* (Princeton: Princeton University Press, 1986)

ROYLE, NICHOLAS, *The Uncanny: An Introduction* (Manchester: Manchester University Press, 2003)

RUTTENBURG, NANCY, *Dostoevsky's Democracy* (Princeton and Oxford: Princeton University Press, 2008)

SASS, LOUIS, *Madness and Modernism: Insanity in the Light of Modern Art, Literature, and Thought* (New York: Basic Books, 1992)
SCHENKER, ALEXANDER M., *The Bronze Horseman: Falconet's Monument to Peter the Great* (New Haven and London: Yale University Press, 2003)
SELTEN, JEAN-PAUL C. J., 'Freud and Dostoevsky', *The Psychoanalytic Review*, 80 (1993), 441–55
SHAKESPEARE, WILLIAM, *The Norton Shakespeare*, ed. by Stephen Greenblatt, Walter Cohen, Jean Elizabeth Howard, and Katharine Eisaman Maus (New York: W. W. Norton, 2008)
SHAPIRO, GARY, *Archaeologies of Vision: Foucault and Nietzsche on Seeing and Saying* (Chicago and London: University of Chicago Press, 2003)
SHATZ, MARSHALL and JUDITH E. ZIMMERMAN, ed., *Vekhi: A Collection of Articles about the Russian Intelligentsia* (Armonk, NY and London: M. E. Sharpe, 1994)
SHLAPENTOKH, DMITRY, *The French Revolution in Russian Intellectual Life: 1865–1905* (Westport, CT and London: Praeger, 1996)
SHNEIDMAN, N. N., *Dostoevsky and Suicide* (Oakville and New York: Mosaic Press, 1984)
SHOWALTER, ELAINE, *The Female Malady: Women, Madness, and English Culture, 1830–1980* (New York: Pantheon, 1985)
SIMONS, JOHN D., 'The Nature of Suffering in Schiller and Dostoevsky', *Comparative Literature*, 19 (1967), 160–73
——'The Myth of Progress in Schiller and Dostoevsky', *Comparative Literature*, 24 (1972), 328–37
SLADE, ANDREW, *Lyotard, Beckett, Duras, and the Postmodern Sublime* (New York: Peter Lang, 2007)
SNODGRASS, W. D., 'Crime for Punishment: The Tenor of Part One', *The Hudson Review*, 13 (1960), 202–53
STRAUS, NINA P., '"Why Did I say 'Women!'"? Raskolnikov Reimagined', *Diacritics*, 23 (1993), 54–65
SWENSON, JAMES B., JR., 'Annotations to "Kant with Sade"', *October*, 51 (1989), 76–104
TAMBLING, JEREMY, *Confession: Sexuality, Sin, the Subject* (Manchester: Manchester University Press, 1990)
TEMKIN, OWSEI, 'The Doctrine of Epilepsy in the Hippocratic Writings', *Bulletin of the History of Medicine*, 1 (1933), 277–322
——*The Falling Sickness: A History of Epilepsy from the Greeks to the Beginnings of Modern Neurology*, 2nd edn (Baltimore and London: Johns Hopkins University Press, 1971)
TERRAS, VICTOR, *A Karamazov Companion: Commentary on the Genesis, Language, and Style of Dostoevsky's Novel* (Madison: University of Wisconsin Press, 1981)
——*'The Idiot': An Interpretation* (Boston, MA: Twayne Publishers, 1990)
——*Reading Dostoevsky* (Madison and London: University of Wisconsin Press, 1998)
THACKERAY, WILLIAM, *The Works of William Makepeace Thackeray*, XV (London: Smith, Elder & Co., 1869)
THOMPSON, DIANE O., *The Brothers Karamazov and the Poetics of Memory*, 2nd edn (Cambridge: Cambridge University Press, 2009)
TURGENEV, IVAN, *Turgenev's Letters*, trans. by A. V. Knowles (London: Athlone Press, 1983)
——*Fathers and Sons*, trans. by Michael Katz (New York and London: W. W. Norton, 1994)
VEITH, ILZA, *Hysteria: The History of a Disease* (Chicago and London: University of Chicago Press, 1965)
VENTURI, FRANCO, *Roots of Revolution: A History of the Populist and Socialist Movements in Nineteenth Century Russia*, trans. by Francis Haskell (London: Weidenfeld & Nicolson, 1960)

Vinokurov, Val, 'The End of Consciousness and the Ends of Consciousness: A Reading of Dostoevsky's *The Idiot* and *Demons* after Levinas', *Russian Review*, 59 (2000), 21–37
Volkov, Solomon, *St. Petersburg: A Cultural History*, trans. by Antonina W. Bouis (New York: Simon and Schuster, 1997)
Vries, Hent de, '"Lapsus Absolu": Notes on Maurice Blanchot's *The Instant of My Death*', *Yale French Studies*, 93 (1998), 30–59
Wachtel, Andrew, 'Dostoevsky's *The Idiot*: The Novel as Photograph', *History of Photography* 26 (2002), 205–15
Wasiolek, Edward, *Dostoevsky: The Major Fiction* (Cambridge, MA: MIT Press, 1964)
—— 'Raskolnikov's Motives: Love and Murder', *American Imago*, 31 (1974), 252–69
—— 'Review of Jacques Catteau's *Dostoyevsky and the Process of Literary Creation*', *Modern Philology*, 89 (1992), 599
Wolf, Peter, 'Epilepsy in Literature', *Epilepsia*, 36 (1995), Supplement 12–17
Wood, Allen W., *Hegel's Ethical Thoughts* (Cambridge: Cambridge University Press, 1990)
Wykes, David, 'Gillray's Guillotines', *Word & Image*, 21 (2005), 213–22
Ziolkowski, Eric J., *The Sanctification of Don Quixote: From Hidalgo to Priest* (University Park: Pennsylvania State University Press, 1991)
Žižek, Slavoj, 'Kant and Sade: The Ideal Couple', *lacanian ink*, 13 (1998), 12–25

INDEX